DETAINED: A WRITER'S PRISON DIARY

For Maxine

For a world
without prisons
and detention
camps

Ngũgĩ
26th may 1989

DETAINED:
A WRITER'S PRISON DIARY

Ngũgĩ wa Thiong'o

LONDON
HEINEMANN
NAIROBI · IBADAN

Heinemann Educational Books Ltd.
22 Bedford Square, London WC1B 3HH
PMB 5205, Ibadan · P.O. Box 45314, Nairobi

EDINBURGH MELBOURNE AUCKLAND
SINGAPORE KUALA LUMPUR
NEW DELHI KINGSTON

Heinemann Educational Books Inc.
70 Court Street, Portsmouth, New Hampshire 03801, USA

ISBN 0 435 90240 7

Grateful acknowledgement is made to Eyre Methuen Ltd
for permission to include an extract from *The Mother*
by Bertolt Brecht, published in 1978 and translated by Stefan Brecht
from the original work, *Die Mutter*, copyright 1957
by Suhrkamp Verlag, Berlin.

Cover design based on a poster by the Ngũgĩ Defence Committee,
London.

Photoset in 10pt Times by GMGraphics, Harrow-on-the-Hill, Middx.
Printed in Great Britain by Richard Clay Ltd., Bungay, Suffolk.

DEDICATION

I would like to thank all those in Kenya, Africa and the world, who fought for my release and for all the political detainees in Kenya. In particular, I would like to mention the university students at Nairobi and some staff members; the Union of Writers of African Peoples; the Pan-African Association, writers and journalists; the London Ngũgĩ Defence Committee; Amnesty International; the International PEN Clubs; the Afro-Asian Writers' Movement; and many other teachers', writers', students' and workers' organisations from all over the world.

There were also many in Kenya, Africa and the world who wrote to Nyambura and the family while I was away; their words and expressions of solidarity cheered them and made them endure. I have not been able to write to all the individuals and organizations. This memoir is my letter to all those friends of Kenya and democracy.

I would like to thank all the patriots who have helped in the preparation of this prison memoir. Thanks also to Adam Matheenge, a fellow detainee at Kamĩtĩ, for allowing me to reproduce his letter from prison.

This book is dedicated to all the people who fight for democracy and particularly:

·To Limuru people; Kamĩrĩĩthũ people; neighbours and family for their tremendous support, encouragement and sometimes defiance; all Kenyan workers and peasants and ex-freedom fighters who fought colonialism with exemplary heroism and are still struggling against neo-colonialism;

To university students who have been at the forefront in the struggle for the democratic rights of Kenyans;

To my children Thiong'o, Kĩmunya, Ngĩna, Ndũũcũ, Mũkoma, Wanjikũ, and Njooki for enduring;

For my fellow detainees at Kamĩtĩ; Wasonga Sijeyo; Martin Shikuku; Koigi wa Wamwere; Simba Ongongi Were; 'Fujika' Mũhoro Mũthoga; Gĩcerũ wa Njaũ; Thairũ wa Mũthiga; Ali Dubat Fidhow; Hadji Dagane Galal Mohamed, Hadji Mahart Kuno Roble; Ahmed Shurie Abdi, Mohamed Nurie Hamshi; Mohamed Abdilie Hadow; Mohamed Dahie Digale; Adam Ahmed Matheenge; Ibrahim Ali Omer; Duale Roble Hussein; and to those in Manyani and Shimo la Tewa; George Anyona; J.M. Seroney; Mwangi wa Mahiinda; L.B. Mwanzia; Washington Juma and Moffat;

And to all the others before us. May these our detentions and this suffering be not in vain!

THE PUBLIC SECURITY (DETAINED AND
RESTRICTED PERSONS (REGULATIONS 1966

DETENTION ORDER

IN EXERCISE of the powers conferred by regulation
6 (1) of the Public Security (Detained and Restricted Persons)
Regulations 1966, the Minister for Home Affairs, being satisfied
that it is necessary for the preservation of public security to
exercise control, beyond that afforded by a restriction order,
over

NGUGI WA THIONGO

(hereinafter referred to as the detained person), HEREBY ORDERS
that the detained person shall be detained.

Date this .... day of December 1977.

(D. T. Arap Moi)

MINISTER FOR HOME AFFAIRS.

Above and right: Pickets outside the Kenyan High Commission, London, 1978

Fear not those who kill the flesh, but fear those who kill the spirit. They cannot kill my spirit even if they kill me as they have killed the others. They will not kill the determination of this country to remain free.

Warŭru Kanja, in a speech in Parliament on Wednesday, 13 November 1980, in which, according to the *Daily Nation* of 14 November 1980, he accused Constitutional and Home Affairs Minister Charles M. Njonjo and the head of the C.I.D., Ignatius Nderi, of being responsible for a plan to eliminate him.

Kweli itashinda namna tunavyoishi
Kweli haihofu tisho wala nguvu ya majeshi,
La uongo lina mwisho, Kweli kitu cha aushi,
Kweli itashinda kesho kama leo haitoshi.

Shabaan Robert: *Masomo yenye Adili*

PREFACE

1

There is no way I could have written this prison memoir without treading on some sensitive toes, since those who were responsible for my detention (or those who were even contemplating my elimination) are still alive and well and still occupying powerful positions of authority and wealth. Although I have a fairly good account of those who were active in calling for the ban on the performances of *Ngaahika Ndeenda* at Kamīrīithū and also of those who fought for my detention to 'teach him a lesson in submission, silence and obedience', I have on the whole avoided mentioning names except in concrete cases when I have had to answer published criticism of my ideological position, be it in books, newspapers, or in the precincts of parliament.

As I am not socially or personally known to most of these individuals, my differences with them are neither private nor personal. They are ideological. These people saw themselves as representing certain social forces; and I as representing others.

I have, therefore, tried to discuss detention not as a personal affair between me and a few individuals, but as a social, political and historical phenomenon. I have tried to see it in the context of the historical attempts, from colonial times to the present, by a foreign imperialist bourgeoisie, in alliance with its local Kenyan representatives, to turn Kenyans into slaves, and of the historical struggles of Kenyan people against economic, political and cultural slavery.

I have confined myself to the period between 31 December 1977 and 12 December 1978. My account starts with 12 December 1978 and ends with 12 December 1978. It is divided into two main sections: my experiences and thoughts in prison; and my letters from prison. In the second section (letters from prison) I have included a letter by another detainee, Mr A. Matheenge, to document my charge that disease was used as a means of torture. Otherwise this is one person's account and I hope that more detainees will write about their prison experiences in post-1963 Kenya in the same way that Mau Mau and pre-Mau Mau detainees have.

The third section (Prison Aftermaths) is sketchy and consists mainly of letters and documents that reveal the collusion between the government and university authorities to deny me employment. This is perhaps meant as a continuation of torture by other means, or as a way to encourage me to seek employment and lucre abroad, an eventuality I have rejected. This collusion to deny me employment is just one of the many things that followed my detention and release. Since I have not included them in the body of the memoir or in the third section, I will here mention a few.

Soon after my release, I was once arrested and falsely charged with drinking after hours. Although I was later discharged by the magistrate, I had already been subjected to a severe beating by the arresting policemen. During the same period (January to May 1979) my family and I were the victims of constant death threats.

I might here also mention the press hostility led by the Hilary Ngweno group of newspapers and especially *The Weekly Review*. I was hardly out of prison when Hilary Ngweno sent one of his reporters to interview me. But he had given her suspiciously leading questions and also instructions on how to go about it, all heavily underlined where Ngweno wanted emphasis:

Interview with Ngũgĩ:
Please show Ngũgĩ the *Nation* report of his interview with them and also specific questions about democracy along the following lines:

(a)   When he says he has learnt about *democracy* from the *peasants* and the people, *what exactly does he mean*?
(b)   Is he still of the opinion (explicitly and implicitly contained in his recent writings and interviews — e.g. with the WR) that what we have in Kenya is *sham democracy*?
(c)   Does he in particular think that to build a *new Kenya*, one must in effect *destroy all bourgeois institutions first*? And do these institutions include *parliament*, a *'free' press*, *churches*, *judiciaries* and all other bourgeois-democratic institutions upon which the Kenyan system of politics is based?
(d)   Given a choice in how to bring about *change* for the

betterment of the *masses* in Kenya, does he believe *evolutionary* processes are as effective in the Kenya context as 'revolutionary' ones?

Due to the experiences Ngũgĩ has had over the past year, some of the above questions may not be easy for him to answer but it is important to get a clear idea of what his *present thinking is*.

(signed) HBN

I looked at the questions and asked the reporter why her employers were interviewing me by proxy? I refused to be interviewed by proxy. She there and then conducted her own interview. This was in December 1978. But the interview was not published until January 1979. In the meantime, Ngweno's Stellascope Newspapers Ltd went on publishing news stories from the interview week by week, thus giving the impression that I was daily rushing to the press. And when at long last the whole interview was published, it was accompanied by the astonishing accusation that I was the only detainee who had not said thank you to the President for releasing me. An ingrate of an ex-detainee, I was once again guilty of the sin of omission.

I could not understand the source of this post-detention hostility, especially coming from a group of newspapers I had always supported because, despite their pro-imperialist line, I saw them as a hopeful assertion of a national initiative. The other newspapers in Kenya (the Nation Group and the Standard Group) are fully owned and controlled by foreign firms. A few months after the above quoted interview, I felt vindicated when I came across a memo by Hilary Ngweno to his staff dated 19 October 1979, in which he had answered one of his own questions about the freedom of the press in Kenya. He was about to close because of a disagreement between himself and the government:

Memo to all staff   Date: 19 October 1979
From: Hilary

As we all know, we are having problems with the government at the moment. Most parastatal organizations have been instructed not to advertise with us any more. As a result, a lot of advertising has been cancelled.

We have not been told why this is being done and all efforts by me to get an explanation have failed so far. What is more important, I do not know what the intentions of the government actually are, whether to kill our newspapers or simply punish us for something we have published.

What I do know is that we cannot continue operating as we are now without advertising. Advertising is what makes it possible for a newspaper to survive or grow; without money from advertising we cannot make ends meet.

It is true that we can exist for a while without advertising from government or parastatal organizations but only for a while, for in due course private advertisers are also going to stop advertising with us for fear they may themselves get into trouble.

This memo is to let you know that at the moment the future of our operations is not bright at all. All of you have personal and family commitments which must come first in your consideration of your own future. For this reason I would like each one of you to know that I sympathise with you over the uncertainty in which this new turn of events has placed you. As I cannot guarantee that you will have a job in two months' time, I would urge those who feel they can best serve their interests by looking for alternative jobs to do so. . .

How can anyone talk about the freedom of the press when that very press is largely dependent on foreign capital for survival? How can it be free when its very survival and growth is dependent on the goodwill and approval of advertisers? Obviously Ngweno was indirectly admitting the primacy of financiers in restricting basic freedoms.

There was an attempt, a subtle attempt, in many of the post-prison interviews, to make me say that things had changed for the better in Kenya after Kenyatta's death, as if Kenyatta solely and alone was responsible for Kenya's neo-colonial mess! I have never tried to analyse the Kenya situation in terms of the morality of individuals and 'tribes', as is the fashion in current scholarship. Capitalism cannot be run on any basis other than theft and robbery and corruption. The situation is much worse in a dependent capitalism, as is the case in Kenya and elsewhere.

In a neo-colony, foreign capital aided by a corrupt bourgeoisie becomes so arrogant that it even pokes its fingers into the noses of a fledgling national capital and growls: 'Out of my way, fellah! Let me and me alone exploit the labour of your workers.' When some of the nationals complain, the owners of foreign capital, i.e., the imperialist bourgeoisie or their spokesmen, act hurt and uncomprehending: 'What's wrong with some of you? We are creating employment for your people. Without us in New York, London, Bonn, Paris, Rome, Stockholm and Tokyo, where would you people be?' Unfortunately, some Kenyans who can see through the holy pretensions of the imperialist bourgeoisie, are not willing to do anything about it, even when they can see the threat to their own national interests. At the height of the debate over the Kenya National Theatre, during the preparatory years for the Second World African and Black Festival of Arts and Culture (1975,1976,1977) I met a young Kenyan industrialist who told me: 'I see that you people are talking about the domination of Kenyan culture by foreign cultural interests. You people don't know what you are talking about. Come to the industrial area and we can tell you where the real domination is.' He was of course right about the primacy of foreign economic domination in Kenya. He could not of course see that cultural domination is precisely a result and a reflection of economic and political domination, and that we were only stating what we believed to be the objective cultural position of this nation in view of the foreign onslaught, but this is not the point. The point was what he was going to do as a result of his knowledge. I asked him: 'But what are you doing about it? Why don't you raise your economic voices against the situation?' He quickly drove away. Democracy and justice can only be achieved when the various interest groups voice their positions and fight for them. Until democratic-minded Kenyans, workers, peasants, students, progressive intellectuals and others, unite on the most minimum basis of a patriotic opposition to imperialist foreign domination of our economy, politics and culture, things will get worse not better, no matter who sits on the throne of power. No country can consider itself politically independent for as long as its economy and culture are dominated by foreign interests.

2

I have been able, since my release, to gather interesting incidents leading to my incarceration:

I am told, for instance, that some time in December 1977, two gentlemen very highly placed in the government flew to Mombasa and demanded an urgent audience with Jomo Kenyatta. They each held a copy of *Petals of Blood* in one hand, and in the other, a copy of *Ngaahika Ndeenda*. The audience granted, they then proceeded to read him, out of context of course, passages and lines and words allegedly subversive as evidence of highly suspicious intentions. The only way to thwart those intentions — whatever they were — was to detain him who harboured such dangerous intentions, they pleaded. Some others had sought outright and permanent silencing, in the manner of J.M. Kariūki, but on second thoughts this was quashed for 'national stability'. And so to detention I was sent!

Many people speculated as to the reasons for this detention. Some in public, some privately. In the absence of any reasons being given on any charges made officially, this speculation was inevitable. Some of it was based on rumour, and some perhaps on concrete facts or on misleading official leakages.

Such seems to be the case with Hilary Ngweno's papers. Thus after my arrest, *The Weekly Review* of 9 January 1978 carried the following:

> Late Wednesday afternoon, however, word was going round that Ngũgĩ had been detained because of the Chinese and other literature found in his possession at the time of the police search in his study.

This particular speculation was apparently based on invention, rumours or false information from officials. My detention order was signed by the then Vice-President, Mr Daniel T. Arap Moi, on 29 December 1977. I was arrested on the night of 30/31 December 1977. My detention could not therefore have been connected with anything found or not found in my study. The invention, or the rumours or the false information, may have had foundations occasioned by the government's refusal to make public my fate. What's surprising is that *The Weekly Review* saw it fit to repeat the speculation even after my release! Incidentally, all publications and manuscripts found were returned, and no charge on banned books was made, a fact the press knew in 1978.

Another speculation is contained in a paper by Ali Mazrui entitled: *The Detention of Ngũgĩ wa Thiong'o: Report on a Private Visit.*

> Ngũgĩ's acknowledgements of Soviet support in the process of his writing a critique of Kenya's economy may have played a bigger rôle behind his detention than many assumed.

This, more likely, was a deliberate invention. I went to Yalta in the Soviet Union in 1975. I was arrested and detained in 1977. My visit was not secret. Even the Kenya ambassador in Moscow hosted a reception for me. Before and after 1975, many Kenyans visited the same country and stayed much longer than I did and with dissimilar consequences. *Petals of Blood* was started in Evanston, Illinois, U.S.A., the bulk of it was written in Limuru, Kenya, the rest in Yalta. I was in Evanston for a year, and in Yalta, for a month; in Limuru for most of my lifetime.

The link between Ali Mazrui's and Harry Ngweno's literary speculations is the obvious attempt, like colonial Somorhough in *The Trial of Jomo Kenyatta*, to bring in a Chinese or a Russian connection in order to gloss over the issues raised.

In this Hilary Ngweno went further than Ali Mazrui. Mazrui defended my right to write without state harassment. But Ngweno was virtually advancing an ideological justification for my detention, and this on the basis that I had never condemned repression in the Soviet Union or North Korea. Thus the same issue of *The Weekly Review*, after rambling on about my literary career (no indication by tone, word or any gesture that *The Weekly Review* was concerned about the state harassment of writers), came back with a bold ideological offensive:

> Part of Ngũgĩ's problem seems to be that as he has moved farther to the left of the country's political ideological spectrum, he has tended to operate in a world which does not allow for objective appraisal of political realities, not only in Kenya but in other parts of the world. A year ago, shortly after a visit to Japan sponsored by a leftist writers' organization, he published an appeal to the South Korean government to

release from detention one of South Korea's poets and authors (viz., Kim Chi Ha). In the same article, Ngũgĩ went out of his way to castigate the repressive regime of President Park Chung Hee, but as in many of his comments on the international scene, he left the impression that the equally repressive regime in North Korea was far more acceptable than the one in South Korea. Ironically Ngũgĩ's article appeared at the same time as North Korea was undergoing one of its most humiliating diplomatic experiences, with dozens of its diplomats from even neutral countries like Denmark* and Sweden being thrown out for indulging in widespread smuggling of cigarettes and liquor, in an attempt to help the sagging foreign exchange position of the North Korea communist regime.

Ngũgĩ, who has been to the Soviet Union on a number of occasions, has never publicly uttered a word against the treatment of writers in the Soviet Union, who for one reason or other have earned the displeasure of the Kremlin authorities. It is as if the whole dissidence movement in the Soviet Union and other communist countries was to Ngũgĩ, as the Soviet and Communist authorities claim, an intellectual embarrassment or nothing but the figment or machinations of the western 'imperialist' forces.

The aim of such speculative journalism, as in *Newsweek* and *Time* magazines, is to shift the debate from the issue of suppression of democratic rights and of the freedom of expression, to a bold discussion and literary posturing about problems of other countries. *They are worse than we are, therefore we are better! In fact we are the best in Africa, the best in the Third World, an African Switzerland.* Any one who says that the worst of another country does not make the bad of ours better (or best) is a heretic. He is a rebel. He is a leftist. He is a socialist. He is a communist. Chain the devil!

*Denmark is a member of NATO.

3

I was, after detention, the subject of all sorts of accusations.

One accusation is very clear in the same write-up referred to above in *The Weekly Review* of 9 January 1978, and can be summed up in one sentence: 'To be a leftist (whatever that means) is a crime.'

A similar accusation is contained in a letter from Ali Mazrui to Mzee Jomo Kenyatta, dated 16 January 1978, asking for the immediate release of all those in detention. After reminding Kenyatta about the fact that some years before, Mazrui and I had sought permission to do a joint biography of Kenyatta, which was refused, Mazrui continued:

> 'In your wisdom, perhaps that decision was right. For one thing, since 1967 Ngũgĩ was Thiong'o has ideologically become more radicalized. Such normative divergence would probably have made a biographer's relations with his subject more complicated. But I believe Ngũgĩ is still a great patriot in his own way, and loves Kenya by his own light. He and I have probably moved further apart since those old days of our deliberations about your biography more than a decade ago. I am basically a liberal, Ngũgĩ has become more of a leftist radical than ever. But I believe ideological differences have not reduced our respect for each other.

Mazrui's letter should be seen in the context of his emphatic call for freedom of expression, for toleration of different ideological positions, and for the release of political prisoners. Professor Mazrui even joined the London demonstration outside the Kenya High Commission demanding the release of political detainees, and he has consistently raised his voice whenever he gets the chance about my fate and plight during my detention and after.

But Ngweno's accusation was followed by very dangerous suggestions: writers, journalists — instead of struggling to extend the frontiers of intellectual and literary freedom — should exercise self-censorship. Against that call for self-censorship, enters the devil, no, the naive ideologue who knows not the limits of liberal dissent. The same *Weekly Review* article continued:

> During the past year or so, Ngũgĩ has acted the part of

ideologue rather than writer and he has done so with increasing inability to relate in the limits of the sphere of an author's operation which is possible in a developing country in areas where ideas, however noble, can be translated into actions which have far-reaching implications to the general pattern of law and order.

What are the limits of the sphere of an author's operations? *The Weekly Review* talked as if this was a norm known by everybody, except of course ideologues. These were the years that I had written and published *Secret Lives*, *Petals of Blood*, and co-authored *The Trial of Dedan Kīmathi* (with Mīcere Mūgo) and *Ngaahika Ndeenda* (with Ngũgĩ wa Mīriĩ) on top of my administrative and teaching duties at the university. Yet I had acted the part of ideologue rather than the writer! For ideology-free writers, turn to *The Weekly Review*!

But quite a few others were not content with accusations: they started attacking me even though they well knew I was not in a position to answer back. One even wrote what amounted to an obituary and referred to me in the past tense! This was before the regime had announced my whereabouts. The attacks were led by the former attorney-general, Charles Mūgane Njonjo. In a speech in parliament on 'the Training of Lawyers', reported in *The Weekly Review* of 23 June 1978, Njonjo suddenly veered from pronouncements on law to denouncement of the Literature Department, and on those who preferred Kenyan names to English ones:

> Regarding the Department of English (incidentally no such department exists) I would like to ask the Assistant Minister who is here today to ensure that we have teachers who have the right qualifications for this department. Some of the people teaching in this Faculty (incidentally a Faculty consists of several departments) think that if you call yourself Kamau wa Njoroge you are a very important lecturer, or a lecturer with a lot of know-how. You no longer call yourself James Kamau. If you want to be promoted higher, it is better to call yourself, Kamau wa Njoroge. . .

The point was not missed. Even *The Weekly Review* was able to point out that this was an aside obviously 'aimed at the former head of the department, the novelist Ngũgĩ wa Thiong'o who is now in political detention'.

There was, of course, every reason to make Charles Njonjo attack me, even while I was in detention. It is not merely a question of background (he is the son of a colonial chief while I am the son of a peasant) but more of a difference in the perception of our rôles vis-à-vis the struggle of Kenyan national culture against foreign imperialist cultures.

Since 1975, I had constantly criticized the domination of our lives by foreign imperialist interests, and especially at the Kenya Cultural Centre and the Kenya National Theatre. I had in particular singled out the concrete examples of The City Players and The Theatre Group, all foreign, all European. Charles Njonjo was the patron of The City Players.

I have also constantly criticized the British chairmanship of the governing council of the Kenya Cultural Centre and the Kenya National Theatre. Montgomery, of British royal ancestry, was the chairman of the governing council. He works in the attorney-general's chambers. He is also the supervisor of elections, and the secretary of the Council for Legal Education.

I am not sure that having an English Christian name would have deterred me from the task of exposing imperialist cultural domin-ation, or spared me the attacks from those not opposed to im-perialism. Only that, as charity begins at home, I had to start by rejecting the slave tradition of acquiring the master's name.

In fact, the most interesting attack on me did not emanate from Charles Njonjo (at least he is forthright and honest about the side he has taken; such a man deserves 'respect' for his unwavering, single-minded and principled defence of his pro-imperialist position even though you may disagree with him); but from petty-bourgeois intellectuals at the university who hide ethnic chauvinism and their mortal terror of progressive class politics behind masks of abstract super-nationalism, and bury their own inaction behind mugs of beer and empty intellectualism about conditions being not yet ripe for action. But at the same time they are scared of openly attacking peasants and workers. So they talk progressive and act conservative; they wear populist intellectual masks in order the better to attack any concrete cases of worker-peasant anti-imperialist struggles. To them, my detention proved them right in their caution and they could now hide their refusal to defend the democratic rights of free expression by openly attacking me. To attack me was safer in those days, perhaps a little remunerative. They could sit down and advance beautifully balanced arguments — footnotes, weighty phrases and all that — justifying my detention. He was a Gĩkũyũ. He was a leftist. He was a communist. But worse, he was a Gĩkũyũ and he wrote about peasants and workers.

In the paper already referred to, *The Detention of Ngũgĩ wa Thiong'o: Report of a Private Visit*, dated 20 April 1978, Ali Mazrui was able to record the views and position of this group of academics:

A number of Ngũgĩ's colleagues at the University of Nairobi do view Ngũgĩ primarily as a Kikuyu. One or two went further than that, asserting that Ngũgĩ himself is partly a Kikuyu nationalist and only partly a Marxist radical. Part of the evidence is drawn from the heavy Kikuyu-centrism of Ngũgĩ's national life. Secondly, it was suggested to me that Ngũgĩ's recruitment policies as head of department included a partiality for Kikuyu candidates. I have not checked this yet, but it was alleged that half the Department of Literature at the University of Nairobi consisted of Kikuyu, and prospects for an increased percentage of Kikuyu were high. Even if Ngũgĩ was not responsible for the favouritism of fellow Kikuyu, it was argued, he did not put up a fight against it. The fourth factor cited concerning Ngũgĩ's Kikuyu-centrism concerned the colleagues he collaborated with. The work he jointly authored had fellow Kikuyu collaborators, although the themes were supposed to be of national significance. The fifth argument used concerning Ngũgĩ's Kikuyu-centrism was his alleged indifference to the teaching of Swahili literature in the Department of Literature at Nairobi, while at the same time supporting the study of oral ethnic literature in the hope that the Kikuyu contribution under his heading would inevitably be largest. Objectively, Swahili literature both written and oral, in Kenya as well as in Tanzania, is by far the most dynamic branch of East African literature alive today. Secondly, Swahili is in any case the national language of Kenya, and the classical literature of Swahili came disproportionately from Kenya, rather than from Tanzania. And yet, although Ngũgĩ's headship at Nairobi did encourage greater study of the literature of the outside world from the Caribbean to India, on the home front Ngũgĩ had allegedly ignored the Swahili heritage, and was beginning to work hard towards giving greater prominence to the literary heritage of the Kikuyu. His own play in Kikuyu which got him into political trouble might have captured the two parts of Ngũgĩ's ideological position — Kikuyu-centrism on one side and radical universalism on the other. All these were allegations by others.

How does one begin to answer such unprincipled attacks? By pointing out that Swahili literature was taught in the Department of Literature since 1969? But being honourable academics they could easily have checked this in the syllabus. By pointing out I was instrumental along with others in the abolition of the old-style English department and the setting up in its place, *the present Department of Literature and the Department of Linguistics and African Languages*?. But being learned men they could have read the Appendix in my book, *Homecoming*! By pointing out the composition of the staff of the Literature Department nationality by nationality and comparing this with the composition of other departments? But being members of the university they could easily have checked the staff lists in the university's annual reports!

No. These attacks had better be passed over in silence. These petty-bourgeois academics fit into the category of intellectuals once described by Karl Marx as geniuses in the ways of bourgeois stupidity!

Against all that was the overwhelming support of the political detainees from our fourteen-million Kenyans — ordinary people, peasants and workers, students — who thronged the streets when they heard about our release. Of course not all the intellectuals mounted these accusations and attacks. There were some who very courageously fought on the side of democratic forces and tirelessly worked for the release of detainees!

There was also the world-wide struggle for the release of prisoners in Kenya from workers, writers and humanist organizations, progressive intellectuals, democratic minded individuals from Africa, Asia, Europe, Canada, Australia, the U.S.A. and Latin America.

My writing this memoir, and letting all these people in Kenya and abroad share my prison experiences, is my way of expressing my undying gratitude to them ALL for their acts and words of solidarity.

SECTION ONE

PRISON NOTES

But, because I tried to extend your liberties, mine were curtailed. Because I tried to rear the temple of freedom for you all, I was thrown into the cell of a felon's jail. . . Because I tried to give voice to truth, I was condemned to silence. For two years and one week (I was) cast into a prison in solitary confinement on the silent system. . . You may say this is not a public question. But it is! It is a public question, for the man who cannot feel for the wife of the prisoner, will not feel for the wife of the working man. He who will not feel for the children of the captive will not feel for the children of the labour-slave.

A worker's representative as quoted by Karl Marx in his article in the *New York Daily Tribune* of 25 August 1852.

Why are we going to live in fear and for how long?

Warūru Kanja, in a speech in Parliament on Wednesday, 13 November 1980, just before his dismissal from a ministerial appointment.

O you with bloodshot eyes and bloody hands,
Night is short-lived,
The detention room lasts not forever,
Nor yet the links of chains.

Mahmoud Darwish, *The Music of Human Flesh*

CHAPTER ONE

1

Warĩĩnga ngatha ya wĩra. . . Warĩĩnga heroine of toil. . . there she walks haughtily carrying her freedom in her hands. . .

12 December 1978: I am in cell 16 in a detention block enclosing eighteen other political prisoners. Here I have no name. I am just a number in a file: K6,77. A tiny iron frame against one wall serves as a bed and a tiny board against another wall serves as a desk. These fill up the minute cell.

It is past midnight. Unable to face the prickly bristles of three see-through blankets on a mattress whose sisal stuffing has folded into innumerable lumps as hard as stones, I am at the desk, under the full electric glare of a hundred-watt naked bulb, scribbling words on toilet-paper. Along the passageway which separates the two lines of Kenyatta's tiger cages, I can hear the heavy bootsteps of the night warder. He is going on his rounds.

At the one end, the passageway leads into a cul-de-sac of two latrines, a wash-room with only one sink and a shower-room for four. These are all open: no doors. At the other end, next to my cell, the passageway opens into a tiny exercise-yard whose major features are one aluminium rubbish-bin and a falling apart tenniquoit-cum-volleyball net hung on two iron poles. There is a door of iron bars at this opening — between the exercise-yard and the block of cells – and it is always shut and locked at night. The block of 'tiger cages' and the yard are enclosed by four double stone walls so high that they have completely cut off any part of the skyline of trees and buildings which might give us a glimpse of the world of active life.

This is Kamĩtĩ Maximum Security Prison, one of the largest prisons in post-colonial Africa. It is situated near three towns — Rũirũ, Kĩambu and Nairobi — and literally next-door to Kenyatta University College but we could as easily have been on the moon or on Mars. We have been completely quarantined from everything and everybody except for a highly drilled select squad of prison guards and their commanding officers.

Maximum security: the idea used to fill me with terror whenever I met it in fiction, Dickens mostly, and I have always associated it with England and Englishmen and with Robben Island in South Africa: it conjured up images of hoards of dangerous killers always ready to escape through thick forests and marshes, to unleash yet more havoc and terror on an otherwise stable, peaceful and godfearing community of property-owners that sees itself as the whole society. A year as an inmate in Kamĩtĩ has taught me what should have been obvious: that the prison system is a repressive weapon in the hands of a ruling minority determined to ensure maximum security for its class dictatorship over the rest of the population, and it is not a monopoly exclusive to South Africa and England.

The menacing bootsteps come nearer. But I know that the prowling warder cannot enter my cell — it is always double-locked and the keys in turn locked inside a box which at five o'clock is promptly taken away by the corporal on duty to a safe somewhere outside the double walls — but of course he can look into the cell through an iron-barred rectangular slit in the upper half of the door. The slit is built so as to only contain the face.

The bootsteps stop. I take my time in turning to the door although I can feel in my bones that the warder is watching me. It is an instinct that one develops in prison, the cunning instinct of the hunted. The face of the warder fills the whole slit: I know nothing so menacingly sinister in its silent stillness as that trunkless face glaring at you through the iron bars of a prison cell.

'Professor. . . why are you not in bed?' the voice redeems the face. 'What are you doing?'

Relief! I fall back on the current witticism in the detention block.

'I am writing to Jomo Kenyatta in his capacity as an ex-detainee.'

'His case was different,' the warder argues back.

'How?'

'His was a colonial affair.'

'And this, a neo-colonial affair? What's the difference?'

'A colonial affair. . . now we are independent. . . that's the difference. . .' he says.

'A colonial affair in an independent country, eh? The British jailed an innocent Kenyatta. Thus Kenyatta learnt to jail innocent Kenyans. Is that the difference?'

He laughs. Then he repeats it. 'The British jailed Kenyatta Kenyatta jails Kenyans.' He laughs again, adding:

'Take it any way you like. . . but write a good petition. . . you might get a hearing this time. . . Your star shines bright in the sky. . . ex-detainee. . .' he chuckles to himself. 'Does "ex-" mean the same thing as "late" — *hayati*?'

'What do you mean?'

'Can I say the late detainee instead of the ex-detainee?'

The tone tells me that he knows the difference and that he is trying to communicate something. But tonight I feel a little impatient.

'You know I no longer teach English,' I say to him.

'You never can tell the language of the stars,' he persists. 'Once a teacher, always a teacher,' he says, and goes away laughing.

In his prison notes, *The Man Died*, Wole Soyinka aptly comments that 'no matter how cunning a prisoner, the humanitarian act of courage among his gaolers plays a key rôle in his survival.' This warder is a good illustration of the truth of that observation. He is the one who in March told me about the formation of the London-based *Ngũgĩ Defence Committee* and the subsequent picketing of the Kenya Embassy on 3 March 1978. He enjoys talking in riddles and communicating in roundabouts. It's a way of protecting himself, of course, but he enjoys seeing a prisoner grope for the hidden meanings.

Tonight, his laughter sounds more direct and sympathetic, or perhaps it is another kind of riddle to be taken any way I like.

Two warders guard the passageway in turns. One sleeps, the other guards. At one o'clock they change places. They too cannot get out because the door between the passageway and the exercise-yard is locked and the keys taken away. Night warders are themselves prisoners guarding other prisoners. Only they are paid for it and their captivity is self-inflicted or else imposed by lack of alternative means of life. One very young warder — a Standard Seven drop-out — tells me that his ambition is to be a fighter pilot! Another, a grandfather, tells me his ambition once was to become a musician.

To hell with the warders! Away with intruding thoughts! Tonight I don't want to think about warders and prisoners, colonial or neo-colonial affairs. I am totally engrossed in Warĩĩnga, the fictional heroine of the novel I have been writing on toilet-paper for the last ten months or so!*

Toilet-paper: when in the sixties I first read in Kwame Nkrumah's autobiography, *Ghana*, how he used to hoard toilet-paper in his cell at James Fort Prison to write on, I thought it was romantic and a little

---

*The novel has now appeared in Gĩkũyũ as *Caitaani Mũtharaba-inĩ* (Heinemann, Nairobi, 1980) and the English translation will appear in 1981 under the title *Devil on the Cross*.

unreal despite the photographic evidence reproduced in the book.
Writing on toilet-paper?

Now, I know: paper, any paper, is about the most precious article
for a political prisoner, more so for one like me, who was in political
detention because of his writing. For the urge to write:

> Picking the jagged bits embedded in my mind,
> Partly to wrench some ease for my own mind,
> And partly that some world sometime may know

is almost irresistible to a political prisoner. At Kamĩtĩ, virtually all
the detainees are writers or composers. Wasonga Sijeyo has
volumes of notes on his life, Kenyan history, botany, zoology,
astronomy and Luo culture. Koigi wa Wamwere has many essays on
politics and culture, several political fables, a short novel, an
autobiography, and a long poem on his prison experience. Gĩcerũ wa
Njaũ has a novel in Kiswahili. Thairũ wa Mũthĩga has a few poems.
Simba Ongongi Were composes heart-rending songs; while Mahat
Kuno Roble, though illiterate, is a highly accomplished poet. And
from Shimo-la-Tewa Prison, I have received two huge manuscripts
of two novels by Mwangi wa Mahiinda. These prisoners have mostly
written on toilet-paper. Now the same good old toilet-paper — which
had been useful to Kwame Nkrumah in James Fort Prison, to
Dennis Brutus on Robben Island, to Abdilatif Abdalla in G Block,
Kamĩtĩ, and to countless other persons with similar urges — has
enabled me to defy daily the intended detention of my mind.

> A flicker, pulse, mere vital hint
> which speaks of the stubborn will
> the grim assertion of some sense of worth
> in the teeth of the wind
> on a stony beach, or among rocks
> where the brute hammers fall unceasingly
> on the mind.

I now know what Dennis Brutus meant. Writing this novel has been a
daily, almost hourly, assertion of my will to remain human and
free despite the Kenya African National Union (KANU) official
government programme of animal degradation of political prisoners.

Privacy, for instance. I mean its brutal invasion. Thus, I was daily
trailed by a warder for twenty-four hours, in waking and sleeping. It

was unnerving, truly unnerving, to find a warder watching me shit and urinate into a children's chamberpot in my cell, or to find him standing by the entrance to the toilet to watch me do the same exercise. The electric light is on the night long. To induce sleep, I had to tie a towel over my eyes. This ended in straining them so that after a month they started smarting and watering. But even more painful was to suddenly wake up in the middle of the night, from a dreamless slumber or one softened by sweet illusion or riddled with nightmares, to find two bodiless eyes fixed on me through the iron bars.

Or monotony: the human mind revolts against endless sameness. In ordinary social life, even the closest-knit family hardly ever spends a whole day together in meaningless circles on their compound. Man, woman and child go about their different activities in different places and they only meet in the evening to recount their different experiences. Experiments done on animals show that when they are confined to a small space and subjected to the same routine they end up tearing each other. Now the KANU government was doing the same experiment on human beings.

At Kamītī, we daily saw the same faces in the same white kūūngūrū prison uniforms; we daily fed on unga and beans in the morning, at noon and at three o'clock; we daily went through the same motions, and this, in a confined space of reliefless dust and grey stones. The two most dominant colours in the detention block were white and grey and I am convinced these are the colours of death.

The government could not have been ignorant about the possible results of these experiments in mental torment: valium was the most frequently prescribed drug in Kamītī Prison. The doctor expected a detainee to be mad or depressed unless proved otherwise.

There was a history to it. I was told a harrowing story about one detainee before my time who had a mental breakdown in that very block. The authorities watched him going down the drain until he was reduced to eating his own faeces. Yet the regime kept him in that condition for two years. This is normal practice in regimes with no popular roots in the masses, and Kenyatta's KANU government was one: but this did not make the horror easier to contemplate.

A week after my incarceration, Wasonga Sijeyo, who had been in that block for nine years but had managed to keep a razor-sharp mind and a heart of steel, eluded the vigilant eyes of the warders then guarding me and within seconds he told me words that I came to treasure:

'It may sound a strange thing to say to you, but in a sense I am glad they brought you here. The other day — in fact a week or so before you came — we were saying that it would be a good thing for Kenya if more intellectuals were imprisoned. First, it would wake most of them from their illusions. And some of them might outlive jail to tell the world. The thing is . . . just watch your mind . . . don't let them break you and you'll be all right even if they keep you for life . . . but you must try . . . you have to, for us, for the ones you left behind.'

Thus in addition to it being an insurrection of a detained intellect, writing this novel has been one way of keeping my mind and heart together like Sijeyo.

Free thoughts on toilet-paper! I had deliberately given myself a difficult task. I had resolved to use a language which did not have a modern novel, a challenge to myself, and a way of affirming my faith in the possibilities of the languages of all the different Kenyan nationalities, languages whose development as vehicles for the Kenyan people's anti-imperialist struggles had been actively suppressed by the British colonial regime (1895-1963) and by the neo-colonial regime of Kenyatta and his comprador KANU cohorts. I had also resolved not to make any concessions to the language. I would not avoid any subject — science, technology, philosophy, religion, music, political economy — provided it logically arose out of the development of theme, character, plot, story, and world view. Further I would use any and everything I had ever learnt about the craft of fiction — allegory, parable, satire, narrative, description, reminiscence, flash-back, interior monologue, stream of consciousness, dialogue, drama — provided it came naturally in the development of character, theme and story. But content — not language and technique — would determine the eventual form of the novel. And the content? The Kenyan people's struggles against the neo-colonial form and stage of imperialism!

Easier said than done: where was I to get the inspiration? A writer needs people around him. He needs live struggles of active life. Contrary to popular mythology, a novel is not a product of the imaginative feats of a single individual but the work of many hands and tongues. A writer just takes down notes dictated to him by life among the people, which he then arranges in this or that form. For me, in writing a novel, I love to hear the voices of the people working on the land, forging metal in a factory, telling anecdotes in crowded matatus and buses, gyrating their hips in a crowded bar before a jukebox or a live band, people playing games of love and hate and fear and glory in their struggle to live. I need to look at different people's faces, their gestures, their gait, their clothes, and to hear the variegated modulations of their voices in different moods. I need the vibrant voices of beautiful women: their touch, their sighs, their tears, their laughter. I like the presence of children prancing about, fighting, laughing, crying. I need life to write about life.

But it is also true that nobody writes under circumstances chosen by him and on material invented by him. He can only seize the time to select from material handed to him by whomever and whatever is around him. So my case now: I had not chosen prison, I was forced into it, but now that I was there, I would try and turn the double-walled enclosure into a special school where, like Shakespeare's Richard II, I would study how I might compare:

> This prison where I live unto the world . . .
> My brain I'll prove the female to my soul,
> My soul the father; and these two beget
> A generation of still-breeding thoughts,
> And these same thoughts people this little world,
> In humours like the people of this world,
> For no thought is contented.

In this literary target I was lucky to have for teachers, detainees and a few warders, who were very co-operative and generous in sharing their different mines of information and experience. For instance, Thairū wa Mūthīga, Gīcerū wa Njaū and Koigi wa Wamwere taught me a lot of Gīkūyū vocabulary, proverbs, riddles and songs; Wasonga Sijeyo was an expert on the nationalist anti-imperialist struggles before 1963 and on the beginnings of land grabbing and foreigners' bribery of former nationalists with token shares in their companies; Gīkonyo wa Rūkūūngū gave me books on rituals of Catholic worship; Simba Ongongi Were taught me some Zairean tunes and words; Mūhoro wa Mūthoga, Koigi wa Wamwere and Adamu Matheenge gave me topographical details of Nakuru; while Gīcerū wa Njaū, Thairū wa Mūthīga and I often discussed women of different careers, especially barmaids, secretaries and engineers, as well as different aspects of social life and bourgeois rivalry in Nairobi. I learnt a lot about business acumen and the whole practice and culture of accumulation from stories and real-life anecdotes narrated to us by the only millionaire in detention, Mahat Kuno Roble.

Not only from conscious discussions and direct inquiries: whis-

pered news of happenings outside the walls would often provide
me with material that I would later weave into the fabric of the
novel. For instance, the main theme and story line emerged when I
learnt that two members of parliament were serving sentences after
being convicted of coffee theft. The shocking news of Professor
Barnard's visit and the generous provision by his Kenya hosts of
public platforms to air his racist pro-apartheid views prompted the
philosophical discussion in a matatu about 'life to come' and the
problems of rival claims to the same heart on the day of resurrection;
it also prompted the satirical depiction of a vision of one robber
character, for a world in which a rich few would ensure their
immortality through the purchase of spare organs of the human body,
thus leaving death as the sole prerogative of the poor.

In the daytime, I would take hasty notes on empty spaces of any
book I might be reading, I would scribble notes on the bare walls of
my cell, then in the evening I would try to put it all together on toilet-
paper.

Sometimes I would be seized with the usual literary boredom and
despair — those painful moments when a writer begins to doubt the
value of what he is scribbling or the possibility of ever completing the
task in hand — those moments when a writer restrains himself with
difficulty from setting the whole thing on fire, or tearing it all into
pieces, or abandoning the whole project to dust and cobwebs. These
moments are worse in prison because there are no distractions to
massage the tired imagination: a glass of beer, a sound of music, or a
long walk in sun and wind or in a starry night.

But at those very moments, I would remind myself that the
KANU-led comprador ruling class had sent me here so that my brain
would turn into a mess of rot. The defiance of this bestial purpose
always charged me with new energy and determination: I would
cheat them out of that last laugh by letting my imagination loose over
the kind of society this class, in nakedly treacherous alliance with
imperialist foreigners, were building in Kenya in total cynical
disregard of the wishes of over fourteen-million Kenyans.

Because the women are the most exploited and oppressed section
of the entire working class, I would create a picture of a strong
determined woman with a will to resist and to struggle against the
conditions of her present being. Had I not seen glimpses of this type
in real life among the women of Kamīrīīthū Community Education
and Cultural Centre? Isn't Kenyan history replete with this type of
woman? Me Kitilili, Muraa wa Ngiti, Mary Mūthoni Nyanjirū? Mau

Mau women cadres? Warĩĩnga will be the fictional reflection of this resistance heroine of Kenyan history. Warĩĩnga heroine of toil . . . there she walks . . .

I am now on the last chapter. I have given myself 25 December as the deadline. 25 December 1978 has a special significance to me. In February or March I had told the other detainees that we would all 'eat' Christmas at home. I had even invited them to a Christmas goat-meat roasting party at my home in Gĩtogoothi, Bibirioni, Limuru. It was said half-in-joke, like so many other prison wagers related to dreams of eventual liberty, but I secretly believed it and inwardly clung to the date though becoming less and less openly assertive about it as days and nights rolled away. Now only twelve days are left. Twelve days to eat Christmas at home. Twelve days to meet my self-imposed literary deadline!

But tonight something else, an impulse, a voice, is urging me to run this last lap faster. The voice is not all that secret. Maybe it is born of the feverish expectation of early release which has been building up in the block for the last four months, though nobody is now sure of its 'ifs' and 'whens'. Maybe it is also born of a writer's usual excitement at seeing the light at the end of a long hazardous tunnel. Or maybe it is a combination of both. But whatever its source, the voice remains insistent.

The heart is willing. The hand which has been scribbling non-stop since about seven o'clock is weak. But the voice is relentless: Write On!

I rise to stretch my legs. I walk to the iron-barred rectangular slit and peer into the passageway. Neither of the two warders is asleep. They are playing draughts, but they are murmuring more than they are playing. I ask the same warder about the time.

'Half-past twelve,' he says, and then adds: 'Why do you want to know the time, Professor?'

'I wanted to know if my star is still shining in the sky,' I answer back.

'You better have some sleep. You might need it.'

No. I don't feel like any sleep tonight. I go back to the desk to resume the race to the literary tape only a couple of paragraphs away.

2

In front of me is a photograph of my daughter Njooki, meaning she who comes back from the dead; or Aiyerubo, meaning she who defies heaven and hell; or Wamũingĩ, meaning she who belongs to the people. Later when I am out of Kamĩtĩ, I will see her and hold her in my arms and learn that she was named Wamũingĩ by the peasant women of Limuru, and Aiyerubo by the Writers of African Peoples in Nigeria, but just now she is only a name and a photograph sent through the post.

She was born on 15 May 1978, five months after my abduction and subsequent incarceration. When her photograph arrived in Kamĩtĩ some time after that defiant break from the chains of heaven or hell, one detainee, Thairũ wa Mũthĩga, had nicknamed her *Kaana ka Boothita*, a post-office baby.

Thairũ spoke a truth. Deep inside me I know that Njooki was a message from the world. A message of hope. A message that somewhere outside these grey walls of death were people waiting for me, thinking about me, perhaps even fighting, with whatever weapons, for my release. A protest, a hastily muttered prayer from the lips of a peasant, a groan, a sigh, wishes of helpless children: such gestures and wishes may today not be horses on which seekers of freedom may ride to liberty, but they do reflect a much needed moral solidarity with a political prisoner, or with the issues for wich he has been jailed. One day these very wishes will be transformed by the organized power and united will of millions from the realm of morality into people's chariots of actual freedom from naked exploitation and ruthless oppression. But just now the mere expression of solidarity and my knowledge of it through Njooki's photograph is a daily source of joyful strength.

In a neo-colonial country, the act of detaining patriotic democrats, progressive intellectuals and militant workers speaks of many things. It is first an admission by the detaining authorities that their official lies labelled as a new philosophy, their pretensions often hidden in three-piece suits and golden chains, their propaganda packaged as religious truth, their plastic smiles ordered from abroad, their nationally televised charitable handouts and breast-beating before the high altar, their high-sounding phrases and ready-to-shed tears at the sight of naked children fighting it out with cats and dogs for the possession of a rubbish heap, that these and more godfatherly acts of benign benevolence have been seen by the people for what they truly are: a calculated sugar-coating of an immoral sale and mortgage of a whole country and its people to Euro-American and Japanese capital for a few million dollars in Swiss banks and a few token shares in foreign companies. Their mostly vaunted morality has been exposed for what it is: the raising of beggary and charity into moral idealism. There is a new-found dignity in begging, and charity for them is twice-blessed; it deflates the recipient and inflates the giver. Nyerere once rightly compared those African regimes who dote on their neo-colonial status to a prostitute who walks with proud display of the fur coat given to her by her moneyed lover. Actually the situation of a comprador neo-colonial ruling class is more appropriately comparable to that of a pimp who would proudly hold down his mother to be brutally raped by foreigners, and then shout in glee: look at the shining handful of dollars I have received for my efficiency and integrity, in carrying out my part of the bargain!

But recourse to detention is above all an admission by the neo-colonial ruling minority that people have started to organize to oppose them, to oppose the continued plunder of the national wealth and heritage by this shameless alliance of a few nationals and their foreign paymasters.

Thus detention more immediately means the physical removal of patriots from the people's organized struggles. Ideally, the authorities would like to put the whole community of struggling millions behind barbed-wire, as the British colonial authorities once tried to do with Kenyan people. But this would mean incarcerating labour, the true source of national wealth: what would then be left to loot? So the authorities do the simpler thing: pick one or two individuals from among the people and then loudly claim that all sins lie at the feet of these few 'power hungry' 'misguided' and 'ambitious' agitators. Note that any awakening of a people to their historic mission of liberating themselves from external and internal exploitation and repression is always seen in terms of 'sin' and it is often denounced with the religious rhetoric of a wronged, self-righteous god. These agitators suddenly become devils whose removal from society is now portrayed as a divine mission. The people are otherwise innocent, simple, peace-loving, obedient, law-abiding, and cannot conceivably harbour any desire to change this best of all possible worlds. It is partly self-deception, but also an attempted deception of millions. Chain the devils!

But political detention, not disregarding its punitive aspects, serves a deeper, exemplary ritual symbolism. If they can break such a patriot, if they can make him come out of detention crying 'I am sorry for all my sins', such an unprincipled about-turn would confirm the wisdom of the ruling clique in its division of the populace into the passive innocent millions and the disgruntled subversive few. The 'confession' and its corollary, 'Father, forgive us for our sins', becomes a cleansing ritual for all the past and current repressive deeds of such a neo-colonial regime. With a few titbits, directorship of this or that statutory body, the privilege of standing for parliament on the regime's party ticket, such an ex-detainee might even happily play the rôle of a conscientious messenger from purgatory sent back to earth by a father figure more benevolent than Lazarus' Abraham, 'that he may testify unto them (them that dare to struggle), lest they also come into this place of torment'. The forgiving father sits back to enjoy international applause for his manifold munificence and compassionate heart. But even when they find that such a detainee is not in a position to play the rôle of an active preacher against the futility of struggle (they may have damaged him beyond any exploitable repair), they can still publicize this picture of a human wreck or vegetable as a warning to all future agitators: he could not stand it, do you think you are made of sterner steel? The former hard-core patriot is physically or intellectually or spiritually broken and by a weird symbolic extension, the whole struggling populace is broken. All is now well in imperialist heaven for there is peace on neo-colonial earth, policed by a tough no-nonsense comprador ruling class that knows how to deal with subversive elements.

The fact is that detention without trial is not only a punitive act of physical and mental torture of a few patriotic individuals, but it is also a calculated act of psychological terror against the struggling millions. It is a terrorist programme for the psychological siege of the whole nation. That is why the practice of detention from the time of arrest to the time of release is deliberately invested with mystifying ritualism. My arrest, for instance.

This could have been effected by a single unarmed policeman or even by a simple summons to Tigoni Police Station. I had nothing to hide. I had done nothing to which I would plead guilty in my patriotic conscience or in a democratic court of law. Indeed I had done nothing that I could not publicly and proudly own up to before the nation and the world. But the police who must have followed me over the years and who must therefore have noted and recorded my mostly solitary, non-violent deeds and habits, nevertheless chose to steal into my house at night with an incredible show of armed might.

It was at midnight on 30-31 December 1977 at Gītogoothi, Bibirioni, Limuru. Two Land-Rovers with policemen armed with machine-guns, rifles and pistols drove into the yard. A police saloon car remained at the main gate flashing red and blue on its roof, very much like the Biblical sword of fire policing the ejection of Adam and Eve from the legendary Garden of Eden by a God who did not want human beings to eat from trees of knowledge, for the stability of Eden and his dictatorship over it depended on people remaining ignorant about their condition. Behind the saloon car were others which, as I later came to learn, carried some local administrative officials and the local corps of informers. These latter remained lurking in the shadows for fear that, even at such a dark hour, the peasants around might recognize them and denounce them to the people.

Armed members of the special branch who swarmed and searched my study amidst an awe-inspiring silence were additionally guarded by uniformed policemen carrying long range rifles. Their grim determined faces would only light up a little whenever they pounced on any book or pamphlet bearing the names of Marx, Engels or Lenin. I tried to lift the weight of silence in the room by remarking that if Lenin, Marx or Engels were all they were after, I could save them much time and energy by showing them the shelves where these dangerous three were hiding. The leader of the book-raiding squad was not amused. He growled at me, and I quickly and promptly took his 'advice' to keep quiet and let them do their work. But I kept on darting my eyes from one raider to the other in case they did something illegal. I soon realized the futility of my vigilance since I was alone and they were all over the study. They could very easily have put banned books or pamphlets if they had wanted to, like the description in a poem entitled 'It's No Use', by Victor Jacinto Flecha. (The translation, by Nick Caistor, appeared in *Index on Censorship*, VIII, 1, London, January/February 1979.)

It's no use
Your hiding deep in the dark well of your house
Hiding your words
Burning your books
It's no use.

They'll come to find you
In lorries, piled high with leaflets,
With letters no one ever wrote to you
They'll fill your passport with stamps
From countries where you have never been

They'll drag you away
Like some dead dog
And that night you'll find out all about torture
In the dark room
Where all the foul odours of the world are bred
It's no use
Your hiding
From the fight, my friend.

Nevertheless, I kept on looking from one to the other and I saw them ferreting among the books by Lenin, Marx and Engels without any more verbal interruptions from me. To the list of the Dangerous Three, they now added Kim Chi Ha, and any book that bore the words 'scientific socialism', plus about twenty-six copies of the offending play, *Ngaahika Ndeenda*. But even then, I could not help musing over the fact that the police squadron was armed to the teeth with guns to abduct a writer whose only acts of violent resistance were safely between the hard and soft covers of literary imaginative reflections.

Abduction. The word needs an explanation. The police took me away under false pretences. The conversation in the sitting-room went something like this:

NGŨGĨ: Gentlemen, can I request that we sit down and record all the books and pamphlets you have taken?

POLICE: We shall do all that at the police station.

NGŨGĨ: Tell me quite frankly: am I under arrest?

POLICE: Oh, no.

NGŨGĨ: In that case, I'll provide you with a table, pen and paper and we can record everything before it leaves the house.

POLICE: We shall do it at the station and you are coming with us.

NGŨGĨ: What for?

POLICE: To answer a few questions.

NGŨGĨ: Am I under arrest?

POLICE: No.

NGŨGĨ: In that case, can't the questions wait until morning?

POLICE: No.

NGŨGĨ: Can you please give me a minute with my wife to sort out one thing or two?

POLICE: It is not necessary. We promise that you'll be back in the morning. Just a few questions.

NGŨGĨ: Can you tell me where you are taking me so that my wife here can know?

POLICE: Kĩambu!

At Kĩambu police station I was pushed into an empty room with bare walls where I was guarded by only one member of the abducting team. Now he smiled rather slyly and he asked me: 'How come that as soon as we knocked at the door, you were already up and fully dressed?'

I had neither the time nor the necessary energy to tell him that I had had a premonition; that I had just returned home from Nairobi after saying a rather elaborate farewell to my lawyer friend, Ndeere wa Njũgi — a strange thing this farewell since he was only going to Langata and I to Limuru; and also, after firmly and repeatedly refusing a beer from another friend, Solomon Kagwe — again a strange thing because he worked in Morocco and I had not seen him for many years; that I had driven from Impala Hotel, Nairobi, to Limuru at a snail's pace, literally not more than fifty kilometres an hour the whole way; that on arrival home, instead of putting on my pyjamas and slipping into bed, I just lay on the cover fully clad, staring at the ceiling and turning over the recent events since the public performances of *Ngaahika Ndeenda* had been banned; that when I heard the knocking at the door and I put on my shoes and went to the window and saw uniformed policemen, I felt as if I had been expecting the scene all along! This I could not tell him, even had I the necessary energy or desire, because a few seconds after his query, a tall slim man came in and standing, staring straight ahead, almost past me, he made the formal announcement: 'I am Superintendent Mbũrũ attached to Kĩambu Police Station and I am under instructions to arrest you and place you in detention. Have you anything to say?' The whole exercise, executed in an emotionless tone, had a slightly comic side: so between Limuru and Kĩambu I was not under police arrest? 'Do your duty!' was all I said.

It was only during the journey to Kilimani Police Station, Nairobi, in a yellow Volvo driven by Superintendent Mbũrũ himself, that I experienced respite from the show of armed terror! Mbũrũ even managed to start a conversation:

'Did your family originally come from the Rift Valley?' he asked.

'No!' I said.

'I have had that impression from reading your books.'

'I only write about it,' I said.

If one had overheard that conversation, one would have assumed that Mbũrũ was only giving me a lift to Nairobi instead of taking me to an unknown destination.

Temporary respite: Mbũrũ did not harass me; he at least had executed his duty decently.

The following morning — it was now Saturday, and the last day of 1977 — soon after being served with detention orders by Mr Mũhĩndĩ whom I later came to learn was an assistant commissioner of police in charge of Nairobi area and also the detainees' security officer, I was suddenly grabbed by some police and roughly put in chains. I was then pushed from behind into the back seat of a blue car with blinds between two hefty policemen armed with a machine-gun and a rifle while a third one, equally well equipped, sat in the front seat beside the driver. I was driven through the heavy traffic in Nairobi streets — Haile Selassie, Ronald Ngala, Race Course, Thika Road, Kamĩtĩ Road — to the gates of the infamous Kamĩtĩ Maximum Security Prison.

The driver almost smashed his way through the heavy closed outer doors of the giant prison. But realizing his mistake, he quickly backed into a small bush, under a tree, car-blinds still drawn, so that none of the people walking about could see who or what was inside the black maria.

It was then that I witnessed something which I had last seen in colonial Kenya during the barbaric British imposed State of Emergency when similar terror tactics were a daily occurrence. The whole area around Kamĩtĩ was immediately put under curfew — and this in the noon of day. I saw innocent men, women and children dive for cover pursued by baton waving warders and within seconds there was not a single civilian standing or walking in the vicinity of Kamĩtĩ Prison. The poor folk had unknowingly made the mistake of peacefully going about their daily chores during the ceremony of detention and no doubt had paid for the pleasure with a few bruises here and there.

The huge prison gates, like the jaws of a ravenous monster, now slowly swung open to swallow me within its walls, which still dripped with the blood of the many Kenyan patriots who had been hanged there for their courageous Mau Mau guerrilla struggle against British imperialism. These had for ever lost their names. They had died as mere numbers on prison files. Up to now, still belonging to nameless numbers, their bones, including Kīmaathi's, lie in that foul place, unwept and unremembered by ungrateful inheritors of the power they paid for with their lives.

Ironies of history: now my turn had come. From Saturday 31 December 1977 I had died to my name of Ngũgĩ. Henceforth I would only answer to a lifeless number on a file among many files. I was later to learn that for a whole two weeks after my abduction, my family and virtually the whole nation were kept in ignorance of my fate. Every police and every government official would plead equal ignorance until my detention was announced in the *Kenya Gazette* of 6 January 1978 (though this issue was held, and not released until 14 January).

Even then my place of detention, as in the case of all other detainees, remained a top secret known only to an initiated few. The KANU government would in fact go to ridiculous lengths to mystify people about our whereabouts: like convening the Detainees' Review Tribunal in Mombasa and flying the detainees there. Yet virtually all the members of the tribunal came from Nairobi, only ten minutes' drive from Kamītī. Or the whole mystery surrounding a detainee's meeting with his family at Embakasi Airport, giving the impression of a flight from afar. And whenever a detainee went out and came in, a curfew was clamped on the whole prison. Why all the mystery, the suspense, the secrecy? Did they really fear that people would storm Kamītī Prison to free detainees by force?

Of course not: the ruling clique in Kenya has the monopoly of all the instruments of anti-people coercive violence, and this they know. But they also know that no force on earth — not even nuclear weapons — can finally put down the organized power of an awakened people. Hence the imperative to bring up people in a culture of silence and fear to make them feel weak before the state. This state assumes the malevolent character of a terrifying super-natural force that can only be placated by supplications of a people on their knees or be appeased by unavengeable gifts of human flesh such as a Pinto or a JM.

The rituals of mystery and secrecy are calculated exercises in psychological terror aimed at the whole people — part of the culture of fear — and at the individual detainee — part of the strategy of eventually breaking him. The first is harder to see, for it can only be understood by delving into history, our history, to trace the roots of current ruling-class culture. That will come later. It is to understand it that I am writing this account. But the latter is easier to see, for it is part of the daily trials of a political prisoner.

The rituals, seemingly petty and childish but rigorously followed to the letter by bemedalled officers and decorated warders, serve to make a detainee feel that he has been completely cut off from the people and hence from that group solidarity — the sense of being one with the people — which alone keeps men and women going even when menaced by truncheons, nailed boots, tear-gas and deathly whistling bullets. He must be made, not just to know, but to actually feel that with the links cut, he is now adrift in an ocean of endless fear and humiliation. He is not introduced into the ocean gradually. He is thrown into it to swim and stay afloat in any way he knows how, or else to plunge into the depths and drown.

During the first month of my prison life, I was daily locked in cell 16 for twenty-two hours. The remaining two hours were distributed to cover the daily chores of emptying the chamberpot topful with shit and urine; of gulping down the breakfast, lunch and supper of porridge, ugali, worm-infested beans and rotten vegetables; and of sunshine and exercise. The other detainees had lived under these conditions for the previous two years; precisely, from September 1975. Everyday I would ask myself: how have they managed to stay afloat?

For the first three weeks of the same month I was also under internal segregation. This simply meant that no detainee was allowed near me. During meals, I would be made to sit apart from the others, often with a warder between us. During my ration of sunshine, I had to sit in my corner often with a watchful warder to ensure that there was no talking contact between me and any of the others.

But since we were all in the same block, it was not easy for the warders to enforce total segregation. The other detainees would break through the cordon by shouting across to me; or by finding any and every excuse for going past where I was sitting and hurriedly throwing in one or two words; or by stopping outside my cell — the other detainees were let out for sunshine in groups of twos or threes, though there were three detainees permanently out under doctor's orders — and through the iron-bar opening they would assure me of their human solidarity. This was always very touching coming from people who were in no better conditions. Sometimes two detainees would stand just far enough away not to be accused of being with me, but near enough for me to hear everything. They would talk to one another about various aspects of prison life, sometimes offering one another advise or hints on how to cope with prison life, but I knew that this was meant for me. And at night, or when inside our cells in the day, there was of course no way of preventing the other detainees from shouting messages and anecdotes through the walls, and I shouting back news of what had been happening in the world up to the time of my arrest.

Despite the efforts of my fellow detainees to break the walls of segregation, the feeling of being alone would often steal into me and I would be seized with the momentary panic of a man drowning in a sea of inexplicable terror. I often felt like those lepers in medieval Europe who had to carry small bells around their necks to announce their leprous presence to the healthy, or those *osu* untouchables in Achebe's novels who had to jump into the bush to let a freeborn pass. In my case I was being denied the social fellowship of even the other political untouchables.

Months later, when I told the other detainees about my feelings during those weeks of January, they laughed and assured me how lucky I was to have had them around me, that the sense of isolation is thousand times more intense for those in solitary confinement.

Mūhoro wa Mūthoga, popularly known as Fujika, told me that his own initiation into prison life at Kamītī was through a six-month solitary confinement in a ghostly cell in what was known as the Isolation Block. Every effort was exerted to make him live and feel the reality behind that name. His only contact was with the warders who brought him food, let him out for an hour of sunshine and exercise, and who guarded the empty silent corridors. One warder always walked on tiptoe. Another would open the cell door, push food inside, and then jump back quickly, shutting the door as if the inmate was a dangerous animal in a cage. Yet another warder, the most liberal, would speak to him words through clenched teeth as if they were being painfully pulled out of his tongue at some cost, and even then the words would come out as whispers. Otherwise the others communicated with him only in gestures. He started doubting himself: could he possibly, unknowingly, have done something more terrible than just asking for application forms from the attorney-general to legally register a new democratic political party? Could he have misread the Kenya constitution, which on paper at least, allowed multi-party formations? The application forms had been sent to him all right. He had sent back the forms plus the constitution of the intended party. In answer, he was arrested and sent to Kamĩtĩ Maximum Security Prison. Maybe *intentions* to form new political parties to represent classes other than the comprador bourgeoisie to whom KANU now belonged had been banned and he had failed to read the relevant gazette!

The detainee told me that he always felt as if he was under a death sentence and he was only awaiting its execution. Gradually he grew into the habit of also speaking in whispers or gesturing whenever he wanted to ask for something. On a few occasions he caught himself walking on tiptoe. When he was finally let out of the six months' ordeal and met the others in the main detention block, he was really scared of them as if they were beings from another world. He started speaking to them in whispers!

I was never myself subjected to this form of torture. I was lucky that my own initiation into prison life took the more mild form of internal segregation. Nevertheless, the constant reminder of my social apartness, this cruel human isolation in the midst of fellow humans, a case really of water everywhere and not a drop to drink, began to tell on me. I became edgy. Voices of warders, even when friendly, would grate on my nerves unpleasantly, and I would suddenly be seized with murderous thoughts. Fortunately for me these thoughts found no physical expression. But they soon had an outlet in words!

3

The first verbal 'victim' was the prison chaplain who one morning came into cell 16 staggering under the weight of two huge Bibles — *The Living Bible* in English and *Ibuku Rĩa Ngai* in Gĩkũyũ — plus a bundle of revivalist tracts from the American-millionaire-supported evangelical missions. He was in a prison officer's uniform of khaki trousers and jumper-coat lined with aluminium buttons and a

decoration of two or three stones on the shoulder flaps. He also
carried the hallmark of all prison officers and warders — a cord over
the left shoulder carrying a whistle hidden in the breast-pocket. But
underneath these symbols of oppression, he wore the holy uniform of
a reverend: a black cloak ending in a white collar round the neck. He
appeared to me, at the moment, the very embodiment of an immense
neo-colonial evil let loose over our beautiful Kenya.

I let him talk and simply held back my tongue in anger.

'Sometimes,' he said, after sitting on the edge of the desk seat with
me on the bed, 'God chastises us for our own good . . . Take Mau
Mau for instance . . . Mau Mau was God's scourge with which he
lashed Kenyans to teach them a good lesson . . . the fruit of this
lesson, well learnt, is the stability we now enjoy and which is the envy
of our neighbours.'

I could hardly believe my ears: Mau Mau, the most glorious
chapter in our nation's long history of struggle was, to this man with
the cloak of a priest beneath a prison officer's uniform, a huge
sjambok with which God had flagellated Kenyans into humble
submission to his eternal will.

'We have all sinned and come short of the glory of God,' he said.
'Who knows, maybe this is a unique God-created chance for you to
meet with Christ. God works in mysterious ways, his wonder to
perform,' he went on.

He did not see the anger seething inside me. He only could see in
my silence a being about to be smitten to the ground by the
thunderbolt of the Lord, like Saul in the New Testament. But to me,
his attempts at word comfort sounded like prayers of thanksgiving for
being chosen to be the earthly instrument of God's mysterious ways
of performing his wonders, and his attempts at converting me, were
trumpets of victory over a fallen foe of imperialist Christendom.

My silence lured him on. He now presented me with the two
Bibles.

'The Bible is the only book in the world containing within its hard
covers a complete library,' he said, fingering each Bible lovingly as
he placed it on the desk. 'Twenty-eight books in one . . . how many
people can boast of a home library that big?'

He then handed to me two religious tracts — *God's City in
Heaven* or some such title — with obvious awe at the American
manufactured weightless leaves of holiness.

Despite my seething anger, I made a hasty retreat before this
onslaught and actually took the leaves. I really felt weak before the

moral certainty of a man who had walked the same path over and over again and hence knows every sharp corner and dangerous bend, every nook and brook on the way, and who knows clearly, from years of experience, where this path leads to: a prisoner's acceptance to forever carry a fascist cross without a murmur of discontent because he has now the spiritual satisfaction of having Christ for a personal saviour.

The visit had been beautifully timed. For over two weeks now I had not engaged in any debate, indeed I had hardly talked to anyone at any length since the night I was abducted from home. I had been denied human company. At the time of his visit, all the older detainees, except Shikuku, had gone to Shimo-la-Tewa Prison in Mombasa to meet the review tribunal. I was totally alone. I felt as if I had been on the run, relentlessly pursued by an invisible silent malignant force which, despite my every effort to outdistance it, had finally caught up with me, and was now transforming me, a free agent able to take decisions, into a passive creature panting and cringing for mercy at the feet of the twin warders of body and soul. My hard anger had now melted into a kind of spiritual lethargy and intellectual torpitude: What's the point of answering back? Isn't it easier, for me, for everybody, but mostly for me, to buy peace with silence?

The priest sensed the uncertainty in his quarry: he now took out his spiritual dagger and went for the kill.

'Let us kneel down and ask God for fogiveness for all our sins,' he commanded, but in a voice tear-bathed in infinite pity and compassion.

Then suddenly, from somewhere in the depths of my being, rose a strong rebellious voice.

'Wake up from your spiritual lethargy and intellectual torpor. Don't let them drug you with this opium, don't let them poison your system with it. It was to make you acutely hunger and thirst for a compassionate human voice that they have kept you near and yet far from human company. If you let him get away with this, you are going to be his prisoner for the rest of your stay here and possibly for ever.'

I felt life astir.

'Hold it!' I cried out. 'Who needs your prayers, your Bibles, your leaves of holiness — all manufactured and packaged in America? Why do you always preach humility and acceptance of sins to the victims of oppression? Why is it that you never preach to the oppressor? Go. Take your Bibles, your prayers, your leaves of holiness to them that have chained us in this dungeon. Have you read *Ngaahika Ndeenda?* Did you ever go to see the play? What was wrong with it? Tell me! What was wrong with Kamĩrĩĩthũ peasants and workers wanting to change their lives through their own collective efforts instead of always being made passive recipients of Harambee charity meant to buy peace and sleep for uneasy heads? Tell me truthfully: what drove you people to suppress the collective effort of a whole village? What has your borrowed Christianity to say to oppression and exploitation of ordinary people?'

I found myself getting worked up as I went along. A few warders had now crowded the door but I did not care. I flayed, right to its rotten roots, his spiritual dependence on imperialist foreigners. What had made him bring me tracts written by Billy Graham? Did he know that this was the same man who used to bless American soldiers in their mission to napalm, bomb, murder and massacre Vietnamese men, women and children in the name of an anti-communist holy crusade? Were there no Kenyans who could write sermons? Why had he not at least paid homage to Kenya's spiritual independence by bringing into prison sermons by the likes of Reverend John Gatũ and Bishop Henry Okullu, men whose liberal sincerity and concern had led them to a measure of patriotism?

The denunciatory vehemence in my voice shook him. The moral certainty had gone. He now became defensive. Avoiding the more earthly issues of oppression, exploitation and foreign control, he said that as a man of God he never indulged in politics. To justify that stand, he quoted the Biblical exhortation to believers to render unto Caesar things that were Caesar's and to God things of God. I quickly quoted back to him the Biblical scene where Jesus had whipped out of God's earthly temple the Pharisee and Sadducee collaborators with Caesar's oppressive conquest.

A little game started. He would refer me to Biblical passages which talked of faith, sin, salvation, grace, life to come; I would in turn refer him to alternative passages where God is cited as having sent his prophets to denounce earthly misrule and oppression of innocents.

'Anyway, we could go on arguing for ever,' he abruptly cut short the heated discussion, 'but I have others to see. You educated people like arguments too much. But remember that you cannot argue your way to Heaven.' He stood up, took back the two huge Bibles and the bundle of Billy Graham and staggered toward cell 11 where Martin Shikuku was on hunger strike.

The second verbal 'victim' was a warder. He was on leave when I was brought to Kamītī. This was his first shift since resuming work. Suddenly, out of the blue, he shouted at me and accused me of dragging my feet in returning to my cell.'We know what you are trying to do, but don't be too clever. This is not the university,' he added, wagging a warning finger at me. This was soon after our supper usually eaten at 3.00 p.m.

The detainees and even the other warders turned their heads. They knew that he had deliberately picked on me as an object on which to display his talents in bullying. Total silence in Kamītī. Everybody froze into his position to watch the drama.

The kind of lethargy I had earlier felt before the spiritual warder again crept in to still my trembling anger: 'I am new in this place . . . shouldn't I buy peace by simply swallowing my anger and pride and slink into my cell? I am down. I must avoid confrontation.'

But another voice, the other voice, quickly intervened: 'You may now be down. But you must always struggle to rise. Struggle for your rights. If you don't pick the glove, if you don't stand to your full height now and stare injustice in the face, you'll never be able to raise your head in this place. It is now, or never!'

I stood up. But instead of going back to the cell, I walked toward the new warder in slow measured steps. I held back my anger. I tried to speak in a controlled voice but loud enough for everybody to hear. I wanted to be firm without shouting:

'You know very well that you did not tell me to go back to my cell. You also know that it is not yet time to go in. To me, even a second of my ration of sunshine is precious and it is my right. I am not begging for more than my due and I have no intention of doing so in future. But whatever the case, never, never shout at me or abuse me. If I have broken any regulation, do your duty, and tell me so politely. I will hear. If I refuse to obey, you should report me to your superiors: the corporal, the sergeant, the chief, officer one, the superintendent or the senior superintendent. But don't add tyranny to the insult and injury of lies and falsehoods.'

He looked about him for support from the other warders. No voice came to his rescue. Suddenly noise and movement returned to the compound. We severally went back to our cells. It was an unwritten rule among detainees never to loudly comment on the results of a showdown between a detainee and a warder, especially when the detainee had won, for fear of uniting the warders into a common determination of vengeance. But I knew, from the relaxed tone of their voices and the ease of their laughter, that they were happy I had stood up to him.

Later, in fact, Koigi was to tell me: 'That warder is a well known bully. If you had not answered him, he would have gone on to spit at you and shit on you. I would like you to watch how he treats Detainee X who in order to avoid conflict dances to their every whim and caprice . . .'

Those two small incidents, and my own internal struggles to know how to react, brought home to me the real message behind what Wasonga Sijeyo had told me about my not letting them break me. They also showed me the tactical meaning behind all those mystificatory rituals.

This: detention and conditions in detention, including the constant reminder of one's isolation, can drive, in fact are meant to drive, a former patriot into a position where he feels that he has been completely forgotten, that all his former words and actions linked to people's struggles, were futile gestures and senseless acts of a meaningless individual martyrdom; yes, reduce him to a position where he can finally say: *The masses have betrayed me, why should I sacrifice myself for them?*

For a detained patriot, breaking through the double-walls of grey silence, attempting, if you like, a symbolic link with the outside world, is an act of resistance. And resistance — even at the level of merely asserting one's rights, of maintaining one's ideological beliefs in the face of any programmed onslaught — is in fact the only way a political detainee can maintain his sanity and humanity. Resistance is the only means of resisting a breakdown. The difficulty lies in the fact that in this resistance he has to rely first and foremost on his own resources (writing defiance on toilet-paper for instance) and nobody can teach him how to rely on them.

But all messages of solidarity, even though through a silent photograph, or through the unwritten word in a letter, are important contributions to his struggle to stay afloat. To a person condemned to isolation, such messages from the outside sound like Joshua's trumpets that brought down the legendary walls of Jericho.

True for me too: Njooki, a picture sent through the post; and Wariinga, a picture created on rationed toiletpaper, have been more than a thousand trumpets silently breaking through the fortified walls of Kamiti Maximum Security Prison to assure me that I am not alone; Wariinga, by constantly making me conscious of my connection with history, and Njooki, by constantly making me aware that I am now in prison because of Kamīrīĩthũ and its people.

But Warĩĩnga and Njooki also keep on reminding me that my detention is not a personal affair. It's part of the wider history of attempts to bring up the Kenyan people in a reactionary culture of silence and fear, and of the Kenyan people's fierce struggle against them to create a people's revolutionary culture of outspoken courage and patriotic heroism.

CHAPTER TWO

1

A colonial affair . . . the phrase keeps on intruding into the literary flow of my mind and pen . . . a colonial affair in an independent Kenya . . . It is as if the phrase has followed me inside Kamĩtĩ Prison to mock at me.

In 1967, just before returning home from a three-year stay in England, I had signed a contract with William Heinemann to write a book focusing on the social life of European settlers in Kenya. The literary agent who negotiated the contract — he was also the originator of the idea — put it this way: 'Theirs is a world which has forever vanished, but for that very reason, many readers will find an account of it still interesting.'

The title? *A Colonial Affair!*

I had agreed to do the book because I strongly held that the settlers were part of the history of Kenya: the seventy years of this destructive alien presence could not be ignored by Kenyans.

Heaven knows, as they would say, that I tried hard to come to terms with the task. I dug up old newspapers and settlers' memoirs to get an authentic feel of the times as the settlers lived it. A writer must be honest. But in the end I was unable to write the book. I could not quite find the right tone. The difficulty lay in more than my uncertainty as to whether or not 'their world' had really vanished. An account of their social life would have to include a section on culture, and I was by then convinced that a Draculan idle class could never produce a culture.

For the settlers in Kenya were really parasites in paradise. Kenya, to them, was a huge winter home for aristocrats, which of course meant big game hunting and living it up on the backs of a million field and domestic slaves, the *Watu* as they called them. Coming ashore in Mombasa, as was clearly shown by the photographic evidence in the 1939 edition of Lord Cranworth's book, *Kenya Chronicles,* was literally on the backs of Kenyan workers. 'No one coming into a new country,' he writes, 'could desire a more attractive welcome. We were rowed ashore in a small boat and came to land on the shoulders of sturdy Swahili natives.' This was in 1906.

By 1956, Sir Evelyn Baring, the governor, could still get himself photographed being carried, like a big baby, in the arms of a Kenyan worker. Thus by setting foot on Kenyan soil at Mombasa, every European was instantly transformed into a blue-blooded aristocrat. An attractive welcome: before him, stretching beyond the ken of his eyes, lay a vast valley garden of endless physical leisure and pleasure that he must have once read about in the *Arabian Nights* stories. The dream in fairy tales was now his in practice. No work, no winter, no physical or mental exertion. Here he would set up his own fiefdom. Life in these fiefdoms is well captured in Gerald Henley's novels *Consul at Sunset* and *Drinkers of Darkness*. Whoring, hunting, drinking, why worry? Work on the land was carried out by gangs of African 'boys'. Both *Consul at Sunset* and *Drinkers of Darkness* are fiction. Observed evidence comes from the diaries of a traveller. In her 1929-30 diaries, now brought out together under the title *East African Journey*, Margery Perham described the same life in minute detail:

> We drove out past the last scattered houses of suburban Nairobi, houses very much like their opposite numbers in England. But here ordinary people can live in sunlight; get their golf and their tennis more easily and cheaply than at home; keep three or four black servants; revel in a social freedom that often turns, by all accounts, into licence, and have the intoxicating sense of belonging to a small ruling aristocracy ... certainly, on the surface, life is very charming in Nairobi, and very sociable with unlimited entertaining; all the shooting, games and bridge anyone could want. And in many houses a table loaded with drinks, upon which you can begin at any hour from 10.00am onwards, and with real concentration from 6.00pm.

And, so, beyond drinking whisky and whoring each other's wives and natives (what Margery Perham prudishly calls social freedom turned 'by all accounts, into licence') and gunning natives for pleasure in this vast happy valley — oh, yes, are you married or do you live in Kenya? — the settlers produced little. No art, no literature, no culture, just the making of a little dominion marred only by niggers too many to exterminate, the way they did in New Zealand, and threatened by upstart 'Gĩkũyũ agitators'.

The highest they reached in creative literature was perhaps

Elspeth Huxley and she is really a scribbler of tourist guides and anaemic settler polemics blown up to the size of books. The most creative things about her writing are her titles — *The Flame Trees of Thika* and *The Mottled Lizard,* for instance — because in them she lets herself be inspired by native life and landscape. Beyond the title and the glossy covers, there is only emptiness, and emptiness as a defence of oppression has never made a great subject for literature.

Their theatre, professional and amateur, never went beyond crude imitation and desperate attempts to keep up with the West End or Broadway. This theatre never inspired a single original script or actor or critic.

In science, they could of course display Leakey. But Leakey's speciality was in digging up, dating and classifying old skulls. Like George Eliot's Casaubon, he was happier living with the dead. To the Leakeys, it often seems that the archaeological ancestors of Africans were more lovable and noble than the current ones — an apparent case of regressive evolution. Colonel Leakey, and even Lewis Leakey, hated Africans and proposed ways of killing off nationalism, while praising skulls of dead Africans as precursors of humanity. The evidence is there in black and white: L.S.B. Leakey is the author of two anti-Mau Mau books — *Mau Mau and the Kikuyu* and *Defeating Mau Mau.*

In art, their highest achievement was the mural paintings on the walls of the Lord Delamere bar in the Norfolk Hotel, Nairobi.* The murals stand to this day and they still attract hordes of tourists who come to enjoy racist aesthetics in art. But the murals in their artistic mediocrity possess a revealing historical realism.

On one wall are depicted scenes drawn from the English countryside: fourteen different postures for the proper deportment of an English gentleman; fox-hunting with gentlemen and ladies on horseback surrounded on all sides by well-fed hounds panting and wagging tails in anticipation of the kill to come; and of course the different pubs, from the White Hart to the Royal Oak, waiting to quench the thirst of the ladies and the gentlemen after their blood sports. Kenya is England away from England, with this difference: Kenya is an England of endless summer tempered by an eternal spring of sprouting green life.

On another wall are two murals depicting aspects of settler life in that Kenya. One shows the Norfolk — the House of Lords as it was

*On 31 December 1980 the Norfolk Hotel was bombed, reportedly by revolutionaries. But the Lord Delamere bar remained intact.

then known — in 1904. Here again are English ladies and gentlemen — some on horseback, others sitting or standing on the verandah — but all drinking hard liquor served them by an African waiter wearing the servant's uniform of white *kanzu,* red fez, and a red band over his shoulder and front. In the foreground is an ox-wagon with two Africans: one, the driver, lashing at the dumb oxen; and the other, the pilot, pulling them along the right paths. The ribs of the 'pushing boy' and the 'pulling boy' are protruding, in contrast to the fully fleshed oxen and members of 'the House of Lords'. But the most prominent feature in this mural is 'a rickshaw boy' with grinning teeth holding up this human-powered carriage for a finely dressed English lady to enter. Oxen-powered wagons for English survival goods; African powered carriages for English lords and ladies. Eleanor Cole, in her 1975 random recollections of pioneer settler life in Kenya, writes:

> Transport in Nairobi in those days was by rickshaw, one man in front between the shafts and one behind, either pushing or acting as a brake. People had their private rickshaws and put their rickshaw men in uniform. There were also public ones for hire.

The other mural depicts the same type of royal crowd at Nairobi railway station. At the forefront, is a well-fed dog wagging its tail before its lord and master. But amidst the different groups chatting or walking, stands a lone bull-necked, bull-faced settler in riding breeches with a hat covering bushy eyebrows and a grey moustache. He could have been a Colonel Grogan or a Lord Delamere or any other settler. The most representative feature about him is the *sjambok* he is firmly holding in his hands.

The rickshaw. The dog. The *sjambok*. The ubiquitous underfed, wide-eyed, uniformed native slave.

In March 1907, Colonel Grogan and four associates flogged three 'rickshaw boys' outside a Nairobi court-house. The 'boys' were later taken to hospital with lacerated backs and faces. Their crime? They had had the intention of alarming two white ladies by raising the rickshaw shafts an inch too high! The rhetoric of the magistrate when later Grogan, Bowkes, Gray, Fichat, and Low were summoned before him for being members of an unlawful assembly, left not the slightest doubt about the sadistic brutality of the deeds of these sons of English nobility and graduates of Cambridge:

From the first to the last it appears to me that out of all the people present assisting at the flogging of these men, there was no one of that number who ever took the trouble to satisfy himself as to whether these natives had ever done anything deserving of punishment at all. There was no trial of any sort nor any form or pretence of trial. These boys were neither asked whether they had any defence or explanation to give, nor does it appear that they ever had any opportunity of making one. Grogan, who ordered the flogging, has himself stated that no plea or defence which they might have made would have diverted him from his purpose. This is a very unpleasant feature in the case and I consider it about as bad as it can be. Yet, in my opinion, it is further aggravated by the fact that the place selected for this unlawful act was directly in front of a court-house.

Sweet rhetoric versus bitter reality: the culprits, all found guilty, were given prison terms ranging from seven to thirty days. Prison? Their own houses where they were free to receive and entertain guests! Elsewhere, in the plantations and estates, the 'bwana' would simply have shot them and buried them, or fed them to his dogs.

In 1960, Peter Harold Poole shot and killed Kamame Musunge for throwing stones at Poole's dogs in self-defence. To the settlers, dogs ranked infinitely higher than Kenyans; and Kenyans were either children (to be paternalisticly loved but not appreciated, like dogs) or mindless scoundrels (to be whipped or killed). In his autobiography, *Words*, Sartre has made the apt comment that 'when you love children and dogs too much, you love them instead of adults'. The settlers' real love was for dogs and puppies. Thus, to hit an attacking dog was a worse crime than killing a Kenyan. And when Poole was sentenced to death, the whole colonial *Herrenvolk* cried in unison against this 'miscarriage of justice'. Peter Harold Poole had done what had been the daily norm since 1895.

In 1918, for instance, two British peers flogged a Kenyan to death and later burnt his body. His crime? He was was suspected of having an intention to steal property. The two murderers were found guilty of a 'simple hurt' and were fined two-thousand shillings each. The governor later appointed one of them a member of a district committee to dispense justice among the 'natives'. The gory details are there in Macgregor Ross's book *Kenya From Within*. Justice in sjambok!

I thought about about this in my cell at Kamĩtĩ prison and suddenly realized that I had been wrong about the British settlers. I should have written that book. For the colonial system *did* produce a culture.

But it was the culture of legalized brutality, a ruling-class culture of fear, the culture of an oppressing minority desperately trying to impose total silence on a restive oppressed majority. This culture was sanctified in the colonial administration of P.C., D.C., D.O., Chiefs, right down to the askari. At Kamĩtĩ, we called it the Mbwa Kali culture.

2

Culture of silence and fear: the diaries and memoirs of the leading intellectual lights of the old colonial system contain full literary celebration of this settler culture. We need go no further than Colonel Meinertzhagen's *Kenya Diaries* and Baroness Blixen's *Out of Africa*.

Meinertzhagen was a commanding officer of the British forces of occupation. But he is far better known in history as the assassin of Koitalel, the otherwise unconquerable military and political leader of the Nandi people. This is what happened. Under Koitalel's inspiring leadership, the Nandi people had waged a ten-year armed struggle against the foreign army of occupation, humiliating British officers, one after the other. Enter Meinertzhagen, a gentleman. Unable to defeat the Nandi guerrilla army, the colonel invited Koitalel to a peace parley on some 'neutral' ground. But only on one condition. Both men would come unarmed. Having been led to believe that the British wanted to discuss surrender terms and guarantees of safe retreat from Nandi country, Koitalel accepted. Put innocence against brutality and innocence will lose. There could be no finer illustration of this than the encounter between Koitalel and Meinertzhagen. Koitalel stretched an empty hand in greeting, Meinertzhagen stretched out a hidden gun and shot Koitalel in cold blood. The incident is recorded in *Kenya Diaries* as an act of British heroism!

Similar deeds of British colonial heroism are recorded in the same diaries.

The scene now shifts to Gĩkũyũ country, where people once again

fought with tremendous courage against the better armed foreign
invaders. So fierce was the struggle that in 1902 Meinertzhagen was
forced to make the grudging but prophetic admission that, even if
they triumphed over the people, this would only be a temporary
victory: the British could never hold the country for more than fifty
years. In one of several battles in Mūrang'a, a British officer was
captured by the national defence army in Mūrūka and was handed to
the people for justice. They killed him. Months later, Meinertzhagen
stole into Mūrūka on a market day, had the whole market surrounded, and ordered a massacre of every soul — a cold-blooded
vengeance against defiant husbands and sons. Thereafter he embarked on a campaign of pillage, plunder and more murder.
Meinertzhagen wrote in his diary: 'Every soul was either shot or
bayonetted . . . we burned all huts and razed the banana plantations
to the ground . . . Then I went home and wept for brother officer
killed.'

Baroness Blixen was the separated wife of the big game hunter-
cum-settler Baron von Blixen. From him she got no children but
incurable syphilis. As if in compensation for unfulfilled desires and
longings, the baroness turned Kenya into a vast erotic dreamland in
which her several white lovers appeared as young gods and her
Kenyan servants as usable curs and other animals. It is all there in
her two books, *Shadows on the Grass* and *Out of Africa*. In the
latter, her most famous, she celebrates a hideous colonial aesthetic in
an account she entitles Kitosch's story:

> Kitosch was a young native in the service of a young white
> settler of Molo. One Wednesday in June, the settler lent his
> brown mare to a friend, to ride to the station on. He sent
> Kitosch there to bring back the mare, and told him not to ride
> her, but to lead her. But Kitosch jumped on to the mare, and
> rode her back, and on Saturday the settler, his master, was told
> of the offence by a man who had seen it. In punishment the
> settler, on Sunday afternoon, had Kitosch flogged, and after-
> wards tied up in his store, and here late on Sunday night
> Kitosch died.

The outcome of the trial in the High Court at Nakuru turned to rest
solely on the intentions of the victim. It transpired by a hideous logic
that Kitosch had actually wanted to die and he was therefore
responsible for his death. In Anglo-Saxonland, it seems colonized

natives have a fiendish desire for suicide that absolves white murderers:

> Kitosch had not much opportunity for expressing his intentions. He was locked up in the store, his message, therefore comes very simply, and in a single gesture. The night watch states that he cried all night. But it was not so, for at one o'clock he talked with toto, who was in the store with him, because the flogging had made him deaf. But at one o'clock he asked the toto to loosen his feet, and explained that in any case he could not run away. When the toto had done as he asked him Kitosch said to him that he wanted to die. A little while after, he rocked himself from side to side, cried: 'I am dead'! and died

Medical science was even brought in to support the wish-to-die theory. This was supposed to be a psychological peculiarity of the African. He wants to die, and he dies. The irony is not Blixen's. She accepts the theory. What, of course, Kitosch said was, 'Nataka kufa which means: 'I am about to die, or I am dying.' But that is not the issue. It is the verdict and the conclusion. The settler was found guilty of 'grievous hurt'. And for a 'grievous hurt' to a Kenyan, the foreign settler got two years in jail, probably on his own farm! It is not recorded how much more grievous hurt he committed later.

The fault is not Blixen's manner of telling the story — all the details are there — but her total acceptance of the hideous theory and her attempts to draw from it aesthetic conclusions meant to have universal relevance and validity:

> By this strong sense in him of what is right and decorous, the figure of Kitosch, with his firm will to die, although now removed from us by many years, stands out with a beauty of its own. In it is embodied the fugitiveness of wild things who are in the hour of need, conscious of a refuge somewhere in existence; who go when they will; of whom we can never get hold.

The African is an animal: the settler is exonerated. Not a single word of condemnation for this practice of colonial justice. No evidence of any discomfiture. And for this, generations of western European critics from Hemingway to John Updike have showered her with praises. Some neo-colonial Africans too. But I err too in saying the

African was considered an animal. In reality they loved the wild game but Africans were worse, more threatening, instinctless, unlovable, unredeemable sub-animals merely useful for brute labour. In *Out of Africa*, Karen Blixen says that her knowledge of wild game was useful in her later contact with Africans!

What of course is disgusting is the attempt by writers like Blixen to turn acts of cold-blooded murder and torture of these 'black suppliers of brute labour' into deeds of heroic grandeur. It makes words lose their meaning or perhaps it is proof that the meaning of a word depends on the user. Galbraith Cole shot dead a Masai national in cold blood. The subsequent trial was a pre-arranged farce, rehearsed to the letter and gesture by all three parties, prosecutor, judge and murderer (all European of course), in such a way that on the records the Kenyan murdered would emerge guilty of unbearable armed provocation. But the settler was too arrogant to hide his murderous intentions behind a glossy mask of lies. As later reported by Karen Blixen, this is how the farce reached a climax of absurdity:

> The Judge said to Galbraith, 'It's not, you know, that we don't understand that you shot only to stop the thieves.' 'No', Galbraith said, 'I shot to kill. I said that I would do so.'
> 'Think again, Mr Cole', said the judge. 'We are convinced that you only shot to stop them.'
> 'No, by God', Galbraith said, 'I shot to kill'.

He was acquitted. But Blixen reported Cole's admission as an act of unparalleled greatness. In a book, *Silence will Speak,* the same literary glorification of the settler culture of murder and torture is shamelessly repeated in 1977 by one Errol Trzebinski.

Robert Ruark, in *Something of Value* and *Uhuru,* was to outdo the Huxleys, the Blixens, the Trzebinskis, in raising the reactionary settler culture of violence to the level of universality, and anybody upsetting it was seen as Hades' harbinger of doom and everlasting darkness.

Meinertzhagen, the soldier-assassin turned writer; Karen Blixen, the baroness of blighted bloom turned writer; Robert Ruark, the big-game hunter turned writer — theirs is a literary reflection of that colonial culture of silence and fear best articulated in a dispatch by an early governor, Sir A. R. Hardinge, on 5 April 1897:

> Force and the prestige which rests on a belief in force, are the

only way you can do anything with those people, but once beaten and disarmed they will serve you. Temporizing is no good . . . These people must learn submission by bullets — it's the only school; after that you may begin more modern and humane methods of education, and if you don't do it this year you will have to next, so why not get it over? . . . In Africa to have peace you must first teach obedience, and the only tutor who impresses the lesson properly is the sword.

Thus the above acts of animal brutality were not cases of individual aberration but an integral part of colonial politics, philosophy and culture. Reactionary violence to instil fear and silence was the very essence of colonial settler culture.

3

This culture of Hardinge, Grogan, Delamere and Meinertzhagen, reflected in the literary works of Blixen, Elspeth Huxley and Robert Ruark, reached its high noon between 1952 and 1962. These were the ten years when the sword and the bullet held unmitigated sway over every Kenyan. It was a period of mass trials, mass murder and mass torture of Kenyans. So brutal were the workings of this culture that even some democratic-minded British were shocked into protest against its anti-human character.

Such was the case, for instance, of Eileen Fletcher, a Quaker social worker, who, after serving for a time as a rehabilitation officer in Kenya, resigned and flew back to England to declare in *The Tribune* of 25 May 1956:

I have just come back from Kenya where I was sent by the British Government. I have seen Emergency justice in oper-ation. And now I can reveal the shocking truth, that I have seen African children, in British jails, sentenced to life imprisonment — for 'consorting with armed persons' and 'unlawful pos-session of ammunition'. In a women's prison, less than a year ago, I saw twenty-one young people — including 11 and 12 years olds — who were all condemned to this inhuman punishment, for supposed 'Mau Mau offences'. All of them, believe it or not, had been convicted by British magistrates.

Similarly, Barbara Castle, a Labour M.P., was to write in horror in *The Tribune* of 30 September 1955: 'In the heart of the British Empire there is a police state where the rule of law has broken down, where the murder of and torture of Africans by Europeans goes unpunished and where authorities pledged to enforce justice regularly connive at its violation.' And in *The Sunday Pictorial* of 31 March 1957, after cataloguing the number of Kenyans hanged, she commented:'With this bloody act, Kenya enters its fourth year of blood, repression, brutalities, mass imprisonment — of the lawless enforcement of unjust law, by agents of its government and of the British Government.'

Barbara Castle was, of course, wrong about what she termed the breakdown of the rule of law. This *was* the rule of law, the colonial rule of law, and it had been in operation, with differing degrees of intensity, since 1895.

Evidence now comes from the horse's own mouth. A secretary for native affairs, A.C.Hollis, on 8 April 1908, wrote a secret memorandum on the miserable conditions in the country's colonial labour camps:

> My first duty on my appointment as secretary for native affairs in June last was to inquire into the labour question. It had recently been reported to His Excellency that a number of Kikuyu had been found dead on the road leading from the railway fuel camps at Londiani to their country. I therefore proceeded to the spot and held an inquiry. A deplorable state of affairs was revealed. It transpired that as voluntary labour was usually not forthcoming, chiefs were called upon to provide labour, and natives were seized by their chief's orders and forced to go and work. The most unpopular kind of work was for Indian contractors on the railway. The men were sent to detested camps where they were badly fed and often beaten and maltreated. They frequently had no blankets given them though the cold at night time was intense, the miserable grass huts provided for their accommodation were neither watertight nor wind-proof, the work of felling trees and breaking stones was uncongenial, and no attempt was made to give them food they were accustomed to in their own homes. Their lives were consequently a misery and their one idea seemed to run away and return to their own country. To prevent this, police guards were stationed at most of the contractor's camps. Many

of the men however succeeded in escaping and hundreds must have died of starvation.

For some years a system of forced labour had been resorted to in various parts of the protectorate and like most wrongful systems matters had gone from bad to worse. At first mild pressure only was used, then the goats were confiscated, and later on armed force had been employed . . .

Exactly thirty years before Barbara Castle, Marcus Garvey had to protest, in words similar to hers, against the 1922 British massacre of Kenyan workers. Only he did not see it as a breakdown of law. He saw it as the logical working out of the laws of colonial conquest by sword and bullet. In a telegram to Lloyd George, dated 20 March 1922, he prophesied what was to happen in 1952:

> *David Lloyd George British Premier Downing St London*
> Four-hundred million negroes through the Universal Negro Improvement Association hereby register their protest against the brutal manner in which your government has treated the natives of Kenya, East Africa. You have shot down a defenceless people in their own native land exercising their rights as men. Such a policy will aggravate the many historic injustices heaped upon a race that will one day be placed in a position to truly defend itself not with mere sticks, clubs and stones but with modern implements of science.

Thus all these eruptions of brutality between the introduction of colonial culture in 1895 and its flowering with blood in the 1950s were not aberrations of an otherwise humane Christian culture. No. They were its very essence, its law, its logic, and the Kenyan settler with his *sjambok*, his dog, his horse, his rickshaw, his sword, his bullet, was the true embodiment of British imperialism. It was not the Barbara Castles and Fenner Brockways who were the true representatives of the empire and the culture it was exporting and nurturing in the colonies: it was Grogan, Delamere, Meinertzhagen, Francis Hall, Peter Poole. They alone understood and tenaciously clung to the aesthetic goals of that culture; submission by terror. They were impatient, and rightly so, with the more deceitful methods of the missionaries and administrators who were trying to educate Kenyans into accepting the same thing: submission. These men were honest and in this lay their crude vigour and perhaps their fascinating simplicity. They went to the heart of their culture, understood and accepted its inevitable brutality where others tried to dress the same logic with biblical homilies, literary flourishes, and rhetorical emptiness about the rule of law. It was their *law*, not anybody else's, to protect their foreign interests by suppressing those of Kenyans, and they knew it.

When one British military commander, Jackson by name, tried and failed to subdue Koitalel's Nandi guerrilla army — long before Meinertzhagen came onto the scene with a sugar-coated bullet — he became almost insane and equated political defiance and military resistance with savagery. In a despatch of 4 May 1897, he tried to cover his military humiliation with words which nevertheless are revealing about the aesthetic goals of that culture — silence, submission, acceptance:

> I have carefully investigated, as far as possible, the reasons for their restlessness and it appears the great cause of the trouble is the hostile attitude assumed by the Chief Lybon, or medicine-man against the government. This man, who has apparently enormous influence over the various surrounding tribes, has declared (war) against the government, and is now busying himself in exhorting the tribes to expel the British. From reliable native information, I find he is endeavouring to bring about a movement against the administration, and numerous pieces of information clearly indicate that combined hostile action against us will undoubtedly begin on the cessation of the present rainy season. The Lybon has lately taken to sending insolent and defiant messages to the Fort, and the fact that no action has hitherto been taken against him has a very bad effect in the eyes of the natives, who say we are afraid of him. I have used every effort to conciliate the tribes and have exercised the greatest forbearance in dealing with them, and at their own request have even gone so far as to make blood brotherhood with many of them; but the ignorance of the people is so extreme that it is impossible to convey to such savages that the occupation of their country is not harmful to them . . .

Really, Mr Jackson! Would you have said with similar equanimity, that the occupation of Britain by Germans would not have been harmful to Britons? In a like vein, Hitler was to be surprised at the savage ignorance of other Europeans to whom it was impossible to convey that the occupation of their countries by blue-eyed blond Germans was not harmful to them.

Arrogance of colonial culture! Its blind self-deceitful ambition is limitless.

4

Obedience of the oppressed to the oppressor; peace and harmony between the exploited and the exploiter; the slave to love his master and pray that God grant that the master may long reign over us: these were the ultimate aesthetic goals of colonial culture carefully nurtured by nailed boots, police truncheons and military bayonets and by the carrot of a personal heaven for a select few. The end was to school Kenyans in the aesthetic of submission and blind obedience to authority reflected in that Christian refrain, *Trust and Obey:*

> Trust and obey
> For there is no other way
> To be happy in Jesus
> But to trust and obey!

Revelry in slavery: it was an aesthetic meant to make Kenyans readily accept, in the words of Jackson, that the occupation of their country by foreigners was not harmful to them.

Even in the 1950s the colonial authorities were still busy trying to teach Kenyans to accept Jackson's aesthetic. In his book *Mau Mau Detainee,* J.M.Kariūki has described the kind of education they were being given in detention camps:

> Attend education classes in their compound. These consisted mainly of the history of Kenya, with especial emphasis on the terrible state of tribal conflict before the arrival of the white man, followed by the story of the arrival of the white man and how he has saved us from barbarism, and finally an explanation of the great benefits he has brought to our country, especially in recent years.

Great benefits indeed: the sword and the bullet; blood, repression, brutality, starvation, carting off the country's wealth to Great Britain!

Fortunately, from Koitalel to Kĩmaathi, there has always been a section of Kenyans who preferred their native 'ignorance' to Jackson's foreign 'wisdom', and went on to lay a firm foundation for Kenya's proud history of resistance against imperialist domination and exploitation. The first prerequisite for this resistance was a rejection of the slave consciousness contained in the colonial culture of imperialism. And it was precisely to deal a blow to the infectious rôle of those patriotic Kenyans who had rejected a slave consciousness that detention without trial was first introduced in Kenya by the colonial authorities.

CHAPTER THREE

1

Detention without trial is part of that colonial culture of fear. It was introduced to Kenya by this racist settler minority, by Jesus-is-thy-Saviour missionaries, and their administrators.

In their book, *Public Law and Political Change in Kenya,* Y.P. Ghai and J.P.W.B. MacAuslan have shown, with detailed evidence and comment, the colonial basis of Kenya's laws — including detention laws, regulations and rules — and their colonial purpose: 'to be a tool at the disposal of the dominant political and economic groups'. Detention was an instrument for colonial domination. In its origins and purpose, it is clearly a colonial affair.

Under the Native Courts Regulations 1897, the commissioner for the East Africa Protectorate (Kenya), Sir Arthur Hardinge — the philosopher of submission by the sword and the bullet — armed himself with powers of preventive detention and restriction of movement of any Kenyan disaffected with the colonial government, or any Kenyan about to commit an offence against the colonial regime, or any Kenyan conducting himself in a manner deemed by the foreign colonial regime to be dangerous to colonial peace and colonial good order. The governor had given himself dictatorial and sweeping powers to detain any Kenyan dissatisfied with the structure of foreign oppression and exploitation. There was, of course, no appeal against the governor's exercise of the powers of arbitrary arrest and detention of Kenyans. Thus the legal groundwork was laid for an oppressive fascist tradition of crimes of thought and intention.

These fascist provisions were strengthened by other colonial laws depriving Kenyans of the basic rights of movement and recourse to even colonial courts. Under the Vagrancy Regulations of 1898, any Kenyan asking for alms or wandering about without employment or visible means of subsistence, could be arrested and detained. (These vagrancy laws exist in an independent Kenya. They are, in turn, based on the 1824 English Vagrancy Statute passed by the British government to control the unemployed veterans of the Napoleonic Wars.) The 1900 Native Pass Regulations empowered the governor to virtually make any rules at any time to control the movement of any Kenyan travelling into, out of, or within the limits of the territory. The Preservation of Order by Night Regulations of 1901 enabled the colonial administrators to impose curfew or any other restriction orders. Finally, under the 1899 Outlying Districts Ordinance, the governor and the other foreign colonial officials could declare whole districts and areas closed to other Kenyans living outside them.

But even before this British colonial fascism was given legal formulation and cover, it was already in operation and it had claimed the freedom and lives of many Kenyan patriots. Waiyaki wa Hiinga, the leading figure in the people's patriotic resistance against the British invasion and occupation of southern Gĩkũyũland — Kabete, as Kiambu District was then known — was among the earliest victims of preventive detention.

Waiyaki was one of several chiefs who were emerging towards feudal lordship status in Gĩkũyũland in the nineteenth century. But Waiyaki also loved his country. Combining political shrewdness and military brilliance, he and his army for many years successfully thwarted the British attempts at penetration and occupation of Dagoretti, Gĩthĩĩga and Gĩthũũngũri, eventually overrunning fortifications at Kĩawariũa. The British were forced to evacuate but managed a safe retreat through the guidance of the treacherous Kĩnyaanjui wa Gathirimũ, later rewarded for this betrayal of his people by being made a paramount chief. The British forces came back, in larger numbers, and built a bigger and stronger garrison, Fort Smith, at Kanyaarĩrĩ near the present Kikuyu station. Fort Smith was immediately besieged by Waiyaki's army. The commanding officer, Purkiss, now resorted to that British treachery which would always prove fatal to many a trusting Kenyan nationalist. He invited Waiyaki to peace talks. Waiyaki was arrested inside Fort Smith on 14 August 1892. But, though now alone and surrounded by bayonets and maxim guns, Waiyaki went on resisting and even bloodied one of his European captors.

They could have killed him there and then, but he was more valuable to them as a political hostage. The British plan worked. Waiyaki's army lifted the siege of Fort Smith.

And now the British decided to keep him a political hostage: on 17 August 1892, they sent him to detention at the coast. This too worked. Waiyaki's army held back, still fearing that any action would bring injury to their beloved leader.

It was then that the British saw his value as a permanent hostage. Thinking that no native from the interior would ever know the truth, they shot Waiyaki and buried him, still breathing, still alive, at Kibwezi. It was a cruel colonial sport, senseless in its sadistic savagery. What of course his British captors did not know was that some *hiingas* (scouts or spies) had followed the convoy and were sending back intelligence reports.

Waiyaki's detention and subsequent murder rekindled the fire of militant nationalism and resistance. His army regrouped and laid another siege of Fort Smith. Evidence comes from a visitor to the fort, Sir Gerald Portal, who was later to write:

> At Kikuyu the European in charge dare not venture f om the stockade without an armed escort of at least 30 to 50 .nen with rifles. He is practically a prisoner with all his p ople; and maintains the company's influence and prestige oy sending almost daily looting and raiding parties to burn the surrounding villages and to seize the crops and cattle for the use of the company's caravans and troops.

Pillage, plunder and murder. That was the British way. But that's another story. Here we are looking at the early detainees and what traditions and forces they embodied in their actions and lives. Waiyaki, one of the first political detainees in Kenya, was also among the first to die in detention, splendidly proud and defiant to the very end. He had rejected a slave consciousness!

Nguunju wa Gakere was another. He was the leading force in the struggle against the British occupation of Nyeri. He fought many brilliant battles against the foreign invaders, compelling Meinertzhagen to admit in his diary: '. . . I must own I never expected the Wakikuyu to fight like this . . . ' He was eventually captured, together with his son, on 6 December 1902 in the battle to capture Nyeri Fort and dislodge the enemy forces. Nguunju wa Gakere was deported to Kismayu where he remained in political detention from 1902 to 1905. Later he was transferred to Mbiri, in Mūrang'a, where he died in detention, in 1907. But like Waiyaki before him, he remained proud and defiant towards the British invaders of Kenya. Like Waiyaki and Koitalel, he rejected a slave consciousness and joined the long line of resistance heroes leading to Kīmaathi in the 1950s.

Kenyan women too played their part: and the most remarkable of them all was Me Kitilili, the leader of the Giriama people's resistance to the British occupation of their country. She was already an old woman when she organized Giriama youth into a fighting force that took the British military machine three years to subdue. Old as she was, she saw very clearly the political character of the armed struggle. She talked to the people about the theft of their land and labour. She talked about the evils of foreign occupation. She pointed out that the only solution was a united people's armed struggle to kick out the foreign enemy.

Towards that noble end, she administered oaths of loyalty and unity to forge oneness among the various Giriama people and other related nationalities. She set up a parallel government and installed Wanji wa Mandoro as its administrative head. In the anti-imperialist oathing ceremonies, the youth swore loyalty to this national government. They swore to never again pay taxes to the colonial regime or to accept the call of forced labour. They also swore to remain steadfast and unwavering in their aim: to drive out the British enemy from coastal Kenya.

Inspired by her vision and courage, the Giriama patriots fought so bravely that the British, refusing to see the political basis of this unity and courage, could only describe this remarkable feat in super-natural terms. Me Kitilili had to be a witch casting a captive spell over her primitive followers. Otherwise how, according to the British, could Kenyans reject foreign rule, domination and oppression? This, anyway, was the opinion of the colonial assistant district commissioner, Arthur M. Champion, who on 23 November 1913, wrote thus to his superiors:

> The witch Me Kitilili and the witch-doctor Wanji wa Mandoro about the end of June, 1913, did stir up sedition amongst the natives of Gallana and Marafa in the district of Malindi and with this object held a large gathering of men determined to make a common cause with disaffected natives of Biria to meat a spell or 'Kiroho' for the purpose of defeating a successful government administration . . . When arrested, Wanji wa Mandoro asserted that he had been appointed chief elder of the Gallana to take precedence over all government appointed headmen. He further asserted that . . . he had held his own council of elders who came from all parts of Gallana to discuss matters and try cases, and that they took fees . . . I would therefore recommend that both the woman Me Kitilili and Mandoro be deported from the district and be detained as political prisoners at His Majesty's pleasure.

The two were detained in November 1913 in Gusiiland, hundreds of miles from the coast, where they faced the torture of inadequate food and covering.

C.E. Spenser, the colonial district commissioner of the then South Kavirondo, was sufficiently moved by the miserable conditions of their detention to appeal to the provincial commissioners of Kisumu and Mombasa to ease the torture:

> These prisoners are old and unable to maintain themselves. I would suggest that they be allowed 10 cents a day each to provide themselves with food . . . I cannot very well return the blankets they are wearing to Mombasa prison until they have been provided with others as I conceive that to leave them without covering in an altitude of 5,500 above sea-level, after a lifetime at the coast, would be equivalent to passing a death sentence on them.

And now comes an even more remarkable feat from this woman. On 14 January 1914, Me Kitilili and her fellow detainee escaped from prison and with help from friendly patriots of the other Kenyan nationalities, they walked all the way back to the coast to continue the resistance. Rewards were announced for any person or persons who would assist in the recapture of this brave Kenyan. She was eventually caught on 7 August 1914, and detained. But she remained proud, defiant and unrepentant to the very end. Me Kitilili had rejected the colonial culture of fear and the slave consciousness it sought to instil in Kenyans.

The detention saga of Arap Manyei, the son of the legendary Koitalel, extends from 1922 to 1962. Before Achieng Oneko and Wasonga Sijeyo, Arap Manyei held the record for the longest-detained Kenyan.

Arap Manyei had continued his father's tradition of uncompromising resistance to foreign domination and oppression. He tirelessly worked to forge political unity among the Nandi and the related Kalenjin peoples. He also sent out feelers for a possible patriotic alliance with Luo and Gusii nationalists. It is possible that he may have also tried a working alliance with Harry Thuku's East African Association. But he was clearly ahead of Thuku and his educated kind for he saw the necessity for armed struggle. He was arrested at Kapsabet in 1922 and he was charged with administering an oath binding the Nandi people to join hands with other nationalities to wage a new war to drive out the British from Kenya. He was detained in Meru for ten years.

In the 1950s he established contact with Mau Mau guerrillas. He started oathing and training parallel Nandi guerrilla units. He was arrested and detained at Mfangan Island in Lake Victoria from 1957 to 1962, just a year before independence. He too remained defiant to the end. Not for him the slave mentality of the colonial culture of fear.

Manyei provides an unbroken link between the early detention of militant leaders of the patriotic armed resistance to foreign invasion at the turn of the century; to those of the early patriotic nationalism of the East African Association leaders like Harry Thuku, Waigaanjo, Mūgekenyi; and of the Mumboist leaders Muraa wa Ngiti, Otenyo, Ongere and others in the 1920s; and those of Mūindi Mbingu, leaders of the Taita Hills Association, and leaders of the Kikuyu Central Association (KCA)— all in the 1930s; to those of Cege Wa Kībacia, Markham Singh and Elijah Masinde (he was the first nationalist to tell the British to get out of Kenya) in the 1940s; to the mass detention of Kau and Mau Mau leaders and activists in the 1950s.

The legal link was the Emergency Powers Colonial Defence Order in Council (1939), itself received from the Emergency Powers (Defence) Act (1939) in Britain. This replaced the 1897 Native Courts Regulations by widening the arbitrary powers of the governor and reducing his accountability. Under this notorious order in council, the colonial governor could assume responsibility to detain, deport and exclude from Kenya any person or persons without recourse to legislature or to the courts.

With the invocation of these orders on 20 October 1952 by Governor Baring, the colonial culture entered its high noon, and detention was an aspect of it, now fully flowered in blood. The British colonial regime embarked on a ten-year programme of mass incarceration of Kenyan peasants and workers in concentration camps like Mackinnon Road, Langata, Manyani, Mageta, Hola, etc., while gathering the remaining millions into fortified concentration villages. It was one of the largest and most brutal mass arrests, incarcerations and displacements of peoples in history, to instil into a community of millions the culture of fear and the slave aesthetic of abject submission to tyranny. The British ruling class had learnt well from Hitler's colonial and racist experiments in Europe. Hitler had himself learnt from the British, who had been the most successful and efficient slave-raiding ruling class of the eighteenth and nineteenth centuries. The cumulative lesson learnt, the oppressive value and profitable significance of concentration camps and mass liquidation of peoples, could not be unlearnt ten minutes afterwards.

So obnoxious were the colonial detention laws, regulations and rules that their immediate abolition by the independent government was one of the top priorities in the now abandoned 1961 KANU Manifesto:

> Much of the current legislation denies the African people their rights and severely restricts their freedom. The Deportation of British Subjects Act has been invariably used to deny the African political and trade union leaders their freedom. Under this Act, the governor is empowered to make a deportation or a restriction order either in lieu of or in addition to the sentence imposed by a court of law against 'undesirable persons'. The preservation of Public Security Ordinance (1959) and the Detained and Restricted Persons (Special Provisions) Ordinance (1959) are other legislation currently employed to detain Africans for eight years without trial. Not only are these leaders detained without trial but they are also detained under conditions which are inhuman. The restriction of our leaders at Lodwar, Lokitaung, Marsabit, Hola, Manyani, suggests that, not only are they to suffer the deprivation of their liberty, but are deliberately confined to areas which are extremely hot, mosquito-ridden and deserted.
>
> KANU is pledged to remove all these undemocratic, unjust and arbitrary practices.

Thus the KANU of 1961, as an instrument of Kenyan nationalism, was totally opposed to the sixty years of colonial culture of repressive violence and mass terror.

2

At independence, the Emergency Powers (Colonial Defence) Order in Council (1939) was repealed as part of Kenyan law. But only on the surface. For the 1939 order in council, itself an enlargement of the 1897 Native Courts Regulations, was in substance adopted in granting emergency powers to the new independent government. It was incorporated in the Preservation of Public Security Act under which comes detention of persons and the restriction of their movements. In fact the only change was in terminology: the word 'Emergency' was deleted because, as the KANU government explained, the word had, 'for us the most distasteful associations of memory . . . We prefer to talk about our public security'. Sweet semantics. The fact is that the Preservation of Public Security Act is a total negation of all the democratic and human rights of Kenyans enshrined in the constitution. It goes against the spirit and substance of the Kenya independence constitution and against the original KANU pledges to remove all these (colonial) undemocratic, unjust and arbitrary practices. Now the cardinal vices of all the colonial detention laws — the unaccountability of the governor to the legislature, i.e. governorial regulations become laws; the waiving of the normal democratic assumption of a person's innocence unless proven guilty; the assumption of a Kenyan's guilt for crimes of thought and intention; the provision that the regulations, promulgated without the legislature are effective notwithstanding anything in the constitution or in any other law inconsistent therewith — were now part of Kenya's 'independence'. As it turns out, the British Governor-General Malcolm Macdonald and others proposed this legal document to suppress nationalist demands regarding the implementation of the 1961 KANU manifesto which by 1965 were seen as a 'Zanzibar-like communist threat'.

Thus by 1966 all the repressive colonial laws were back on the books. The Christian refrain of yesteryear was amplified ten times and more: trust and obey for there is no other way to be happy in Colonel Jesus except to trust and obey.

3

What happened between 1961 and 1966 to make KANU reintroduce all these undemocratic, unjust and arbitrary practices?

Before independence, there were two main parties representing opposing interests. The Kenya African Democratic Union (KADU) was then the main political instrument of foreign interests and accommodation of imperialism. It was the black front for most of the interests previously catered for by the European colonist associations: from the Grogan–Delamere conventions in the 1920s to Blundell's supposedly multi-racial New Kenya Group in the 1960s. Like Muzorewa's African National Council in the fictitious Zimbabwe-Rhodesia, KADU was backed internally by the white settlers and externally by the British imperialist bourgeoisie.

KANU was then an anti-imperialist movement representing Kenya's national aspirations. It was the constitutional inheritor of all the previous anti-colonial Kenyan organizations. The resounding beating it gave KADU in pre-independence elections was an indication of the support of expectant millions.

The historical situation is well summed up in an unsigned pamphlet dated 13 November 1979 and widely circulated in Kenya and much quoted in the press during the 1979 General Elections in a paragraph that stated:

> Before 1965 Kenya's mortal enemies were the British colonial settlers and their Kenyan supporters. Their chief supporters were grouped in KADU. KANU fought them hard and defeated them resoundingly. But they regrouped cunningly and joined KANU with Kenyatta's knowledge and approval and slowly turned KANU against its own founders (and) fighters — killed them, jailed them, detained them. In alliance with foreign interests and the Kenyatta clique they murdered the militant KANU spirit.

But KANU was a mass movement containing within it different class strata and tendencies: peasant, proletarian, and petty-bourgeois. Leadership was in the hands of the petty-bourgeoisie, itself split into three sections representing three tendencies: there was the upper petty-bourgeoisie that saw the future in terms of a compradorial alliance with imperialism; there was the middle petty-bourgeoisie which saw the future in terms of national capitalism; and there was the lower petty-bourgeoisie which saw the future in terms of some kind of socialism. The upper petty-bourgeoisie can be branded as comprador; and the middle and lower petty-bourgeoisie can be branded as nationalistic. The internal struggle for the ideological dominance and leadership of KANU from 1961 to 1966 was mainly between the faction representing comprador bourgeois interests, and the faction representing national patriotic interests. The faction representing the political line of comprador bourgeoisie was the one enormously strengthened when KADU joined

KANU. This faction, led by Kenyatta, Gĩchũrũ and Mboya, also controlled the entire coercive state machinery inherited intact from colonial times. The patriotic faction was backed by the masses but it did not control the central organs of the party or the state and it was the one considerably weakened by KADU's entry. But the internal struggles continued with unabated fury.

The struggles were primarily over what economic direction Kenya should take. The comprador bourgeoisie which had been growing in the womb of the colonial regime desired to protect and enhance its cosy alliance with foreign economic interests. It is now a fact of Kenyan history that just before and immediately after independence, the foreign economic interests with their various local branches and enterprises embarked on a calculated campaign of recruiting new friends from among politicians, administrative cadres, the new university graduates, the up-and-coming African petty-bourgeois businessmen by offering them token, but personally lucrative, shares and directorships in their local companies. The friends were, in return, to ensure the unrestricted freedom of the foreign economic interests to make profits, meaning of course the freedom to continue, unmolested, their age-old exploitation of Kenyan peasants and workers. Politically, this meant the common identity of the interests of the comprador bourgeoisie and those of the western imperialist bourgeoisie in all domestic, African and international affairs.

The nationalist bourgeoisie wanted a national economy even though its nature and forms were not clearly defined. But they wanted to at least restrict the freedom of foreign economic interests to exploit Kenyans where, when, and how they liked. They wanted a fair deal for the masses in land distribution and resettlement, in education, in negotiating deals, loans and contracts with foreign investors. Politically this meant non-alignment in international affairs; a pro-African position in pan-African affairs; and a patriotic nationalist anti-imperialist democratic line in domestic affairs.

In the section on education and culture, this pre-Kenyatta platform declared:

> In the past it has been the policy to educate a relatively small number of children on the grounds that the country does not possess the money to build the schools necessary to accommodate all the children. We firmly believe that it is better to educate all the children in huts than to waste huge sums on

expensive buildings only for a part of the numbers of those who need education . . .

KANU is strongly opposed to the practice of eliminating students by the process of examinations . . .

KANU is concerned at the present wastage when children are thrown out of school at standard IV and at KAPE levels. Not only is this wastage expensive but it brings with it numerous social problems as well as risk to security and stability. KANU believes, therefore, that in the interim period before enough facilities for higher education can be provided, all children who reach the KAPE level and cannot go further for any reason should be compulsorily required to attend a technical or vocational school for two years. Such a programme would, in addition to meeting other factors, accelerate the pace of our efforts to create a pool of skilled and semi-skilled labour . . . The children of Kenya must be taught to build their motherland and to love her rather than be allowed to develop a slavish mentality under a stilted education.

Education should instil the love of one's motherland and way of life. It should train the youth to love the freedom of their mind and body. It must foster pride in one's country so that one would want to build one's country into a great nation. It is KANU's contention that the present educational system does not make the African student take his rightful place in the fight for freedom. In other words it has not created that yearning for freedom of the individual and one's country that must necessarily be the result of a good education. What we see is the desire among the educated to compete with the local European in the superfluities of life. KANU appeals to the educated youth of Kenya to come away from their comforts so as to lead their suffering brethren into freedom.

But by 1966, the comprador bourgeois line, led by Kenyatta, Mboya and others, had triumphed. This faction, using the inherited colonial state machinery, ousted the patriotic elements from the party leadership, silencing those who remained and hounding others to death.

Economically this was reflected in the accelerated purchase of more token shares and directorships in foreign economic enterprises and the abandonment of even lip-service to nationalization. What little was nationalized earlier on was systematically turned into tax-financed private property.

Politically, it was reflected in the KANU government becoming a virtual mouthpiece of Anglo-American interests at international forums and in its down-grading relationships with anti-imperialist countries and liberation movements. In the case of China, all books and other publications, irrespective of content, published by Peking Foreign Languages Press, were banned. There is evidence that the American ambassador in the early 1960s, William Attwood, was instrumental in this banning. (See William Attwood's *The Reds and the Blacks,* a book that should be required reading for all Kenyans who seek to know why we are where we are. However, the book is banned in Kenya and is not available to Kenyans.)

In Africa, the comprador-led KANU government took a less and less pro-Africa position, culminating in that shameful act of allowing Kenyan territory to be used by Israeli Zionist commandos to strike against Uganda and in its tacit support for the Muzorewa–Smith regime in Zimbabwe.

In domestic matters, the comprador bourgeoisie abandoned democracy and any lip-service to Kenya's history of struggle, by the 1969 official mass oathing ceremonies meant to psychologically rehabilitate home-guards among the Aagĩkũyũ, Embu and Meru and by extension all those in the other nationalities who had played the rôle of home guard. Now all those who had remained 'neutral' or had sold out during the years of anti-imperialist struggle, or those who had strenuously opposed independence, were transformed into instant nationalists who had all fought for Uhuru in their different ways, however dubious and treacherous. In schools, the children were taught colonial history which glorified the rôle of traitors — Kĩnyaanjui wa Gathirimũ, Mumia, Karũri wa Gakure, Lenana, Wangoombe wa Nderi, Wambũgũ wa Mathagamia, Wangũ wa Makeri — and other collaborators with the enemy. Thus, for instance, at Lenana High School, one of the top government schools in Kenya, all the houses, and the school itself, are named after traitors like Mumia and Kĩnyaanjui.

Ideologically, the ascendancy of the comprador bourgeoisie was reflected in the change of the KANU constitution and manifesto, in effect turning the party into the opposite of what it was in 1961. The crowning glory of this turnabout was the KANU sessional paper no.10 called *African Socialism,* which is now widely recognized as the work of an American professor then in Mboya's employ at the

Ministry of Economic Planning.

KANU had changed from a mass nationalist party to a moribund bureaucratic machine catering, when necessary, for the alliance of a few home and foreign financiers. The call for a patriotic education which would instil a love for one's motherland and way of life — meaning of course a patriotic national culture which would lead the youth away from useless Euro-American superfluities — was now met with embarrassed silence or with derision and laughter. KANU had thus finally become the organ of the home-guards and the comprador bourgeoisie. By 1977, only the name remained, a hollow echo of its patriotic origins.

4

Now a comprador bourgeoisie is, by its very economic base, a dependent class, a parasitic class in the *kupe* sense. It is, in essence, a *mnyapala* class,* a handsomely paid supervisor for the smooth operation of foreign economic interests. Its political inspiration and guidance come from outside the country. This economic and political dependency is clearly reflected in its imitative culture — excrescences of New York, Los Angeles and London. For this class, as Frantz Fanon once put it, has an extreme, incurable wish for permanent identification with the culture of the imperialist bourgeoisie. Here this class faces insurmountable difficulties and contradictions. For to truly and really become an integral part of that culture, they would have to live and grow abroad. But to do so would remove the political base of their economic constitution as a class: their control of the state of a former colony and hence their ability to mortgage a whole country and its people for a few million dollars. So this class can only admire that culture from an undesirable distance and try to ape it the best they can within the severe limitations of territory and history, but with the hope that their children will be fully uninhibited and unlimited in their Euro-Americanism.

They will order suits straight from Harrods of London or *haute couture* from Paris; buy castles and estates abroad and even build seaside and country villas there; now and then go on holidays abroad to relax and shop and bank. At home, they will meticulously groom,

Kupe, tick; *mnyapala*, overseer

with the country's precious and hard-earned foreign currency reserves, a privileged elite caste of imported foreign experts and advisors, at the same time setting up a school system reproducing what they assume obtains abroad. They will send their children to the most expensive boarding schools abroad, or else approach EEC countries to build worthwhile international-class *lycées* at home for the super-elite children of the super-wealthy.

But the members of a comprador bourgeoisie of a former settler colony count themselves lucky; they don't have to travel and reside abroad to know and copy the culture of the imperialist bourgeoisie: have they not learnt it all from the colonial settler representatives of metropolitan culture? Nurtured in the womb of the old colonial system, they have matured to their full compradorial heights, looking up to the local Europeans as the alpha and omega of gentlemanly refinement and ladylike elegance. With racial barriers to class mobility thrown open, the deportment of a European gentleman— rosebuds and pins in coat lapels, spotless white kerchiefs in breast pockets, tail-coats, top-hats and gold-chained pocket watches — is no longer in the realm of dreams and wishes. Thus in a very recent book edited by Elspeth Huxley, *Pioneer's Scrapbook*, there is an approving comment about this cultural imitation:

> Henry Scott died . . . on 11 April 1911 and was buried at Kikuyu. He was succeeded in the following year by Dr J.W. Arthur, who had come to Kikuyu in 1907: a man of great personal charm and driving force, who exercised a tremendous influence over the younger Kikuyu. His habit of wearing a rosebud or carnation in his lapel is perpetuated by some of the leading politicians of the present day who were small children at Kikuyu in the late twenties.

Lady Eleanor Cole, wife of the infamous Galbraith Cole, in her otherwise dry, humourless, random recollections of settler life in Kenya, writes enthusiastically about the social scene in the Nairobi of 1917:

> Nairobi was very social and people gave formal dinner parties, at which the women were dressed in long skirted low-necked gowns and men in stiff shirts and white waistcoats or in uniform. Men and women were carefully paired, and you were

taken to dinner on the arm of your partner. There were strict rules of precedence, and woe betide the hostess who ignored them.

She is describing the Nairobi of 1917, but she could as easily have been describing Nairobi of the 1970s; only the latter Nairobi's wastefulness behind the feudal formality surpasses the former in sheer opulence.

The most popular columns in the old settler papers, *The Sunday Post* and *The Kenya Weekly News*, were the social pages listing who was who at this or that function at this or that club or at so and so's residence. The columns used to make hearts flutter, in tears or joy depending of course on whether or not one was included. Those who appeared more regularly, especially at functions in exclusive clubs and residences, were regarded with envious awe and admiration by the less fortunate aspirants. After independence, the columns ceased to be, as did the two newspapers.

Well, the columns are now back in the glossy bourgeois monthlies *Viva* and *Chic* and in the Aga Khan-owned tabloid, *The Daily Nation.* They are even more popular. The columns are still a cause for joy or sorrow to many an expectant lady and gentleman. Only that this time, among the main European and Asian actors are to be found upper-crust Kenyan blacks holding, on their gentlemanly arms, ladies bedecked with gold and diamonds holding a goblet of liquor.

Lessons learnt in the Hardinge school of philosophy. First through the bullet and the sword. Then through the more 'humane' and 'modern' methods. The character and the behaviour of the more successful pupils would have pleased Governor Hardinge and all the other tutors, from Eliot to Malcolm Macdonald, in that famous school of colonial philosophy. First the gun, cow them; then the pen take their minds prisoner; then filter them and pick out the token loyalists and bribe them numb with some semblance of power and wealth. And see the results.

Thus, the settler played golf and polo, went to horse-races or on the royal hunt in red-coats and riding-breeches, a herd of yapping and growling hounds on the chase. The black pupils now do the same, only with greater zeal: golf and horses have become 'national institutions.

The settler prostituted women, as when Karl Peters publicly hanged his African mistress because she preferred the company of her Kenyan brothers to his own. His pupils today have gone into the whole game with greater gusto: tourism, as practised today, can only thrive on the virtual prostitution of the whole country, becoming a sacred industry with shrines, under the name of hotels and lodges in all the cities and at the seaside. The modern-day Karl Peters need not use the gun to deter rivals. The name of the game now is money.*

The settler built exclusive betting clubs, drank neat whisky on the verandah of his huge mansion, or indulged in countless sun-downers and cocktail parties. Their pupils continue the process: gambling casinos and strip-tease joints get full state support and legal encouragement.

The settler despised peasant languages which he termed vernacular, meaning the languages of slaves, and believed that the English language was holy. Their pupils carry this contempt a stage further: some of their early educational acts on receiving the flag were to ban African languages in schools and to elevate English as the medium of instruction from primary to secondary stages. In some schools, corporal punishment is meted out to those caught speaking their mother tongues; fines are extorted for similar offences. Men at the top will fume in fury at fellow Africans who mispronounce English but will laugh with pride at their own inability to speak a single correct sentence in their own African languages. In some government departments, the ability to speak the Queen's English, exactly like an upper-class English gentleman, is the sole criterion for employment and promotion. But since few, if any, Africans can speak the language exactly like those native to it, only Englishmen get employed or promoted to critical positions of authority.

The settler loathed any intellectually challenging literature or any genuine creative expression, beyond imitations of sugary comedies from London performed by amateurs wearing robes flown from

* I was too hasty when I wrote this. The *Standard* of 1 October 1980 carried this report: 'American sailor Frank Joseph Sundstrom, who admitted killing a Kenyan, Monicah Njeri, in her Mombasa flat after an evening of sex, was yesterday discharged on the condition that he signed a bond of shs. 500 to be of good behaviour for the next two years.' Sundstrom, who was with the U.S.S. *La Salle*, which was then paying a good will' visit to Kenya, was tried before a white judge, L.G.E. Harris, and a white prosecutor, Nicholas Harwood. The government has granted military facilities to the U.S.A., and the *La Salle* was visiting Kenya from the U.S. Middle East fleet poised to suppress any genuine anti-imperialist nationalist uprisings in the area. The massive anger of Kenyan people at the judgement forced the retirement of Justice Harris, but a whole four months or so after the infamous judgement and even then with full benefits.

abroad to give the whole tear-jerking acrobatics a touch of the real thing. To him, African culture was a curious museum-piece or an esoteric barbaric show for the amusement of tittering ladies and gentlemen desiring glimpses of savagery. Their comprador pupils too hate books and they loathe any theatre or music that challenges their betrayal. If a certain book is in vogue, they will buy it and ask their wives or children to go through it and tell them briefly what the fuss is all about. They also loathe African culture except when it can be used to rationalize their betrayal. But they will invite a few traditional dancers to do acrobatics for visitors from abroad, later summing up the whole show with polite applause and patronizing wonder: how do these people manage such bodily contortions?

The settler built goodwill churches to thank a white God for delivering the white race from the toils of Adam and invited his African labourers to share in the joyful tidings. The settler believed in charity to passively grateful African serfs: a bit of the plunder back to the plundered? Here these dutiful pupils surpass themselves in their singular zeal to execute the same. Charity donations and church-going become 'national' imperatives and moral yardsticks for political acceptance. The cult of ostentatious godliness is raised to new ethical planes. The propertied few compete in donating money for erecting several churches in a rural village that cannot boast of a single decent primary school, much less food or water. The imperialist evangelical drive of colonial missions is now led by the state and its wealthy blacks, with the same message: trust and obey. Spiritual leaders are trotted out in a string to calm rising disgust by promising future bounty for obedient souls. There is a pathetic side to the whole exercise in apemanship exhibited by these successful pupils of Hardinge's school of philosophy:

In the 1950s a blue-blooded settler memsahib whose education never went beyond riding Arab ponies and bashing the keys of the piano, sought and found solace for her early widowhood in joining the anti-Mau Mau, anti-communist, Moral Rearmament crusade. Accompanied by a MRM team flown from its headquarters in Switzerland, paid for by the financial gnomes of Zurich, she visited schools and colleges and detention camps showing pro-imperialist religious films like *The Forgotten Factor, Freedom, The Crowning Experience,* in which anti-colonial guerrillas suddenly give up the armed struggle for liberation on learning about the presumed transforming power of the four moral absolutes of honesty, un-selfishness, purity and love. Her theme? Give up guns for holy kisses

Beware of godless communism.

Well? Soldierly religious words never die. In the 1970s the same words reappear in speeches by a senior cabinet minister, intellectual conqueror of universities in Africa and abroad, at fund-raising ceremonies for more and more goodwill churches. His theme? Beware of godless communism! This foreign ideology is against our African traditions. We are Christians and capitalists by birth and ancestry.

Thus far for the modern and humane features of Hardinge's school of philosophy. Playing golf and polo, gambling at modern casinos and horse-races, ogling at naked women in strip-tease clubs, creating a modern happy valley for moneyocrats from Germany and America, televising ostentatious displays of well-groomed holiness and Churchillian extravaganzas at weekends, speaking English with an upper-class English accent, all these seem harmless imitations although far reaching in their consequences. They can be fought if there's democracy. Reality is anyway more powerful than a million imitations.

Unfortunately, it is the repressive features of colonial culture — Hardinge's sword and bullet, as the only insurance of continuing their life-style — that seem to have most attracted the unqualified admiration of the compradors. The settler with the *sjambok* lording it over a mass of 'pulling and pushing nigger boys', that figure so meticulously preserved on the walls of 'The Lord Delamere' in the Norfolk Hotel, seems the modern ideal for the post-colonial ruling class.

How else can it be explained that the 1966 laws of detention, sedition and treason, reproduce, almost word for word, those in practice between 1951 and 1961 during the high noon of colonial culture?

Submission through the sword and the bullet! And only later is it possible to achieve the same through the modern 'peaceful' methods of churches, schools, theatres, television, cinema, colonial history, junk literature — all run, supervised and approved by foreigners!

The fact is that the comprador bourgeoisie would like to resurrect the imagined grandeur and dubious dignity of colonial culture. The unilateral arbitrary arrest and detention of Kenyans opposed to imperialist culture was a major step towards reconstruction of the new colonial Jerusalem, where people would for ever sing in unison: Trust and obey, for there is no other way, to be happy amidst us, except to trust and obey.'

'Arise colonial Lazarus' is their celebratory call to divine worship at the holy shrines of imperialism:

> Our father in Europe and America
> Hallowed be thy name
> Thy kingdom come
> Thy will be done
> In our wealthy Africa
> Our willing and welcoming Africa
> As it was done in the colonial past.
> Give us this day our daily dollar
> And forgive us our failures
> Help us triumph over those that challenge you and us
> And give us grace and aid and the power to be meek and grateful
> For ever and ever, Amen.

CHAPTER FOUR

1

Colonial Lazarus raised from the dead: this putrid spectre of our recent history haunted us daily at Kamĩtĩ Prison. It hovered over us, its shadow looming larger and larger in our consciousness as days and nights rolled away without discernible end to our sufferings. We discussed its various shades and aspects, drawing on our personal experiences, often arriving at clashing interpretations and conclusions. Who raised colonial Lazarus from the dead to once again foul the fresh air of Kenya's dawn?

To a mistaken few, this was a proof that human nature, white, black or yellow, never changes; it remains evil. To others, it was a case of the mysterious biological nature of the ruling nationality. To a few, it was merely an act of God: 'Shauri ya Mungu tu' as Mzee Duale Roble Hussein used to put it during our walks on the side-pavements. Yet to others, it was a case of civilian weakness and indiscipline: if only the military . . . ? For a few others, it was clear that this was one other result of the battle of classes and their interests, the fundamental feature behind all the vicissitudes of Kenyan history. But we all shared a common feeling: something beautiful, something like the promise of a new dawn had been betrayed, and our presence and situation at Kamĩtĩ Maximum Security Prison was a logical outcome of that historical betrayal.

Irretrievable loss: had we really come to this? Was prison our destiny as a Kenyan people? Fated always to plunge back to the days of Hardinge and Eliot, of Delamere and Grogan, only hours after being tantalized with glimpses of new dawns? What of the million dead and maimed? Was it only to enable a depraved few to carry on the colonial philosophy of Hardinge, Baring and Renison that countless poor men, women and children had sacrificed their lives?

Back in our cells, each detainee would struggle against mounting despair — the inevitable outcome of bitter reflections — churned over and over in the mind. For here one had no helper except one's own experiences and history. That, I would say, was the real loneliness of prison life. In the silence of one's cell, one had to fight, all alone, against a thousand demons struggling for the mastery of one's soul. Their dominant method was to show continually that there was only one way of looking at things, that there was only one history and culture which moved in circles, so that the beginning and the end were the same. You moved only to find yourself on the same spot. What was the point of making the effort? We were all the children of Sisyphus fated for ever to roll the heavy stone of tyranny up the steep hill of struggle, only to see it roll back to the bottom.

But wait, I shouted back at the demons of dispair. The African Sisyphus had another history, a beautiful history, a glorious history and most Kenyan people were its best illustration. It is the history of Kenyan people ceaselessly struggling against Arab feudalists and slave dealers; against Portuguese marauders who opened up Africa to her four-hundred years of devastating encounter with European domination, and later against British predators trying to embrace Kenya with claws and fangs of blood; yes, a history of Kenyan people waging a protracted guerrilla war against a British imperialist power that used to boast of its invincibility to man or God; the history of Kenyan people creating a resistance culture, a revolutionary culture of courage and patriotic heroism. The culture of the defiant Koitalel and Kĩmaathi. A fight-back, creative culture, unleashing tremendous energies among the Kenyan people.

Economically, this energy found its creative expression in the many industries set up by Kenyan people in times of national crisis. The Lumboko and Chetambe fortifications, built by the Bukusu people around Mount Elgon during their resistance against the British invasion of their country, still stand to this day as a living memorial to their courage and genius.

During the Mau Mau war for national independence, the guerrillas set up underground clothing and armament industries in the cities and upon the mountains. People who only the other day were just carpenters, plumbers and bicycle repairers, now turned their skills into manufacturing pistols, rifles and bombs under very difficult conditions. And they had triumphed.

Politically, this energy found creative expression in the sheer organizational efforts and abilities which enabled Koitalel to sustain a ten-year guerrilla struggle against vastly superior British might, a feat repeated by Kĩmaathi in the 1950s. What is fascinating is how quickly the needs of the struggle compelled such leaders to see the imperative necessity of greater unity among the various nationalities. Koitalel tried to forge a political alliance with the Luo and Baluhya peoples; Me Kitilili's oath was an attempt to unify coastal

nationalities and clans; and Kīmaathi attempted a grand political
alliance of Kenyan people to oust the imperialist enemy.

In literature, the energy found creative expression in the many
patriotic songs, poems, plays and dances over the years, giving rise to
a great patriotic literary tradition of Kenyan poetry and theatre.
There was for instance the Ituīka, a revolutionary cultural festival
among the Aagīkūyū which was enacted every twenty-five years
both as a ceremony transferring power from one generation to the
other; and as a communal renewal of their commitment to a struggle
against tyrants, as their forefathers the Iregi generation had done.
The Iregi was a generation of revolutionary rebels, who had
overthrown the corrupt dictatorial regime of King Gīkūyū, established ruling councils and established the procedure for handing over
power, an event commemorated in the Ituīka festival of music,
dance, poetry and theatre. The last such festival was held towards
the end of the nineteenth century. The next, due in about 1930, was
banned by the colonial overlords as a threat to public peace and
order.

There were also during the 1930s Mūthīrīgū dances and songs,
voicing people's rejection of forced labour, their disgust with cultural
imperialism, their uncompromising opposition to political oppression, and their strong condemnation of Kenyan collaborators with
colonialist enemy occupation. The songs and dances were banned
and many Mūthīrīgū artists were hounded to prison. But even behind
prison bars, they went on singing their patriotic poetry of protest and
commitment to freedom, ending with the chorus:

Gīthaka, Gīthaka giīkī
Gīthaka, Gīthaka giīkī
Twatigīirwo nī Iregi.

Land oh this our land
Land oh this our land
Left to us by Iregi.

The Mumboist anti-imperialist movement among the Luo and
Gusii nationalities and the anti-imperialist *Dini ya Musambwa* gave
rise to poetry, and many of the singers and composers were detained,
exiled or hounded to death. But they kept on creating new songs and
new dances. Even an artist like Mabiro Kimolai of Sibou was
arrested in 1913 when his silent art became the cry of the people.

Finally, there was the whole Mau Mau writing and publishin industry in the 1940s and 1950s. Volumes of songs, poems and pros were published. Many more songs and poems were simply commi ted to memory and were sung and recited in most homes or wherev two or more people had gathered. A people's theatre flourished awa from the stifling confines of walls and set fixed stages. Once agai the colonial overlords banned these publications; they banished th authors, composers and publishers to detention camps, prisons an cruel deaths. But even behind the barbed wire and stone walls of th colonial Jericho, they went on composing new songs and singing o a collective patriotic defiance that finally brought those wa tumbling down:

> Tūtiūragia gūthaamio
> Kana gūtwarwo Njeera
> Kana gūtwarwo icigīrīra
> Toondū tūtigaatiga
> Gūtetera ithaka/Wīyaathi
> Kenya nī būrūri wa andū airū.

> We are not afraid of detention
> Or of being sent to prison
> Or of being sent to remote islands
> For we shall never give up
> Our struggle for Land/Freedom
> Kenya is an African people's country.

The period produced some romantic figures, like the legendar Maraanga wa Gītoonga who would not leave his guitar behind as l went to fight in the forest.

This culture generated courage, not fear; defiance of oppressio not submission; pride in self and in one's country, not coward acceptance of national humiliation; loyalty to Kenya, not its betray to imperialism. And it was precisely in reaction to the people history as change and the revolutionary culture it generated, that th colonial rulers had tried to humiliate Africa's Sisyphus into accep ing the oppressor's view of history — that all efforts to change th reality would end in futility.

The colonial culture of silence and fear, then, was primarily reaction to the Kenyan people's revolutionary culture of outspoke courage and patriotic heroism. For instance, Hardinge's philosop of the sword and the bullet was a reactionary reply to the people's philosophy of struggle and resistance against foreign occupation. Put it this way: would Hardinge have called for the use of the bullet if there had been no armed resistance? Would he have tried to force submission if there had been no defiance? In the same vein, the Ituĩka revolutionary cultural festival and the Mũthĩrĩgũ dances and songs were suppressed because they obviously carried the aesthetic line that struggle to change an oppressive status quo was a good thing. In their turn, the foreign missionary churches intensified efforts to promulgate colonial religions and cultures that carried the aesthetic line of the beauty of revelling in slavery. The colonial regime built more church and government schools — after suppressing people's own institutions of learning like Gĩthũũngũri Teachers' College, the Kikuyu Karĩng'a and Independent schools which taught pride in self and country — to propagate, unchallenged, the godly ideals of happiness in submissive obedience.

Finally, the institution of British theatre in Kenya in the 1950s was a reactionary response to the resurgence of a popular dance and theatre following the return of embittered Kenyan soldiers from the European-generated Second World War. The colonial regime had cause for alarm. The anti-imperialist Mũthuũ dances had spread in central Kenya like fire across a dry plain. In Nyeri, Kĩmaathi had started the Gĩcamu theatre movement with its base in Karũna-inĩ. Patriotic dance and theatre had become a common feature in all the people's own schools. The British countered this by starting theatre clubs for British plays and players: the Little Theatre in Mombasa in 1948; the Donovan Maule Theatre in Nairobi in 1949; and similar clubs in Nakuru, Eldoret, and Kitale at about the same period. In 1952 the colonial regime, in concert with the British Council, started the British Kenya National Theatre. Here an annual schools' English drama festival was started, with the British Council as the main donor of prizes for deserving African children. During the same period, a European drama and music officer was appointed to control the growth of African theatre in all Kenyan schools. In places like the Alliance High School, the performance of Shakespeare became an annual ritual attended by colonial governors and applauding administrators. But it was Shakespeare trimmed to fit into trousers manufactured by the British Council. Evidence for all this comes from another horse's mouth. In *Race Against Time*, Richard Frost, former head of the Empire Information Service and the British Council's first representative in East Africa, offers fantastic revelations about the deliberate manner in which the whole imperialist cultural programme was put into force. Thus of the establishment of the British Kenya National Theatre, built under direct instruction from the Colonial Office to meet the urgent need for fostering improved race relations through an organization which would aim, in the first place, at establishing primarily cultural facilities, Frost writes:

> The National Theatre was built where it was because those who planned the scheme, including Thornly Dyer, the architect who designed the Parliament Building and conceived the master plan for Nairobi, wanted to build the National Theatre in the 'snob' centre of Nairobi. The instruction given by the Secretary of State to the British Council Representative was to build a National Theatre and Cultural Centre where people of culture and position could meet. At that time no Africans were able to live anywhere near the site which was selected, but that site was chosen because it was hoped that in due time the residential *apartheid* would be brought to an end and Muthaiga, Westlands, the Hill and other areas, which were then open only to Europeans, would become districts where leading people of all races would live.

And on the Kenya Drama Festival Richard Frost is even more forthright about its cultural basis for creating a Kenyan colonial elite:

> The Kenya Drama Festival, which has an offshoot in the Schools Drama Festival, was the result of a plan put into operation in 1951. The British Council had to win the goodwill of Europeans and do what it could to help them to keep at a high standard the cultural heritage of Britain. Drama was a cultural activity enjoyed by both actors and audiences and it was also an activity in which Africans and Asians engaged. It was hoped that through the theatre the goodwill of the European community could be gained, European cultural standards could be helped, and, later on, members of the different races could be brought together by participation in a common pursuit which they all enjoyed.

Apart from schools, the Moral Rearmament team toured detention camps showing pro-imperialist films and plays, while at the same time trying to organize theatre groups among the political prisoners to stage nice Christian plays about prodigal sons and forgiving fathers. They even recruited their own writers from among the political prisoners. In *Mau Mau Detainee*, J.M. Kariũki has described this pro-imperialist theatre and writing:

> Benjamin was a very clever and able man and an expert at writing booklets in Kikuyu. He was a co-operator, but a most subtle one. He never beat anyone and he always treated the other detainees well. He composed a skilful pamphlet on 'confession' which was given to us all. He also produced sketches and plays in which the man who had confessed was always richer or surpassed in some way the man who remained hardcore. The warders and the softcore liked these very much. We condemned them as the Wamarebe Plays.

Empty Tins Theatre: what an apt description of imperialist and pro-imperialist theatre and culture!

Kenyan people's theatre survived this reactionary onslaught. In Nyeri, Theuri started a theatre group on the ruins of those banned by the British. He staged plays in the Gĩkũyũ language. In schools like The Alliance High School, some students rebelled against the cult of Shakespeare in British Council trousers and started writing their own plays in Kiswahili. These they took to the villages around Nairobi and to African locations in Nakuru, the heartland of settler culture. In the forests and the mountains, the Mau Mau guerrillas continued their patriotic dances, songs and theatre with one main theme: death to British imperialism; bury the white imperialist and his black running dogs. Well, their theatre called a dog a dog and not by any other name.

See now the dialectical workings of history: it was the British invaders who actually became terrified of the people's vigorous culture of revolutionary courage and optimistic determination. The indomitable strength and resilience of Kenyan popular culture had struck terror, fear and panic among the foreign settlers who felt stalked by naked insecurity on every side. They now ate, drank and even made love in uniforms of newly sharpened bayonets and nailed boots. By the 1950s, in the very high noon of their reactionary culture, their homes had become virtual fortifications complete with ramparts, moats, spikes, sirens, drawbridges, while bloodhounds, Mbwa Kali, kept guard at the gates of the erstwhile paradise.

Raise colonial Lazarus from the dead? The fact is that the heirs of this, the current ruling class, have also been caught in the dialectical net of history. Thus in Kenya today, the Kenya of colonial Lazarus raised from the dead, it is not the peasants and workers who walk about in abject terror. Why should they? They possess no stolen property to disturb their nightly sleep lest the owner should knock at the door. Their sole fear is that the police or the General Service Unit (GSU) will molest them.

On the contrary, it is the comprador minority propertied class and its foreign friends that now walk the streets stalked by naked insecurity from every side. Their homes, like those of the settler minority whose culture they have chosen to emulate, have become virtual fortifications complete with guns, sirens, electronic surveillance and bloodhounds, *Mbwa Kali!* The neo-colonial resurgence of this *Mbwa Kali* culture was concretely demonstrated in 1979, when the guards of the American-owned Del Monte fruit company in Thika set their dogs on innocent Kenyan children and killed one girl and maimed the other. Their fear is such that they cannot even fully trust the coercive machinery of their state for total security. Might not that soldier or that policeman one day remember that he too is a worker of peasant origin, now earning a miserable Judas pay to suppress members of his own class? So they go for supplementary protection from foreigners. Foreign-owned security companies — like the London-based British Securicor guards or the Israeli-run Ossica — are doing a lucrative business in Kenya as hired security officers in a vast ministry of fear. *The Weekly Review* of 11 January 1980 says:

> Good security is expensive, but the cost of no security is higher. Awareness of this fact has resulted in the proliferation of over 90 security firms throughout Kenya that employ no fewer than 20,000 people — as home guards, factory guards, guards for business premises and guards who escort cash in transit.
>
> Even though these firms might never be able to guarantee absolute security of property from theft, the call for guards grows. Home guards have even become a much-sought-after status symbol among affluent Kenyans. Not surprisingly many security firms tend to concentrate their home-guard services in Nairobi's posh residential ares to satisfy the high demand. But

residents in a number of housing estates in the city also pool their resources to hire watchmen . . .

Securicor (Kenya) Limited is the biggest such organization. It was formed in 1969 when it acquired a number of small local security firms complete with staff and assets. In those days operations were confined to Nairobi and Mombasa and the Securicor pay-roll contained about 2,000 names. Today the company employs more than 4,500 people and has 19 branches in different parts of Kenya . . . Securicor Kenya is part of the British Securicor group, the largest industrial security organization in Great Britain and one of the biggest on the whole of the European continent . . .

Foreign-run private armies to protect foreigners and a handful of Kenyans from the wrath of fellow Kenyans: what an irony of history!

The culture of silence and fear had achieved a dialectically opposite effect. Kenyan people had rejected the view of history which the colonial and neo-colonial gods had tried to impose on rebellious Sisyphus. Why should I accept it?

2

In my cell, number 16, continuously thinking about the beauty of our history, I became more and more convinced that in their vindictive agitation for the banning of our theatre efforts at Kamĩrĩĩthũ and in their feverish clamour for my incarceration, the comprador bourgeoisie and their foreign friends had been driven by fear. True to their colonial cultural inheritance, they were mortally scared of peasants and workers who showed no fear in their eyes; workers and peasants who showed no submissiveness in their bearing; workers and peasants who proclaimed their history with unashamed pride and who denounced its betrayal with courage. Yes, like their colonial counterparts, they had become mortally afraid of the slightest manifestation of a people's culture of patriotic heroism and outspoken indomitable courage.

Eliud Njenga, the then Kĩambu district commissioner who presided over the banning of the public performances of *Ngaahika Ndeenda*, voiced the general panic of this class when, in an interview with *The Nairobi Times*, he claimed that on top of the play raising the best-be-forgotten issues of the patriotic rôle of Mau Mau guerrillas and the traitorous rôle of home-guards during the struggle for Kenya's independence, it was also calling for a class struggle.

He was of course wrong about the latter. The play, as I was to afterwards try to explain to the Detainees' Review Tribunal (chaired by a British ex-judge) of July 1978, could never have called into being what was already there. Classes and class struggle were the very essence of Kenyan history. The play did not invent that history. It merely reflected it — correctly.

But the D.C. was expressing a deeper fear: the comprador bourgeoisie believed in the magic omnipotence of an imperialist colonial culture. Why else raise a putrid corpse from the grave? But here were ordinary peasants and workers at Kamīrĩĩthũ showing up the putrescent impotence of that borrowed culture. Moreover, they were acting it out to thunderous applause from appreciative thousands who had trekked on foot and in hired matatus and buses from all parts of the country. Was Kamīrĩĩthũ becoming a revolutionary shrine?

3

Kamirĩĩthũ! It is difficult for me to conjure up in adequate literary terms the different images I have of Kamirĩĩthũ. The name is a diminutive form of Mĩrĩĩthũ, meaning a flat place on which rests a pool of water defiant to drought.* Little Mĩrĩĩthũ is bound by three sloping ridges that make it look like a rectangular trough which is open on one of its smaller sides facing Maanguuũ marches. In my youth, all the sloping ridges were strips of cultivated fields with a few people's homesteads scattered about. A few Swahili *majengo*-type houses were built on the flat murram trough, away from the pool. It was a path through Kamirĩĩthũ that in 1947 I daily followed to Kamaandũra school, about two miles from home.

It was at Kamĩrĩĩthũ that I first saw Nyambura and thought her the most beautiful woman I had ever seen, and vowed there and there that she would one day be my wife. That this came to pass several years after I am sure had nothing to do with that boy's vow, but it had everything to do with the fact in the new Kamĩrĩĩthũ to be, our two

---

*A trans-Africa highway has now been built through Kamirĩĩthũ and has for ever drained the defiant pool.

homes were separated by only a street. Njooki, my daughter whose photograph kept me company in prison, was named after Nyambura's mother. But the Kamīrīīthū peasants called the child Wamūingī, meaning that she belonged to them, she belonged to all Kamīrīīthū.

As part of Limuru, Kamīrīīthū is crucial to Kenya's history of struggle. Some KCA leaders, like Johana Wakīraka, came from that area. The lands at Tigoni and Kanyaawa, where in the 1920s people had been ejected by force to make room for more European settlement, are only a few yards away from Kamīrīīthū. A railway-line divided the stolen lands where the settlers soon set up the Limuru Hunt, the Limuru Golf-Course, the Limuru Racecourse, the Limuru Farmers' Corner — all high-class cultural rendezvous — from the African reservations of cheap labour and sex. I have tried to describe the lanscape in *Weep not, Child* where Kipanga town obviously stands for Limura, or Rūūngai as the town was popularly known. One of the valleys described in *Weep not, Child* originates from Kamīrīīthū.

When in 1948 I left the mission-run Kamaandūra School for the Gīkūyū Karīng'a School at Maanguuū, I never visited Kamīrīīthū except once briefly in 1953, when as a newly circumcised youth complete with my initiate's robe of white cloth decorated with several safety pins and one cent pieces, I went across it, through the cultivated fields on one of the ridge slopes, and on to Tharūni and Ndīiya on the edges of Maasailand to visit other *riika* initiates to sing and dance the stick dance called *waine*.

That was in fact my very last impression of old Kamīrīīthū when in 1955 I went from my home village overlooking Limuru town to Alliance High School, Kikuyu, hidden in the guardroom of a goods train through the friendly efforts of Chris Kahara, then a railway official. I had no movement pass. The year before, my elder brother, Wallace Mwangi, had joined the Mau Mau guerrilla army after a dramatic escape from police custody. Many home-guard loyalists would never forgive me for what some thought a miscarriage of educational justice: a brother of a Mau Mau 'terrorist' securing a place in one of the then top African schools in colonial Kenya?

I came back after the first term and confidently walked back to my old village. My home was now only a pile of dry mud-stones, bits of grass, charcoal and ashes. Nothing remained, not even crops, except for a lone pear tree that slightly swayed in sun and wind. I stood there bewildered. Not only my home, but the old village with its culture, its

memories and its warmth had been razed to the ground. I walked up
the ridge not knowing whither I was headed until I met a solitary old
woman. Go to Kamĩrĩĩthũ, she told me.

Kamĩrĩĩthũ was now no longer the name of a trough with a defiant
pool of water surrounded by a few Swahili houses, but the name of a
new 'emergency village' on one of the sloping ridges next to the path I
used to follow on my way to Kamaandũra. I walked through the new
village asking people for my new home and passed through the
present site of Kamĩrĩĩthũ Community Theatre. All around me, I saw
women and children on rooftops with hammers and nails and poles
and thatch, building the new homes because their men were in
detention camps or away with the people's guerrilla army. Many
critics have noted the dominance of the theme of return in my novels,
plays and short stories, particularly in *A Grain of Wheat*. But none
has known the origins of the emotion behind the theme. It is deeply
rooted in my return to Kamĩrĩĩthũ in 1955. The return of Mau Mau
political detainees was to come later.

Initially, the village was a riotous mass of smoking straw
mushrooms. Later in 1956 or 1957, when the decision was taken to
turn the emergency concentration villages into permanent features to
facilitate the creation of an African landed middle class through land
consolidation and the enclosure system, while retaining the villages
as permanent reservoirs of cheap labour for both the 'white'
highlands and for the new African landlords, the village was
expanded with slightly better planning. The yeomen were later
allowed to build homes in their enclosures and they quit the villages.
The landless remained. Four acres of land were set aside for a youth
centre. A mud-walled barrack-type building was put up there. That
was all.

Kamĩrĩĩthũ has not changed much from its emergency origins.
Poverty is still the king. Many families live on village paths. And of
course Kamĩrĩĩthũ is still a reservoir of cheap labour for the new
Kenyan landlords and Euro-American multi-nationals who, at
independence, replaced the former British landlords in the sprawling
green fields of tea and coffee around Tigoni and beyond. To be
wealthy in Kenya today is incomplete without land in Limuru. The
golf-course and the race course remain. The Limuru Hunt is still the
big event of the Year. Every weekend, a troupe of unemployed youth
from Kamĩrĩĩthũ go to the premises of Tigoni Golf Club to offer their
services as caddies for the local and foreign golf-playing tycoons.

During the emergency, the youth centre at Kamĩrĩĩthũ was the meeting place for boys and girls to dance *erithi* and *nyangwĩcũ* and other dances of the period. After independence, the centre came under Limuru Area Council and a few carpentry classes were started. In 1974, the Limuru Area Council was disbanded. The centre had now nobody to look after it. But it remained . . . a four classroomed barrack with broken walls, occupying about a quarter of an acre with the other four and three-quarters making a grazing ground for a few solitary cows and goats. The village children also found a good common ground for their games of wrestling and dice-throwing. They also used it as a toilet and the stench was overpowering. There has never been any health programme for this village of more than ten thousand souls.

The only major cultural activity on this grass in Kamĩrĩĩthũ occurred in 1976 when the University of Nairobi Free Travelling Theatre, run by the Department of Literature, performed some plays including extracts from *The Trial of Dedan Kimathi* written by Mĩcere Mũgo and myself. Otherwise the centre was dead to real culture.

It was through the tireless efforts of a community development officer, Njeeri wa Aamoni, that a new committee made up of concerned villagers was formed to revive the centre and run it on a self-help basis. That was how I came to join the new management committee under the chairmanship of Adolf Kamau, a peasant-farmer, and later Ngigĩ Mwaũra, then a sales director with a motor vehicle company. Karaanja, a primary-school teacher from the village, was the secretary. But the majority of the committee members were peasants and workers from the village.

The committee changed the name of the youth centre to Kamĩrĩĩthũ Community Education and Cultural Centre, reflecting a new ambitious programme for uplifting the place and change the lives of the villagers through what we called a Harambee of sweat. The committee decided that money was not the basis of development. Human hands and brains were the basis. Co-operative labour, not money and Harambee charity handouts, was going to develop the centre along several broad lines and phases: adult education (adult literacy, continuing education, etc.); cultural development (music, dance drama, etc.); material culture (furniture, basketry, leather-work, music crafts — all the material objects daily used by the community); and health. The centre was going to be run on a democratic collective decision-making basis, all of us drawing on our different experiences in identifying and tackling problems. Each problem area would come under a sub-committee. Initially, two sub-committees were set up for education and culture, with provision for more to deal with community health and material culture.

I was elected the chairman of the cultural committee, and Ngũgĩ wa Mĩriĩ, a researcher in adult literacy at the University of Nairobi, the chairman of the education committee. The first programme was literacy; the centre started with a class of fifty-five workers and peasants in June 1976, and by the end of the year all could read and write in Gĩkũyũ language. We had established roots.

We were now ready to venture into cultural activities. Here most of the peasants and workers were quite clear as to what they wanted. Some had already participated in or seen concerts and playlets by a group of workers at St Lwanga Catholic Church at Kamĩrĩĩthũ. Others had seen the plays of the University of Nairobi Free Travelling Theatre. Yet others had been to the controversial Kenya National Theatre in Nairobi in October 1976, and had seen the Kenya Festac'77 Drama Group's performance of the complete version of *The Trial of Dedan Kimathi* as brilliantly directed by Seth Adagala. Now they wanted similar efforts at Kamĩrĩĩthũ!

Plays would serve three main purposes. They would serve as entertainment and collective self-education; they would form follow-up reading material for the new literates; and they would raise money to finance the other programmes, material culture and health for instance, and to meet the day-to-day expenses like chalk, writing materials and electricity bills. That was how in December 1976 Ngũgĩ wa Mĩriĩ and I came to be given the task of producing a working script. The script had to be ready by March 1977.

We could not meet the March deadline. But by April 1977, an outline of the script of *Ngaahika Ndeenda* was ready. For the next two months the peasants now added to the script, altering this and that. Reading of the final working script and rehearsals started on 5 June 1977. The actual performances would commence on 2 October, the twenty-fifth anniversary of the declaration of the State of Emergency in Kenya and the beginning of the Mau Mau armed struggle.

The six months between June and November 1977 were the most exciting in my life and the true beginning of my education. I learnt my language anew. I rediscovered the creative nature and power of collective work.

Work, oh yes, work! Work, from each according to his ability for a collective vision, was the great democratic equalizer. Not money,

not book education, but work. Not three-piece suits with carnations
and gloves, not tongues of honey, but work. Not birth, not palaces,
but work. Not globe-trotting, not the knowledge of foreign tongues
and foreign lands, not dinners at foreign inns of court, but work. Not
religions, not good intentions, but work. Work and yet more work,
with collective democratic decisions on the basis of frank criticisms
and self-criticism, was the organizing principle which gradually
emerged to become the corner-stone of our activities.

Although the overall direction of the play was under Kĩmani
Gecau, the whole project became a collective community effort with
peasants and workers seizing more and more initiative in revising
and adding to the script, in directing dance movements on the stage,
and in the general organization.

I saw with my own eyes an incredible discipline emerge in keeping
time and in cutting down negative social practices. Drinking alcohol,
for instance. It was the women's group, led by Gaceeri wa
Waigaanjo, who imposed on themselves a ban on drinking alcohol,
even a glass, when coming to work at the centre. This spread to all the
other groups including the audience. By the time we came to perform,
it was generally understood and accepted that drunkenness was not
allowed at the centre. For a village which was known for drunken
brawls, it was a remarkable achievement of our collective self-
discipline that we never had a single incident of fighting or a single
drunken disruption for all the six months of public rehearsals and
performances.

I saw with my own eyes peasants, some of whom had never once
been inside a theatre in their lives, design and construct an open-air
theatre complete with a raised stage, roofed dressing-rooms and
stores, and an auditorium with a seating capacity of more than two-
thousand persons. Under a production team led by Gatoonye wa
Mũgoiyo, an office messenger, they experimented with matchsticks
on the ground before building a small working model on which they
based the final complex.

The rehearsals, arranged to fit in with the working rhythms of the
village, which meant mostly Saturday and Sunday afternoons, were
all in the open, attracting an ever-increasing crowd of spectators and
an equally great volume of running appreciative or critical commen-
taries. The whole process of play-acting and production had been de-
mystified and the actors and the show were the gainers for it. The
dress rehearsal on Sunday, 25 September 1977, attracted one of the
biggest crowds I have ever seen for a similar occasion, and the same

level of high attendance was maintained for the next four Saturdays and six Sundays.

Furthermore, the whole effort unleashed a torrent of talents hitherto unsuspected even by the owners. Thus before the play was over, we had already received three scripts of plays in the Gĩkũyũ language, two written by a worker, and one by a primary school teacher. One unemployed youth, who had tried to commit suicide four times because he thought his life was useless, now suddenly discovered that he had a tremendous voice which, when raised in a song, kept its listeners on dramatic tenter-hooks. None of the actors had ever been on a stage before, yet they kept the audiences glued to their seats, even when it was raining. One of the most insulting compliments came from a critic who wrote that the orchestra was professional and had been hired from Nairobi. Another insulting compliment came from those who heatedly argued that simple villagers could never attain that excellence; that the actors were all university students dressed in the tattered clothes of peasants. Another equally insulting compliment came from a university lecturer in literature who argued that the apparent effortless ease of the acting was spontaneous: after all, the villagers were acting themselves. The fact was that all the actors and musicians, men, women and children, came from the village, and they put in more than four months of conscious disciplined work. Some of our university lecturers and those other critics, in their petty-bourgeois blindness, could never conceive peasants as being capable of sustained disciplined intellectual efforts.

For myself, I learnt a lot. I had been delegated to the rôle of a messenger and a porter, running errands here and there. But I also had time to observe things. I saw how the people had appropriated the text, improving on the language and episodes and metaphors, so that the play which was finally put on to a fee-paying audience on Sunday, 2 October 1977, was a far cry from the tentative awkward efforts originally put together by Ngũgĩ and myself. I felt one with the people. I shared in their rediscovery of their collective strength and abilities, and in their joyous feeling that they could accomplish anything — even transform the whole village and their lives without a single Harambee of charity — and I could feel the way the actors were communicating their joyous sense of a new power to their audience who too went home with gladdened hearts.

Before long, we had received one delegation from Gĩkaambura village, in Kikuyu; and another from Kanyaarĩrĩ, on how they too could start a similar community cultural project. Another group of teachers came from Nyaandaarwa North and they too wanted to start their own Kamīrīīthū.

Then suddenly the KANU government, through its district commissioner at Kīambu, struck with venom. In a letter to the chairman of Kamīrīīthū Community Educational and Cultural Centre dated 16 December 1977, he withdrew the licence for further performances of *Ngaahika Ndeenda* and he thus plunged a three-year-old communal vision into a sea of sorrow and depression. He later elaborated on the reasons for banning further performances by citing public security. He should have more truthfully cited the public insecurity of a few individuals who thought their reservoir of cheap labour and sex was threatened by the new confidence generated among the villagers by the new theatre.

The comprador bourgeoisie could have their golf, polo, cricket, rugger, tennis, squash, badminton; their horse and motor-races; their royal hunt; their German, American, French, English, Italian theatre, cinema, music, concerts; their swimming pools and expensive sauna and massage clubs; their choice of expensive drinks after an easy day's work; their gambling casinos and striptease joints with white nudes imported from Soho, Las Vegas and Stockholm; their endless cocktail parties with the participants featured in the socialite pages of *Viva, The Daily Nation* and *Chic;* but the peasants with clods of clay had no right to a theatre which correctly reflected their lives, fears, hopes, dreams and history of struggle; had no right to their creative efforts even in their own backyards. The foreign imperialist church with its eternal call for submissive trust and blind obedience, and the foreign-owned breweries of mass soporiferous drinks were now their only legalized cultural alternatives.

These men who had so callously razed the Kamīrīīthū people's cultural effort to the ground (some like the D.C. Kīambu had not even bothered to see it) had acted in the dog-in-the-manger tradition of those 'faceless faces of important men' once described by Sylvia Plath:

> It is these men I mind:
> They are so jealous of anything that is not flat!
> They are jealous gods.
> They would have the whole world flat because they are.

They might of course be flat but they had the power of the police truncheons and the law courts, of the bullet and the prison, and woe

unto them that challenge the legalized necessity of flat lives!
the law courts, of the bullet and the prison, and woe unto them that
challenge the legalized necessity of flat lives!

A problem remained. The play's performances had been duly
licensed by the office of the same district commissioner, Kīambu.
Everything at the centre had been done in the open, including the
play-reading sessions, the selection of actors and all the rehearsals.
Kamīrīīthū Community Education and Cultural Centre was itself
legally registered as a self-help project with the Department of
Community Development of the Ministry of Housing and Social
Services. In its official submissions to the UNESCO general
assembly in Nairobi in 1976, the KANU government had made a
very strong case for integrated rural development with culture,
including rural village theatres as a central core, and this had been
accepted. Indeed a senior cabinet minister in the KANU government was then the current president of UNESCO. Now a popular
people's play had been refused further performances by a government which had hosted UNESCO and endorsed its cultural policies,
and no satisfactory reason was forthcoming!

How now to deceive the nation and the whole world? Incarcerate
the whole village? Detain a whole community? But there had been no
riots, no drunken brawls, no open defiance of any existing laws. On
the contrary, the crime rate and drunkenness in the village had
markedly fallen for the duration of the play's run! Besides, detaining
a whole village would severely drain a necessary reservoir of cheap
labour. Who would now pick tea-leaves and coffee beans? Who
would cultivate the fields for a pittance?

There was of course an easier way. What right had a university
professor to work with ragged-trousered workers and tattered
peasants and even 'pretend' to be learning from a people whose
minds we have decreed should never rise above the clods of clay they
daily break? What is he really up to? Let us thwart his intentions —
whatever they are. Incarcerate the clever fellow!

That was how it came to pass that at midnight on December 30-31
1977, I was taken from my home and led in chains to Kamītī
Maxiumum Security Prison. I had entered political detention. For a
whole year I was to remain in cell 16 wrestling with multifarious
demons in the dry wilderness of Kamītī Prison, contemplating the
two dialectically opposed traditions of Kenyan history, culture and
aesthetics. They had raised colonial Lazarus from the dead. Who
will bury him again?

CHAPTER FIVE

1

The wrestling with demons in the stony and dusty wilderness of Kenya's detention camps since 1895 has produced two types of political prisoners: those who finally succumbed and said 'Yes' to an oppressive system; and those that defied and maintained 'Never!'

The demons led the acquiescent type down the abyss of despair to a valley of white bones. There, they allowed him a glimpse of African Sisyphus endlessly labouring to push up the rock of oppression, only to see it roll back to the original spot. This is your black fate, the demons told him, and waited for his reactions. They saw that he believed this vision of despair. They let him be overwhelmed by the vision of doom. They would then graciously offer mediation services. Then suddenly or gradually, depending on how they read his character and the situation outside the stony wilderness, they showed him the only way to personal salvation: 'Resist Not Evil'. He took that way out. This type of detainee came out of the wrestling match a broken soul ready to denounce in both words and deeds his previous stands and actions.

Harry Thuku was the greatest threat to colonial settlerdom in the 1920s. As the leader of the East African Association, he inspired the workers to organize to fight against forced labour, female and child slavery, high taxation without even a little representation, low wages, and against the oppressive *kipande* that the workers were obliged to carry with chains around their necks. Unlike some labour leaders, who, like Mboya, later came to deceive workers that trade unionism could be divorced from politics, Harry Thuku clearly saw that the solution to the workers' problems lay in politics. The economic emancipation of the worker was through political struggle and never through apolitical trade unionism. Thus the East African Association further demanded that Kenya must not be a colony; that elections to the legislative council should be on a common roll; and that all the stolen lands should be returned to the rightful owners. Harry Thuku strenuously fought and exposed the divisive ideology of racism, rejecting, for instance, the white settlers' attempts to divide Asian and African workers. This was the Harry Thuku who could write so movingly about the emerging unity of workers of different nationalities and religious faiths. He wrote in the workers' newspaper *Tangazo:*

> I was very delighted to be travelling to the meeting at Ng'enda because I was accompanied by the school-teacher, Samuel Okoth, a Christian from Maseno; and two Muslims, their names were Abdullla Tairara and Ali Kironjo. We were very pleased at our trip for we travelled as brothers. And I saw no difference between the Kavirondo and the man from Kikuyu, or even between the Christian believer and the believer in Islam.

Thus, the 'famed' traditional rivalry between Aagĩkũyũ and the Luo people was clearly a later colonial invention. The fact is that, right from the beginning, the two nationalities had the biggest working-class elements. The unity of Mũũgĩkũyũ worker and the Jaluo worker (because of their numbers) was always a threat to imperialism in Kenya, and Harry Thuku understood this. Unfortunately so did the foreign settlers, and the long line of Kenyan collaborators with imperialism. They had to create artifical rivalry as they still do.

This was the Harry Thuku who on being threatened by the colonial regime with the choice of either losing his well-paid job at the treasury or giving up political struggle, promptly and proudly replied: 'I choose politics.' This was indeed the Harry Thuku who could see that colonial chiefs, like Kĩnyaanjui, were like dogs: 'They bark at the sound of other dogs, when their masters want them to, and also when they want to be fed by the government.'

Not surprisingly, his arrest on 14 March 1922, brought about one of the biggest workers' mass protests and demonstrations in the streets of Nairobi. The colonial regime, true to its cultural traditions, responded to the workers' demands for Thuku's release with mounted troops and rifles. One-hundred-and-fifty workers, including their leader Mary Mũthoni Nyanjirũ, were ruthlessly massacred while at the Norfolk Hotel's 'house of lords', the settlers joined in the massacre and cheered and drank whisky at the sight of the workers blood. This Harry Thuku has already moved into patriotic heroic legends and I have treated him as such in the early chapters of my novel *A Grain of Wheat.*

But after nine years of lonely detention at Kismayu, Lamu and

Marsabit, where he was constantly indoctrinated by the demons in the physical form of district commissioners, he came back, joined the militant KCA (the political successor to his banned East African Association) and he, having succumbed, immediately tried to turn it into a colonial instrument.

Fortunately, Jesse Kariũki and the other KCA leaders saw through him: this was a different Thuku from the one for whom women workers had composed a praise song, nick-naming him *Mũnene wa Nyacĩng'a*. In people's politics, there is no room for sentimentality. It can prove fatal and treacherous to a movement, and the KCA leaders had grasped this. They threw him out.

Harry Thuku wasted no time in acting out his new chosen rôle of colonial messenger. He formed a loyalist Kikuyu Provincial Association to fight against the Kenya nationalists:

> Every member of this organization will be pledged to be loyal to His Majesty the King of Great Britain and the established government and will be bound to do nothing which is not constitutional according to the British traditions or do anything which is calculated to disturb the peace, good order and government.

This colonial zombie, a total negation of his earlier pre-detention self, could years later write admiringly about colonial chiefs whom earlier he had correctly described as dogs:

> Some of the bravest people during Mau Mau were the Christians; many were murdered because they refused to take the oath. And if they were forced they would go and confess it the next day. Chief Njiiri was like this too. When the Emergency broke out, he hoisted the Union Jack in the centre of his village, and I remember one meeting with Sir Evelyn Baring where I was present when Njiiri asked for permission to go into the forest and fight 'these evil people' himself.

He should have added that the same chief was later to smash his radio set to pieces when in 1961 he heard that Kenyatta and the Mau Mau leaders were to be released from detention to return home as nationalist leaders of Kenya's independence.

In his autobiography published in 1970, Harry Thuku shows not the slightest awareness of his divided loyalties. The colonial aesthetic of submissive trust had done its work. Harry Thuku was broken by nine years of detention and had said 'yes' to colonial culture.

Jomo Kenyatta was another terror of the same colonial settler-dom and imperialism in the 1930s and 1950s. This was the Kenyatta who, as a KCA delegate in London, could write in *The Sunday Worker* of 27 October 1929 words still ringing with contemporary relevance in today's anti-imperalist struggles:

> The present situation means that once again the natives of the colony are showing their determination not to submit to the outrageous tyranny which has been their lot since the British robbers stole their land . . . (Kenyans) have found themselves constantly denuded of their land, and compelled by means of forced labour to work the vast natural wealth of their country for the profit of their interloping imperialist bosses. Discontent has always been rife among (Kenyans) and will be so until they govern themselves . . .Sir Edward Grigg talks of 'agitation' there is agitation, an agitation that meets a hearty response from robbed and maltreated Africans, and will not cease until we are our own rulers again.*

Recalling the 1922 massacre of Kenyan workers outside the Norfolk Hotel, he wrote a strong denunciation in *The Daily Worker* of January 1930 with the prohetic words that Kenyan people will never forget these imperialist atrocities:

> I was in the crowd myself and saw men, women and children killed, and many others lying in agony. It was a most terrible massacre of people who were quite unarmed and defenceless and the people of Kenya will not forget. †

*This and most subsequent extracts from speeches by Kenyatta are taken from Murray-Brown's book *Kenyatta*.

†After the bomb blast at the Norfolk Hotel on New Year's Eve 1980, a European journalist, Brian Tetley, wrote an article for *The Sunday Nation* of 4 January 1981 in which, recalling the gory massacre of Kenyans by foreigners at the Norfolk Hotel in 1922, he remarked: 'There was a reason, however bad, for this tragedy'. Thus the massacre of Kenyans by foreigners is understandable; the bomb blast is not.

Or later in 1934, in his contribution to Nancy Cunard's anthology, *Negro:*

> Kenya is the most important British colony in East Africa . . . During the past thirty five years (our) people have been robbed of their best land and are reduced to the status of serfs forced to work on their own lands for the benefit of the white 'owners', and even in some circumstances to work without pay or food . . . The soul of the African is stricken nigh to death by confiscation of its ancestral lands, the obstruction of its free development in social and economic matters, and its sub-jugation to an imperialist system of slavery, tax-paying, pass-carrying, and forced labour. This policy of British imperialist robbery and oppression aroused the greatest alarm and anxiety amongst the Kenyan Africans, the outcome of which was the revolt of 1922, when defenceless Africans, men, women and children, were shot down by these filibusters.

Yes, this was the Kenyatta who could castigate in the strongest possible terms the colonial culture of golf, polo and whisky. He condemned the seduction of African girls 'to satisfy their (the colonialists') bestial lust . . .' concluding that colonialist 'civilization is all in the interest of capitalist greed and imperialist exploitation'. He wrote in the 1933 issue of Marcus Garvey's *The Negro Worker,* that: 'The missionaries . . . are agents of the imperialists who teach Africans that they must tolerate all oppression and exploitation in order that they shall have a good home and better conditions in heaven when they die.'

In the November 1933 issue of *The Labour Monthly,* Kenyatta might almost have been talking about the Africa of the 1980s when he wrote the following prophecy:

> Perhaps many will ask: what can we do against an imperialist government which is armed with machine guns, aeroplanes and guns, etc? My answer to that is we have learnt examples from other countries. And the only way out is the mass organization of workers and peasants of various tribes, and by having this unity we shall be in a position to put up a strong protest against this robbery and exploitation.
>
>   There, all Kenyan Africans must fight for their liberation. We cannot forget how we have been exploited and oppressed

through these solemn 'pledges'. Let none of our countrymen have any faith in these imperialist hypocritical 'promises' which mean nothing but the oppression and exploitation of the masses. In this fight we shall have the support of all who are oppressed by the British slave empire — the Indians, the Irish, the South Africans — all these people are revolting against this damnable empire whose days are numbered.

With the support of all revolutionary workers and peasants we must redouble our efforts to break the bonds that bind us. We must refuse to give any support to the British imperialists either by paying taxes or obeying any of their slave laws! We can fight in unity with the workers and toilers of the whole world, and for a free Africa.

Good morning, revolution! The Kenyatta of the 1930s was talking about the imminent inevitable collapse of the old British Empire, falling to the united blows of its enslaved workers and peasants. Yes, Kenyatta was talking about a liberated Kenya, concretely meaning the liberation of all the workers and peasants of all the Kenyan nationalities from imperialist economic exploitation and political and cultural oppression. More, he was talking of a free Africa — in 1933!

This was the Kenyatta of 'the burning spear', of whom the Kenyan masses then rightly sang as their coming saviour. This was the Kenyatta reflected in my novel, *Weep not, Child*, about whom the peasant characters whispered at night. The remnant of this Kenyatta could still, in 1952 at the Kapenguria trial, denounce imperialist justice and reject any and every abject accommodation.

In saying this, I am asking for no mercy at all on behalf of my colleagues. We are asking that justice may be done and that the injustices that exist may be righted.

Following the tone he set, the rest of the Kapenguria six stood luminously splendid in their defiant rejection of imperialist justice. 'Impose any sentence you like!' they all said, and they were jailed.

What happened to that Kenyatta during the ten years of prison life in lonely dusty places? In the prisons, reading only the Bible and the Koran, with the district commissioner constantly calling him to private audiences away from the other four, did the demons, in the ghostly forms of Ross, Hooper, Barlow and Arthur — all the early missionaries who used to write to him in the 1930s urging him to return to church fellowship and give up 'extreme' politics — did these now visit him and, raising him from the valley of dry bones, show him the escape route from the ceaseless, fruitless labours of African Sisyphus? Did they then take him to the mountain-top and show him all the personal glory accruing to him who would kneel before the god of imperialism and offer prayers of devotion, sprinkled of course, with occasional nationalist slogans borrowed from past memories? Evidence of such visitations now comes from the work of a die-hard settler. Michael Blundell was the leader of the settlers and a leading architect of ways and means of suppressing Mau Mau and African nationalism. In his settler memoirs, *So Rough a Wind,* he describes secret visit to Kenyatta in detention:

> We had a long talk together, especially on the land problems of the poorer Kikuyu, with which he had always been so concerned. When I was leaving to get into my car, he asked me why the Europeans disliked him so much. I thought it best to tell him the truth; that they associated him with the evil side of Mau Mau and considered that he had planned and initiated the movement, with all its horrors and murders; and felt that he hated them and would not treat them fairly if he ever achieved power. He asked me what he should do as this was a wrong analysis of his feelings, although he was determined that Africans were the leaders and first-class citizens in their own country. I replied that I could not help him, that I firmly believed the new African world needed the best of the Europeans and that only he could correct, by his speeches and actions, the impressions which many Europeans sincerely held about him. He took no offence at this straightforward talk, but nodded his head, grunting away the while, which is a habit of his when considering anything.

Did Kenyatta enter into some secret agreement with the British while he was in detention? Or did he merely act on the advice of the likes of Michael Blundell?

At any rate, the Kenyatta who came out of detention in 1961 was talking an entirely different language from the one he used to talk when he was 'the burning spear' of nationalistic politics. The new Kenyatta now went to Nakuru, the heartland of white colonial settlerdom, on 12 August 1963, soon after the KANU victory and he actually asked the erstwhile imperialist murderers and sadistic rapists to forgive him for whatever wrongs he had done them, just as Blundell had asked him to do:

> If I have done wrong to you it is for you to forgive me. If you have done wrong to me, it is for me to forgive you . . . We want you to stay and farm this country.

But to the Kenyan workers and peasants and the Ma u Mau stalwarts he was talking a tough language of threats almost as if they were now his main enemies. Indeed his assurances to the settlers and imperialist foreigners about their special protected rôle in an independent Kenya was a slap in the face to the many Kenyans who had fought precisely to get imperialists off the back of Kenya's economy

> The government of an independent Kenya will not be a gangster government. Those who have been panicky about their property — whether land or buildings or houses — can now rest assured that the future African government will not deprive them of their property or rights of ownership.

It was this Kenyatta, now preaching 'forgive and forget' who, as an earlier Bishop Muzorewa, sent the army inherited from colonial times to hunt down the remaining Mau Mau guerrillas, describing them as 'these evil men, vagrants'.

This action was of course quite consistent with the anti-Mau Mau denunciatory line he had taken in 1952 and at Kapenguria: 'The (colonial) government, instead of joining with us to fight Mau Mau they arrested all the leading members of KAU (Kenya African Union).' What was surprising was the ready swiftness with which he went about eliminating the fighters. It is interesting that throughout his life as prime minister and president of an independent Kenya, he never allowed the remains of Kīmaathi to be removed from Kamīti Prison to a symbolic shrine of honour. It is interesting too that Kenyatta never allowed a single former militant associate of KAU and Mau Mau pre-detention days near him. Recent evidence seems to prove that in fact Kenyatta never believed totally in liberation and nationalism but rather in a form of association.*

*See Maina-wa-Kēnyatti, 'Mau Mau, the peak of Kenyan nationalism', in *Kenya Historical Review*, vol. 5, no. 2, 1977, and Kaggia, *Roots of Freedom*.

This deliberate and conscious effort to remove Mau Mau and other patriotic elements from the central stage of Kenyan politics always reached ridiculous heights during the commemorative month of October, in which Kenyatta was usually spoken of as the sole, single-handed fighter for Kenya's independence. It was as if such others as Kaggia, Oneko and the millions of dead and detained had been wiped off the face of known and written history.

For administration and for political advice, the new Kenyatta relied more and more on those who used to be actively anti-Mau Mau, or on colonial chiefs and sons of colonial chiefs. The sole remaining symbol of Mau Mau militancy to occupy a place of national importance after independence was J.M. Kariūki. He too was finally murdered in 1975.

In Kenyatta's officially collected speeches, *Harambee,* all his post-detention anti-imperialist, anti-explotation, and anti-oppression statements and articles were deliberately excluded. His other book, *Suffering Without Bitterness,* was written by two British journalists. Indeed, the new Kenyatta, like Harry Thuku before him, could now only cite personal accumulation as the sole criterion of one's moral and political worth. The evidence is there for all the world to see. It is contained in that now famous attack on Bildad Kaggia, at Kandara, on 11 April 1965, only a year and five months after independence:

> We were together with Paul Ngei in jail. If you go to Ngei's home, he has planted a lot of coffee and other crops. What have you done for yourself? If you go to Kubai's home, he has a big house and has a nice shamba. Kaggia, what have you done for yourself? We were together with Kūng'ū Karūmba in jail, now he is running his own buses. What have you done for yourself?

Here independence was interpreted as a golden opportunity for personal gain. Anyone who did not grab was lazy. In fact there has now grown up a clan of Kenyans who, following the colonial tradition of European settlers, pride themselves on their hard work and efficiency. But this 'hard work and efficiency' consists of a small commission fee for every ten million shillings they let go out of the country on the shoulders of foreign investments. Seen in terms of grabbing wealth, then the European settlers had been a most efficient and hard-working lot, for they had gone about it day and night. It is interesting that in his Kandara attack on radical nationalism, the point of departure or reference is not KCA or KAU or Mau Mau but prison. It was as if Kaggia had broken some collective resolution agreed to in detention!

Because of his revolutionary KCA-influenced past; of his Pan-African associations with Kwame Nkrumah, C.L.R. James, Paul Robeson, George Padmore, and W.E. Dubois; of his KAU patriotic nationalistic phase; of the cult of revolutionary anti-imperialist personality built around him while he was in detention; of his consummate, almost instinctive sense of political opportunism, the new Kenyatta went on fooling his peasant admirers who always thought that he still concealed behind his gold-dyed beard and hypnotic eyes, a master-plan for Kenya's final deliverance from external and internal exploitation. 'Our Kenyatta knows what he is doing', was the general ambiguous attitude even when they felt uneasy about the influx of imperialist Europeans in an independent Kenya. They were of course right. Kenyatta was too much of a political opportunist not to know what he was doing. But for most Kenyans, the truth that this was not the Kenyatta of patriotic Kenyan nationalism came to light with the callous, brutal murder of J.M. Kariũki and the subsequent official cover-up. This Kenyatta had finally said 'Yes' to the colonial culture of fear at Lodwar, Lokitaung and Maralal.

In the novel *A Grain of Wheat,* I tried, through Mũgo who carried the burden of mistaken revolutionary heroism, to hint at the possibilities of the new Kenyatta. But that was in 1965-6 and nothing was clear then about the extent to which Kenyatta had negated his past, nor the sheer magnitude of the suffering it would cause to our society today.

2

The negation of a previously progressive position in the type of detainee as exemplified by Thuku and Kenyatta cannot entirely be attributed to their lonely wrestles during imprisonment with the demons of surrender. In the case of both Thuku and Kenyatta, the roots of their political about-turn lay in their petty-bourgeois class positions (the result of missionary education) which they never quite transcended by fully and consciously immersing themselves in the fortunes of the peasantry and working class. In his book, *Revolution*

and Counter Revolution in Germany, Engels has aptly described
the social basis of the vacillating character and psychology of the
petty-bourgeoisie:

> Its intermediate position between the class of larger capital-
> ists, traders, manufacturers, the bourgeoisie proper so-called,
> and the proletarian or industrial class, determines its charac-
> ter. Aspiring to the position of the first, the least adverse turn of
> fortune hurls the individuals of this class down into the ranks of
> the second . . . Thus eternally tossed about between the hope of
> entering the ranks of the wealthier class, and the fear of being
> reduced to the state of proletarians or even paupers; between
> the hope of promoting their interests by conquering a share in
> the direction of public affairs, and the dread of rousing, by ill-
> timed opposition, the ire of a government which disposes of
> their very existence, because it has the power of removing their
> best customers; possessed of small means, the insecurity of the
> possession of which is in the inverse of the amount —this class
> is extremely vacillating in its views.

Kenyatta was always torn between the power and might of
imperialism and the power and might of the masses. He was
therefore strong or weak depending on which individuals or groups
were closest to him: pro-imperialist, or anti-imperialist.

Kenyatta, for instance, was very strong in the 1930s when he was
close to KCA, radical pan-Africanists, or radical nationalists. But
towards the end of the 1930s, he had lost touch with Kenyan based
anti-imperialist nationalist organizations and two people — Professor Malinowski and Mbiyū Koinange — had come into his life
reinforcing the reactionary tendencies of his own class. Professor
Malinowski led him down the easy paths of cultural nationalism
through a study of anthropology, which culminated in the public-
ation of *Facing Mount Kenya* with its obvious attempts to hold back
the political bitterness which progressive Africans necessarily felt
then. Nevertheless, Kenyatta's previous KCA-influenced, radical
anti-imperialism was strong enough to leave a mark on the general
political tone of *Facing Mount Kenya.*

Mbiyū Koinange has never really condemned imperialism. His
politics have never gone beyond the call for an end to the colour-bar
in acquiring land, in the holding of public office, and in social life. He
remained the educated son of an enlightened chief, but with a strong

admiration for mystical feudalism. In 1933, Mbiyũ was defending British colonialism in Kenya:

> It is an undeniable fact that the natives of Africa have benefited by British administration, for, regardless of its failures in some respects, the British Government has shown a desire for fair play in its dealings with the Natives.

This was at a time when even his own father was demanding the return of the stolen lands, and Kenyatta was calling for the violent overthrow of British imperialism not only in Kenya but in the whole of Africa. The decisive intervention of the university-educated Mbiyũ in the life of the virtually self-educated Kenyatta at certain strategic moments in 1938, 1946 and 1963, has been disastrous for Kenya's nationalism and modern history.

In the only book that he has published, *The People of Kenya Speak for Themselves* (1955), Mbiyũ was at pains to prove the blessings of multi-racialism if only the colour-bar would end in Kenya. This may not have been surprising in the 1950s. What is surprising is that in 1979, he allowed a reprint of the book. On page 75 of the reprint appears the following: 'The Kenyan people, without settler domination, would be of infinitely more value and service to the British Commonwealth of Nations than all the mess settlers have created both in Kenya and in the eyes of the world. The people of Kenya, free from settler domination, would make a powerful contribution to the British people. . . .'

For Thuku, similar interventions came in the form of selected friendly priests and 'objective' colonial district administrators who called on him to give advice on the basis of a carefully packaged 'human' equality.

Nevertheless, prison detention, by removing a Thuku and a Kenyatta from the mainstream of the people's struggles, was the essential first step for the total repudiation of former militance making them say 'Yes' to that which only yesterday was most repugnant to their seemingly patriotic selves.

3

The other type of detainee, typified by Waiyaki wa Hiinga, Nguunju wa Gakere, Me Kitilili and Arap Manyei, never repudiated their former militant political stands. Led down the ladder of despair by the demons of surrender they turned their eyes away from the valley of white bones, but, instead of futility in the labours of the African Sisyphus, they saw their people's history and culture of struggle and determination whence they had gained the strength to say 'No' to the colonial culture of fear and its aesthetic of submissive silence. They were sure that a million hands united in struggle would finally break the rock of oppression. They as individuals could go, but the struggle would continue and they would for ever be part of it. Detention could not then break their spirits, it could at most only break their bodies. So they remained firm, defiant and strong. In the zenith of colonial culture, this kind of detainee was labelled a hard-core Mau Mau.

Now to the original list of Waiyaki, Me Kitilili, Arap Manyei, and Mau Mau hard-core anti-imperialists, we may now add two more detainees, Makhan Singh and J.M. Kariūki. The list grows with time.

The positive contribution of Kenyan workers of Asian origin to the struggle for independence has been deliberately played down by European colonialists and their Kenyan intellectual sympathisers and chauvinists of all shades. From 1893, the Indian workers, Indian labour leaders and progressive Indian newspaper editors, have contributed a lot to Kenya's anti-imperialist struggle.

But the name of Makhan Singh, a remarkable Kenyan of Asian origins, is synonymous with the growth of a modern workers' movement and progressive trade unionism. We see him in successive stages as the able and dedicated general secretary of the Indian Trade Union, the Labour Trade Union of Kenya, and the East African Trade Union Congress. Like Thuku in the 1920s, he correctly saw the economic emancipation of workers in political terms. Strikes, which mean the organized temporary withdrawal of the workers' labour power from the market, were legitimate weapons of political struggle. Indeed the right to strike was a worker's basic human right: it was only a slave who had no right to bargain for what he should be given for the use of his labour power. If a worker is unable to strike, then he is in the position of a slave. One of the resolutions proposed by Makhan Singh and adopted by the Trade Union Congress at Kaloleni Hall in Nairobi on 23 April 1950, was a demand for the complete independence and sovereignty of the East African territories, as the only way in which workers could get a fair economic deal. On 1 May 1950, Makhan Singh wrote:

The call of May Day 1950, in the middle of the twentieth century, is that the workers and the peoples of East Africa should further strengthen their unity, should become more resolute and thus speed up the movement for freedom of all the workers and peoples of East Africa.

He was arrested on 15 May 1950, and tried before R.S. Thacker under the prosecution of A.G. Somorhough, the same colonialist duo that was to later sit in judgement over the Kapenguria six. In the colonial court, Makhan Singh carried himself with calm dignity, answering all the racist provocation of the prosecution with a progressive political line that further maddened Thacker and Somorhough. When, for instance, he told the Kangaroo Court that the British government had no right to rule Kenya, that the country should have a workers' government with a parliament freely elected by the people and only answerable to the country's workers and peasants through their organizations, the settler magistrate was so outraged that he took over the rôle of prosecution:

THACKER: Where would you get your judges, for instance?

SINGH: From the people of this country.

THACKER: There is no single African qualified in law?

SINGH: The new government will give opportunities for training people to become judges, lawyers, magistrates, etc.

THACKER: In the present stage of the African, you would be content to appoint him a judge or magistrate?

SINGH: Of course. If before the advent of the British they were able to judge about matters, even now they can do it.

Chain this devil, said the magistrate, and it was done!

Makhan Singh was detained in Lokitaung, Maralal and Dol Dol for eleven-and-a-half years from 5 June 1950 to 22 October 1961. During that time, he was constantly visited by the demons in the physical form of prison officers, district commissioners, and other colonial agents, who tried to pressure him into agreeing to leave Kenya and be rewarded for it, or to recant and start working against the Kenya workers' movement and progressive nationalism, with rewards of course, but he refused. After his release, he resumed his patriotic activities in the workers' movement. His book, *Kenya's*

Trade Union Movement to 1951, is, up to now, the only patriotic treatment of the emergence of modern Kenya.

It is clear that even Makhan Singh, of Asian origin, derived his strength to say 'No' from his roots in the progressive aspects of Kenyan people's culture. In an article he wrote for *The Daily Chronicle* of 12 February 1949, he urged Kenyans of Asian origin to forge common links with native Kenyans. 'The main task before us,' he wrote, 'is to forge a strong unity among ourselves and with Africans for the common cause of democractic advance in this country.' He advocated the establishment of common schools for all Kenyans. 'Learn the language of the people — Swahili. Teach the best of your culture, learn the best from African culture. This way lies our salvation and this is the way out!'

J.M. Kariũki has written an account of his own wrestling with demons in more than fourteen detention camps all over Kenya. His autobiography, *Mau Mau Detainee,* is an important contribution to the Kenyan literature of struggle, and I have written about it in my book *Writers in Politics* (Heinemann Educational Books, London). In Manyani, the European camp commandant sadistically tortured Kariũki to make him sign a statement of submissive acquiescence and betrayal. But Kariũki said 'No'. 'I was given the strength to endure all these things,' he was later to write, 'because I knew that I was right . . . This is the sort of strength that no amount of beatings can weaken.'

Even the glamorous easy riches of independence — for the lucky few —could not deflect him from the path of struggle, and he remained one of the bitterest critics of the post-independence betrayal of Kenyan people. It took more than a flag and more than an anthem to make a nation, he kept on reminding Kenyatta and the entire KANU leadership. We do not want to create a Kenya of ten millionaires and ten million beggars, he would add, in stern naked contrast to Kenyatta's refrain: What have you done for yourself?

He had dared to say 'No' and he paid for his patriotic consistency with his life at Ngong Hills on 2 March 1975.

4

Makhan Singh was a communist. He said so both before and after his detention. As such, he was opposed to capitalism. J.M. Kariũki was a nationalist. He was not necessarily opposed to capitalism. All

he advocated was to free national capitalism from foreign control
and to build a welfare state in which 'everyone will have an
opportunity to educate himself to his fullest capabilities, in which no
one will die or suffer through lack of medical facilities and in which
each person will earn enough to eat for himself and his family.'

But what they both shared was a common national patriotic
tradition that goes way back to the very early detainees — Me
Kitilili, Waiyaki, Nguunju wa Gakere — who all had said 'No' to the
colonial culture of fear and rejected its aesthetic of blind trust and
obedience to foreign economic, political and cultural occupation and
encirclement. On the contrary, they had rooted themselves in the
people's revolutionary culture of outspoken courage and patriotic
heroism, the kind of courage that Kariũki once experienced when as
a youth he took the Mau Mau oath of resistance and struggle. He
wrote in *Mau Mau Detainee*:

> My emotions during the ceremony had been a mixture of fear
> and elation. Afterwards in the maize I felt exalted with a new
> spirit of power and strength. All my previous life seemed
> empty and meaningless. Even my education, of which I was so
> proud, appeared trivial besides this splendid and terrible force
> that had been given me. I had been born again and I sensed
> once more the feeling of opportunity and adventure that I had
> on the first day my mother started teaching me to read and
> write. The other three in the maize were all silent and were
> clearly undergoing the same spiritual rebirth as myself.

Armed with the new power given him by his total identification with
the resistance culture of his people, he was able to face detention and
all the temptations in the stony wilderness. Detention could not
break him. Only death. But that came later. Not at the hands of a
colonial commandant in a colonial detention camp but at the hands
of those who had inherited the colonial power.

A colonial affair . . . a neo-colonial affair . . . what's the difference?
In 1953 he was taken from his own small hotel in Nakuru to more
than fourteen concentration camps for seven years of torture. In
1975 he was detained as he was leaving a prominent foreign-owned
hotel in Nairobi to a death camp at Ngong after hours on con-
centrated torture!

5

Yes, No. Ndio, La. Two of the tiniest words in any language. But yes or no, one had to choose between them. To say 'Yes' or 'No' to unfairness, to injustice, to wrong-doing, to oppression, to treacherous betrayal, to the culture of fear, to the aesthetic of submissive acquiescence, one was choosing a particular world and a particular future.

It was not, of course, very cheering to know that most of those who had said 'No' to the culture of fear and silence, had ended dying untimely deaths buried alive in desert places or left on hillsides for hyena's midnight feasts. Nor was it particularly cheering to contemplate that I was now in detention under a regime headed by an ex-detainee who had finally given in to years of imperialist blackmail and bribery. Would a political yes-man ever recognize the rights of a political no-man and the human and democratic legitimacy and necessity of that position? Would he, in other words, release a detainee who dared say 'No' when he himself had said 'Yes'?

Wasonga Sijeyo's position was a source of both strength and despair. He had refused to renounce his pre-1969 anti-imperialist and anti-exploitation views and he was now entering his tenth year at Kamītī. Others were in their eighth, seventh, fourth or third years and I was only just starting. That Wuodh Sijeyo looked cheerful and strong in spirit was a source of hope; but that he was now in his tenth year with no visible signs of release was a source of despair. I know a time came when virtually all the eighteen detainees silently said: Let them at least release Wasonga Sijeyo, then there's hope for us too!

If release for those who said 'No' depended on the length of years, what hope was there for us who were novices? I am not trying to write a story of sentimental heroism. I am only a stammerer who tries to find articulate speech in scribbled words. Pen and paper have so far been my only offensive and defensive weapons against those who would like to drown human speech in a pool of fear — or blood. Besides, I would hate to court unnecessary martyrdom. But I searched every corner of my mind and heart to see if I could find a speck of wrong-doing in joining hands with Kamīrīīthū peasants and workers in our open democratic venture of building our village, and I could find not the slightest trace of wrong to challenge my conscience.

If release depended on duration of stay, I was in for a long spell. If it depended on saying 'Yes' then I was equally in for a long spell in Kamĩtĩ or any other prison in Kenya. For right from the beginning I was determined never to renounce Kamĩrĩĩthũ — there was really too much of Limuru and Kenyan history in that tiny village! I was equally resolved to always speak truthfully and proudly about our collective aims and achievements at Kamĩrĩĩthũ Community Education and Cultural Centre. I would never, for as long as I lived, and for as long as I was sane, disown the heroic history of Kenyan people as celebrated in *Ngaahika Ndeenda,* or be a conscious party to the historical betrayal mourned and condemned in the same drama. My involvement with the people of Kamĩrĩĩthũ had given me the sense of a new being and it had made me transcend the alienation to which I had been condemned by years of colonial education.

So I was intellectually reconciled to the possibility of a long stay in prison. If Wasonga Sijeyo was the yardstick, then the earliest release date I could think of was 1988. Nought thought for comfort. Besides, intellectual acceptance was one thing: emotional reconciliation to the stark reality was another. I had to find ways and means of keeping my sanity.

Writing a novel was one way. I had planned to finish the Gĩkũyũ version by the end of 1978. In line with my new thinking on Kenya's national languages, I would embark on a Swahili version in 1979. Gĩkũyũ was the language of my birth: Kiswahili was the all-Kenya national language of communication, besides its roots in the culture of Kenya's coastal nationalities. Kiswahili was Kenya's transnational language. In 1980, I would attempt an English version. English was a foreign language, but it was an important language in the history of Kenya. Thereafter? Maybe I would find other things to occupy myself with. Besides, one could never really tell how long a novel would take to write. *The River Between* had taken me one year; *Weep not, Child,* two; A Grain of Wheat, about three; and *Petals of Blood,* about six years. Maybe the new novel, translation included, would take me many years. Or it might never be completed. For I would write in a language that I had never used before in writing novels, and also under prison conditions where one had to keep on playing a game of write-and-hide, with inquisitive warders prying and prowling constantly.

But writing aside, I knew, in my heart of hearts, that my sanity depended on my being able to continually say 'No' to any and every manifestation of oppressive injustice and to any and every infringement of my human and democratic rights, a 'No' that included

etention itself. I would seize any and every occasion to denounce
etention without trial. Yes or No . . . two great words in their own
ay but the greatest of them was No when spoken in sound or silence
r action against oppression.

In Kamītī prison, one of the most oppressive and offensive
ractices to human dignity was the chaining of detainees before
iving them medical treatment or allowing them to see their wives
nd children. Those who had the misfortune of being hospitalized
eceived even worse treatment. Even in the operating theatre, their
egs and hands were chained to bed frames while armed policemen
nd prison warders stood on guard night and day.

The other detainees had told me about this, and I dreaded the
rospect of this unnecessary humiliation. It was not so much the
haining — one had no power to resist if it was forced on one — that I
inded most: it was the expectation and requirement of a detainee's
wn co-operation in his slavery that I found most repugnant. Co-
perate in my own chaining as the condition for getting medical
eatment that I was entitled to, and as the condition for a five-minute
lance at my wife in the presence of an over-armed escort?

Then my dental problems started. The prison doctor recom-
ended that I see a dentist at Kenyatta National Hospital.
oreboding seized me. I could not delay the confrontation.

CHAPTER SIX

1

Jela ilimshinda, or *alishindwa na jela,* meaning that prison defeated him or more frequently that he was defeated by prison, is an expression often on the lips of warders, discrediting any detainee who had physically or mentally broken down within the double-walled compound, almost as if they — the warders — were some neutral referees in a gladiatorial contest between the prison and the prisoner, a contest that the defeated had freely and willingly entered with the sure-to-win braggadocio of a Muhammad Ali.

The expression is, of course, a cover-up for any fatal or near-fatal ill-treatment of a political detainee: the moral accountability for the disablement is thus thrown back onto the victim, like Karen Blixen's magistrate holding the murdered Kitosch responsible for his own death because he had moaned in pain, 'Nataka kufa', 'I am about to die'.

But the warders' assumption of a contest between prison and prisoner with cheering or jeering forces behind each contains a grain of truth. A narration of prison life is, in fact, nothing more than a account of oppressive measures in varying degrees of intensity and one's individual or collective responses to them. For even assuming that one was getting the best possible food, the best possible accommodation and the best possible health facilities, the fact of being wrongfully held in captivity at the presidential pleasure, the very act of forcible seizure of one's freedom for an indefinite period whose termination is entirely dependent on somebody else's political fears, is in itself torture, and it is continuous to the last second of one's detention. All other forms of torture, not excepting the physical, pale besides this cruellest of state-inflicted wounds upon one's humanity.

The detaining authorities are not of course content to just inflict the wound: they must keep on twisting hot knives into it to ensure its continued freshness. This takes various forms: physical beating with the possibility of final elimination; strait-jacketing to ensure total bodily immobility; sleeping on cold or wet cement floors without mat or a blanket so the body can more easily contract disease; denial of news or books to weaken the intellect; bestial food or a starvation diet to weaken the body; segregation and solitary confinement to weaken the heart; such and more are the sadistic ways of prisons and detention camps. One or a combination of more than one of these instruments can be used to keep the wound fresh. And for the duration of the presidential pleasure, the stony dragon remains deaf to all human cries and groans from its captives.

Saint Man in a deadly combat with the stony dragon: not for comfort the thought that nobody can tell beforehand how he or she will cope with the unsought-for combat. Nobody knows how long the president's pleasure might last. Nobody can tell how he or she will physically, intellectually and spiritually survive the hot knives of torture. Many factors come into it: stamina; the occasional measure of fairness and humaneness in the warders and prison officers; the extent of the determination by jailers to break their victim; and the degree of a prisoner's awareness of and commitment to the cause that brought him to jail. More important are the moral standards and principles born of that awareness and commitment which the political prisoner has set for himself, like the African poet of Arabia, Anitar, who once wrote that despite captivity in slavery:

> I will not leave a word for the railers
> And I will not ease the hearts of my enemies
>   by the violation of my honour.
> I have borne with misfortune till I have
>   discovered its secret meaning . . .

But even when such a prisoner might have all these ideals, it is still difficult for him to tell beforehand his bodily or mental reactions to certain forms of torture. Some people can cope with any amount of physical torture; others, any amount of psychological torture; yet a few others, can withstand all. Whatever the case, he can only tell this at the hour of trial.

At Kamĩtĩ, disease and family were the two most frequent means of tormenting political detainees. First, disease. It was the most dreaded hydra in Kamĩtĩ Prison. 'Whatever you do,' the other detainees had told me, 'try not to be ill . . . Here they wait until disease has fully percolated through your system before treating you . . . and even then, they treat you not to cure, but to have it on record that they treated you.'

One detainee used to suffer from swollen veins. His laments

would be met with indifference or with the ready explanation that he was malingering. Then suddenly he would be whisked off to Kenyatta National Hospital, in chains, under heavy guard, for surgery. Two days later he would be back in the block, still in chains, but with bleeding cuts. The laments would start all over again. This game of treatment-without-a-cure had gone on for seven years. He was still hospitalized at Kenyatta National Hospital when news of his freedom reached him.

Another detainee had a wound in the anus: advanced piles. He bled a lot. He had to lie sideways. Eating was torture because of thoughts of the pain to come. He had been arrested a week before he was due for an operation by a top specialist at Kenyatta National Hospital. His terror was that the wound might extend to his intestines. On arrival at Kamītī, he had reported his critical condition. It was not until six months later that they took him to hospital for an operation. He could hardly walk. But they put him in chains, plus an armed police and prison squad. At the time of his release on 12 December 1978, he was still uncured.

My own observation was that at Kamītī, every detainee suffered from one or more diseases: headaches, backaches, toothaches, eye and skin ailments, anything. And the warders had only one explanation, malingering, although there was no work to be avoided. The prison doctor, an old man who had been in prison all his working life had only one explanation: depression. The standard prescription for everything, headaches, stomach-aches, toothaches, broken backs and hips, was anti-depression tablets —Valium, mostly. 'It's just the effect of jail,' he would say 'you'll soon come out.' He normally met complaints with the chilling threat: 'I can even inject you with water or worse and get away with it. You think you are more important than Kenyatta whom I used to treat with water at Lodwar?'

The most notorious case of disease as punishment was Shikuku's. Martin Shikuku used to be a populist, vocal member of parliament who had made a national reputation for raising awkward issues in the House of the Honourables. He was an active member of the J.M. Kariūki committee whose findings and final report virtually incriminated the Kenyatta regime in the murder of J.M. He also proposed and won a motion for a select committee on corruption, causing much hatred from the big ones who proceeded to quash the committee. Then one day in October 1975, he made a passing reference to the effect that parliament should not be killed the way

KANU had been killed. He was detained. I had mentioned his detention and that of Seroney in my novel *Petals of Blood,* so I was naturally curious to see him. One day, soon after my arrival in Kamītī, I entered his cell. I found him seated on the bed. There was a yellow plastic pail near him. Between every two sentences, he would vomit into the pail. Each time he belched, he would vomit into the pail. He had to eat about fifteen times a day so that on vomiting something would remain behind to sustain his life. He had been in that condition for two years. I was shaken by this revelation. He was really a very sick man although he took it all philosophically. 'That which is hidden under the bed will one day come to light,' he had told me. I could never have believed the scene in a supposedly independent Kenya. Why keep a sick man in prison just to prove to him that KANU was not dead, that what he thought was death was simply the party's style of life?

I was then under internal segregation and the warder ordered me back to my cell. I was looking through the iron-bar slit in my door when suddenly I saw somebody crawling along the corridor, using the walls for support. What apparition was this? It was Shikuku again. He had come to ask me a few questions about the outside. Now I learnt that on top of his minute-after-minute vomiting, the man could not walk without support. There was something wrong with his hips. To the warders? He was malingering. To the doctor? He was simply depressed. Although he could not walk without some support, Shikuku used to be chained to his bed in hospital, with armed police and warders guarding all the exits and entrances night and day. He remained in that tortured condition, the doctors unable to cure him, the authorities unwilling to let him go home and seek his own cure, until 12 December 1978. The instructions to the stony dragon concerning the detained combatant would seem to have been: if you miss his *will,* don't miss his *body.* Break his *will* or break his *body* or both.

Not surprisingly fear of illness was itself another kind of disease infecting all the detainees at Kamītī. There was also the fear of being poisoned under the pretext of being treated. I too caught the fever. What I dreaded most was a possible recurrence of my asthma. In Dakar, Senegal, in 1968, I had nearly lost my life after a very severe attack, my inability to speak French hindering my frantic efforts to get a doctor or any medical help. The timely arrival of Ali Mazrui in my hotel had saved me. At home in Limuru, I always kept some quick relief tablets in readiness. At Kamītī prison, I was lucky. Not once did I get such an attack; not even bronchial wheezes. But the fear remained.

It was the toothache that caught me unawares. The extreme lower right-side molar had a hole and I started experiencing difficulties in eating. The right side was really very painful and woe unto the whole mouth should a grain of salt lodge itself in the hollow. But when the doctor recommended that I see a dentist at Kenyatta National Hospital, I was seized with panic.

Two principles had suddenly clashed inside me: the necessity for bodily fitness for my physical survival in the combat; and the necessity to make a stand over the issue of chains for my spiritual survival in the combat.

2

It is the paramount duty of every political detainee to keep physically fit. Any bodily disablement can considerably weaken his will or forever damage him. He who survives the deadly combat can always live to fight another day. There is also the saying, told me by one detainee as a piece of homely advice, that when a cow is finally pinned to the ground and tied with ropes to a slaughterhouse it cannot refuse to be slaughtered. We in detention were that cow and we had no choice but to do whatever was dictated by the whims of our captors.

But a human being is not a dumb beast. Even the cow does not acquiesce in its own slaughter. It goes down kicking to the last breath. In the same way, a political prisoner must always stand for certain principles if he is going to survive the trials of the stony dragon. He must be ready to protest against wrongs even in prison. He must keep on insisting on his constitutional rights, however few and whatever they are, and on his democratic and human rights.

Now my own feelings were that once the authorities had detained a person, they carried the entire responsibility for any diseases afflicting that person for the simple reason that such a person was not in any position to take care of himself medically. I felt that it was wrong, it was criminal in fact, to torture people with disease, to use it to extort information or confession, to use it as a means of vindictive humiliation, or of breaking a person's will. I strongly felt that if for some reason or other the authorities were unable to take a prisoner to hospital outside the compound, then in all democratic and human fairness they had to bring a doctor into the compound. Even prisoners of war are given full and fair medical treatment without conditions.

But in Kenya, at Kamĩtĩ in particular, it was a different story. Crawl on your hands and feet so that we can treat you. Co-operate in your own chains of humiliation without a murmur of protest so that we can take you to hospital. Kneel, beg, if not, die or become crippled for ever. Quite apart from that, I had resolved that, at the earliest possible moment, I would make my feelings known about the whole business of chaining political detainees, people who had never been convicted in a court of law, who never had any history of physical violence, escape or attempted escape.

The same detainee who had advised me on the necessity for passivity at a slaughterhouse, told me that chains on the innocent were beads of honour and a detainee should never be afraid of them. No. Chains were beads of humiliation. But I was not afraid of them. After all, I had come to Kamĩtĩ in them. Even if I had been chained and dragged through the streets of Nairobi or of my village, I would never have allowed the intended humiliation to touch my heart because I had done no wrong whatsoever. I had merely chosen sides in the class struggle. To write for, speak for and work for the lives of peasants and workers was the highest call of patriotic duty. My only regret was that for many years I had wandered in the bourgeois jungle and the wilderness of foreign cultures and languages. Kamĩrĩĩthũ was my homecoming.

Nevertheless, I had resolved that while I would not make any physical resistance to the wearing of chains — that way lay suicide — I would equally not willingly or co-operatively put out my hands for chaining. I would at least say 'No'. I would kick even though I was tied to a slaughterhouse.

This, I knew, might involve me in certain difficulties. The tendency is for a police officer or a prison warder or officer to take such a protest as a personal affront or as a defiance of his own personality. I had to keep on reminding myself that when the time came, I should protest politely but firmly. I should state my case without rudeness to the executing authority, for my being at Kamĩtĩ was not a directly personal thing between him and me.

For a long time before the dreaded day, I keenly felt this clash of principles. I wished that the battlefield had not been my health. But I equally felt that if I did not say 'No' to this oppressive requirement at the earliest opportunity, I would never thereafter be able to say 'No' over the same issue or any other acts of blatant oppression.

Then the hour suddenly came. Thursday, 15 June 1978. Over three months after my initial complaint of toothaches. At Kamītī a detainee was told he was going out only a few minutes before the police armed escort was due to arrive. The detainee was then required to change from his prison uniform, *kūūngūrū*, into his civilian clothes, otherwise kept under lock-and-key in the chief warder's office.

It was about ten in the morning. I changed as required. I walked through the compound toward the gates. Was it worth resisting the chains? I have said 'No' to oppression several times in my life and I have always experienced the same sensation of agonizing fears and doubts. I feel foolish, childish even . . . why disturb the currents?

As a boy, I used to pick pyrethrum flowers for one of the very few African landlords in pre-independence Limuru. The landlord on whose land we lived as *ahoi* had an orchard of pears and plums. Once, some children went into the orchard and picked a few plums. The landlord's wife came to know about it. In the evening, after she had weighed our flowers from a spring balance, she announced that we would all lose our day's pick in punishment for the stolen plums. It was a collective punishment. But of course if we squealed and pointed out the culprits, or if the offenders gave themselves up voluntarily, then the innocents would be spared. We were all angry because of the collective punishment and its severity: lose a whole day's labour because of a few 'stolen' plums? She called out each person's name: own up to the crime, squeal, or lose your day's work! She was met with non-committal silence.

My heart was beating hard. Gīkūyū pre-colonial culture, the remnants of which still governed our lives, was very strict about the relationship between a child and a grown-up. I remember, for instance, being admonished by my mother for telling a grown-up, to his face, that he was lying. A grown-up had the right to thrash a child who was rude to him, even if he was the one who had initiated the action resulting in the rude exchange. And if the grown-up should report this to the parents . . . woe to the 'rude' child. I now believe that the oppressive reactionary tendencies in our pre-colonial peasant cultures are only slightly less grave than the racist colonial culture of fear and silence and should be fought, maybe with different weapons, but fought all the same. But I had not then worked this out.

I felt cold panic inside me. I knew I would raise a dissenting voice. I was stung by the injustice of it all, and although I could not reverse it, I had no intention of suffering in silence. In our home, we depended on every single cent that we could collect from the sale of our labour. We had sweated in the sun, without a meal or a glass of water all day, and here she was, going on about morality and enforcing it by robbing us of our hard-earned money without so much as a blink. 'You claim you are saved,' I shouted at her in tears. 'Is this what you mean by Christian salvation? Cheating and robbing us? This is theft! This is theft!' She came to my home the same night and reported what she called this 'terrible abuse from a mere child' and urged my mother to beat me. My mother, a peasant living on the estate of the landlord, just looked down. She did not say anything. But she did not beat me.

I had felt the same cold panic each time I knew I would join the chorus of those at the university who used to protest against the annual European-supervised beating of innocent students, an annual ritual of violence fully sanctioned by the KANU government. The worst such ritual was in 1974 when women were raped and others had their limbs broken, their blood left spattered all over the whitewashed walls of the different classrooms. In 1969, I had resigned from the university in protest. I was outraged by the silence of most lecturers and professors, a silence which I took for complicity with the fascist evil. But in 1974 more lecturers had joined in the protest and had made their feelings publicly known.

What I most remembered in these past incidents was that unpleasant cold foreboding that always preceded my every 'No' to oppression, but it was always a sign that I would not hold back the voice of protest. So when now the prison warder asked me to raise my hands for the ceremony of chaining and I felt the same kind of foreboding I knew I would refuse. Which I did!

The warder, also in civilian clothes — going out for a detainee was a civilian ceremony all round — could not believe his ears. He called the others. Still I refused.

He reasoned with me, trying to prove to me that the chains meant nothing: 'Be a man and carry the chains!'

I thought this a strange way of proving my 'manhood', and if the chains were nothing, why was I required to wear them? I still refused.

Kimeto, the police superintendent in charge of escorting detainees in and out of Kamĩtĩ, intervened. He was tall with a partiality for straw hats which he carried with a conscious swagger, probably in imitation of an American F.B.I. detective he had once seen on television.

'Listen!' he said, standing arms akimbo, measuring his voice for all to hear clearly. 'Even Kenyatta was once chained, and he accepted it.'

'I am not Kenyatta!' I said.

'So you refuse to go for medical treatment?'

'Would I have so promptly put on my civilian clothes if I was not eager to go? After all, it is I who have the toothache. It is you who is refusing to take me to hospital.'

'Then we have to chain you.'

'I don't want to be chained. I don't see why you must chain an innocent political detainee.'

'You are refusing to go to hospital.'

'No. It is you who are refusing to take me. I am not faster than all the bullets you and your team are carrying. Why anyway chain me as a condition for medical treatment? If you are finding it difficult to take me out to see a dentist, and I am not insisting on going out, why don't you bring a dentist here?'

'Take him back to the cell!' he shouted, disgust written all over his detective face. 'We shall see if he will cure himself.'

I was never treated though I kept on complaining about it. I even complained to the commissioner of prisons, Mr Mutua, on the only occasion that he visited the compound. I pointed out that it was wrong to use disease to torture political detainees.

I also wrote a letter of protest to Mr Mūhīndī Mūnene, the detainees' security officer, seeking, at the same time, his intervention to secure me dental treatment inside the compound. It had been done before, I later came to learn, so there was nothing in the regulations which said that a dentist could not come into Kamītī. Nor was there a regulation requiring chaining as a condition for medical treatment outside Kamītī. And if there was, it was unjust and criminal. Not all detainees, I came to learn, were chained!

Mr Mūnene never replied. And the Detainees' Review Tribunal under Justice Hancox, before whom I raised the matter in July, never did anything about the use of disease to torture political detainees. One got the impression that the next stage for the authorities in that line would be to actually infect detainees with certain diseases if natural ones failed. In fact, any detainee who contracted a disease and was taken to hospital or was treated in prison had always that additional fear. What if, having got there, the

,overnment quack 'mistakenly' injected strychnine, causing death iot in combat or in defiance, but prostrate in a ward bed? Considering Kenya's recent history and the general official attitude oward disease, this fear was not without foundation.

Fortunately for me, the abscess gradually healed. Must have been he medicine of willpower. At any rate, it gradually ceased throbbing xcept when something hard — like a grain of salt or a piece of bean ir *ugali* —lodged inside.

But this was not the end of the chains affair. The next act was later o be played out on the occasion of a scheduled family visit six nonths after my abduction and subsequent incarceration.

3

3ecause of the intensity of emotion attached to it, the family can be ised to break the political backbone of an unsuspecting detainee. Any forcible separation from loved ones is of course very painful. 3ut even more painful is the sense of utter helplessness. There is iothing he can do about it. Such a person feels that there was iomething left unsaid, a sentence cut in the middle, a melody abruptly stopped. It now feels as if even a minute's brief reunion would enable the unsaid to be said, the sentence or the melody completed. If only . . . if . . . if . . .

In my case, I had left Nyambura four months pregnant, and now a child, whom I could only see through the courtesy of photography and the post office, had been born. A visit would enable me to see her. I was also eager to know how the others — Thiong'o, Kĩmunya, Ngĩna, Ndũũcũ, Mũkoma and Wanjikũ — were doing at school and how they were taking the whole thing. My mother also. In 1955 she had to bear three months of torture at Kamĩrĩĩthũ home-guard post because of my elder brother who had joined the Mau Mau guerrillas. Throughout the 1950s she had to carry the burden of not knowing if he would come out of the mountains, and later out of detention, alive. In 1974 she lost her youngest son, Njiinjũ, through a car accident. I knew that she would now be very concerned about the loss of yet another. A visit would reassure her. As for Nyambura, I was keen to erase from my mind my last image of her: standing in the inner corridor of our house at Gĩtogoothi, pregnant, bewildered, but silent in perfect immobility. 'Give me the keys of the car!' were her last words before they took me away. She had seen what I was not able to see: that they were taking me away for a long spell.

Now, a woman who may not understand why her husband or son was arrested, or who may not sympathize with the cause, can easily be approached directly or indirectly — through a third or fourth party that is — and be fed, by a sympathetic tone and voice, with stories of her husband's or son's arrogance or stubbornness in prison; of how he has spurned all the government's moves for reconciliation and co-operation. Your husband/son is behaving as if *he* is the *government* and the government his child, she will be told, earnestly. It might then be suggested to her that a letter from her, just a few lines urging him to co-operate, would work miracles and hasten his release. Examples of those already released can be quoted: 'Is your husband/son bigger than so and so who agreed to co-operate and was immediately released? Look at him now. He is the director of this and that government crop marketing board, or this and that parastatal corporation. Why cannot your husband/son agree to come out of prison and play the same kind of constructive rôle?'

Before she is aware of what is happening, the tables are turned and subject/object relationships are reversed. It is her husband/son who is now stubbornly clinging to the prison walls despite several magnanimous government pleas. Gradually she will be put in a position where she may think that she is actively working for and aiding his release by writing him letters gently, lovingly rebuking him for his non-co-operation. She might even add stories of family suffering and how his presence is urgently needed if the home is not going to fall apart. An exchange of letters (his censored, of course) might start here but these will only widen the gulf of mutual incomprehension.

On the side of the detained person, stories of his wife's moral conduct in his absence might be leaked to him. If he is a man of property, he may be allowed to know how everything he has spent so much toil and sweat and years to build is going to ruins.

There was a warder who, whenever it was his turn to guard us at night, would come to my door and he would literally insist that it was I who was refusing to leave prison. 'You know the government cannot bring you here for nothing . . . just own up . . . confess everything . . . and you'll see yourself home tomorrow . . . but go on demanding to know why you were detained . . . and my friend, you will be here forever.' The warder knew Limuru area very well and I often wondered what stories such a person might be releasing about my stubborn refusal to be 'free'.

When a detainee therefore gets a chance to see his wife and family, he is very eager to seize the time because, even though he has no privacy with them, he can reassure his family and give them the heart and spirit to endure the trials to come. He can also gain strength and spirit from that brief supervised encounter. The unsaid words may not all be said, the sentence and the melody may remain incomplete, but another word will have been added, another note will have been sung.

What I found disgusting in these family visits were the elaborate lies in the whole surreal exercise. First the family, and not the detainee, had to apply for a visit through the detainees' security officer, or through the Ministry of Home Affairs. Depending on the whims of the concerned authorities — there really seemed to be no rational basis for granting or denying these visits — the family would be notified to call at the necessary police station early in the morning of a particular day. They would then be driven to the airport and ushered into a waiting-room. They would wait for hours.

Meanwhile, at Kamĩtĩ, the 'lucky' detainee would be given half-an-hour's notice to get ready to see his dear ones. He would quickly change into his civilian clothes (released from custody for the purpose), rush to the gates for the usual chaining ceremony, be welcomed by a contingent of armed policemen, and be driven in a blinds-drawn police vehicle to the door of the waiting room.

There his chains would be removed and he would be ushered into the waiting-room for a five-minute chat with his wife surrounded on all sides by security men and civilian-clad prison warders. Then he would be whisked out of the room, back into chains, and be driven back to Kamĩtĩ, under heavy escort, to resume life in his prison uniform. Thus the detainee, without knowing it, had participated in a gigantic lie to his family and to the entire Kenyan nation. The family would now spread the lie that their relative had come by plane from a distant place. He was in civilian clothes, therefore he was not really in prison, and probably was not being treated badly after all.

I used to look at the faces of the detainees just before and after the visits. On going, they were all smiles. On coming back, they were all depression. They would carry their private grief on their faces for a few weeks more before hiding it inside and resuming the communal, contourless monotony of prison life. A family visit was not really a celebration of a cherished contact, it was more a renewal of the sorrow of separation.

But my main concern, even for the cherished family visits at the airport rendezvous, was still with the chains one was required to wear. Either they allowed me to see my family without chaining me as a condition, or they did not allow me to see them. At any rate, I was determined that, while I would participate in the charade of putting on civilian clothes, I certainly would not willingly accept the chains. I still had not yet developed wings faster than the bullets they all carried in their guns.

When the day and the hour finally came, again unexpected, just half-an-hour or so for changing clothes, I found that all the prison officers in charge of the compound were present. Plus the police contingent led by the escorting police superintendent with his American swagger, straw hat, and his arms akimbo stance. Most of the other detainees had crowded into the compound. Now one of the prison officers came to my cell and shut the door behind him. He started lecturing me, as to a little child, about the virtues of family visits and how much good it did to all those concerned.

'Imagine all the little ones coming all that way and finding out that their daddy has refused to see them. I know you may want to prove to all these other detainees that you can stick to your principles. Principles are all right. But it is your wife and children you are going to see and you shouldn't care a damn how these others are going to view it. Some of these detainees, and I am telling you this in confidence, have only themselves to blame for their non-release . . . so obstinate . . . Now these chains, they are really nothing, nothing at all . . . Just be a *man* . . . I would not want you to lose all the sympathy *some* people have for you . . . '

I listened to his monologue with all its suggestive hints, vague promises and veiled threats all harmonized into an avuncular plea for me to show common sense and willingly accept the chains. I politely thanked him for his advice and concern, but I reiterated my position that I would not accept wearing chains as a condition of seeing my family. It was almost a repetition of the earlier scene. I walked to the gates. I refused to wear the chains. They refused to let me see my family.

For weeks after, I was literally trembling inside, wondering what lies had been fed Nyambura and the children. I was not particularly worried about how my peasant mother would take it. I knew that from her experiences during the British-imposed state of emergency, she would never believe the police version of events.

But Nyambura? And the children? It was a terrible three weeks, with some of the detainees reproaching me in silence — as if I had taken the joke too far — while a few others told me so to my face. How dare you refuse to see your family? How do you think they will take your stubborn refusal? Why increase their misery?

With these, I would patiently go over the arguments. I would tell them that I had not refused but that I had not been allowed. I would reiterate my strong feelings about the chaining of political detainees. I would explain the necessity of struggling for democratic and human rights even in prison. I would explain the importance of a truly democratic Kenya in which the different classes and nationalities would freely debate the past, present and future of our country without fear or favour or flattery. This democratic Kenya would not be given to people on a silver platter by the ruling minority class. It had to be struggled for. Kenyan people, wherever they were, under whatever circumstances, had to keep on insisting on certain irreducible democratic and human rights. If we did not do this, if we all succumbed to the culture of fear and silence, Kenya would have merely moved from a colonial prison into a neo-colonial prison, while the more than seventy years' struggle was precisely to release Kenyan people from the imperialists' economic, political and cultural prison altogether. What was the real gain in moving from one prison, run by white guards, into the same prison now run by black guards? The difference was one of form and not of substance. The point really was to change the economic, political and cultural substance, and this would never be possible without a struggle for democracy. This struggle was not a mere verbal abstraction. It had to begin where each Kenyan was: in our homes, in our schools, in our places of work, even in prisons and detention camps.

There were a few, though, who understood my position, and they told me so. They even told me that chaining political detainees was a recent development. It had not always been the practice. When it was first introduced by Lokopoyet, they had tried to organize a collective stand against it but a few detainees had got cold feet at the very last minute and had readily jumped into the chains. They pointed out that, as a result of that disunity, they were now all exposed to extreme danger, especially when they travelled to Mombasa by air, because even in an aeroplane they were still in chains!

But my main worry was still Nyambura and the children. I knew

that I could never write down my version of events because this
would certainly be censored by the police and the prison authorities.
Then suddenly one day I received a letter from her. It was the best
gift I could have got from anybody. I shut myself in my cell and
studied every word and every line and every paragraph to get at the
unstated message. The letter, written after the airport fiasco, was in
reply to another I had written months before on receiving news of
Njooki's birth. Now she referred to that letter and deliberately
avoided references to the visit. Not a word of rebuke. No complaint.
That in itself was a vote of confidence . . . I read it over and over
again:

> Greetings from *your big family*. We are safe and sound. The
> children are still growing. Particularly our new baby. She is
> now very big. You surprised me in your last letter. Do you
> mean that you don't know all my mother's names? She is called
> Njooki but as you know that means being born again. So in the
> light of this, my mother has two names: *Njooki, and*
> *Wamũingĩ. Very many friends of ours have been coming to see*
> *the baby.* We miss you a great deal but we hope one day we
> shall be able to eat, laugh, discuss matters that concern us, and
> live together.
>
> *As you can see I have decided to write a rather long letter*
> *since unless things are relaxed we may not be able to see each*
> *other for a long time to come.* So what I am now most
> concerned with are the exact reasons for your detention. *When*
> *you were detained, we only gathered from the local and the*
> *international press that you are a political detainee. I hope*
> *that you are being treated like a political detainee. What*
> *gives me courage is because I know you are there not because*
> *of any crime you have committed. What gives me strength is*
> *my knowledge that you are not a criminal.*
>
> I hope you received the books and the money I sent through
> Mr Mũhĩndĩ. Some books were returned to me but that is all
> right, I understand.
>
> I have sent a pair of sandals and two pairs of underwear.
> Hoping to read from you soon.
>
> Mrs Zirimu sends her greetings.
>
> > Salamia Wengine,
>
> > Nyambura

(italics mine)

Nyambura's previous letters had been very brief, businesslike to the point of coldness. I could of course guess the source of their rigidity and hesitancy. She did not want to give anything that might conceivably be used against me. But this last letter was relaxed, informative, and had even ventured into political questioning. And that so soon after the visit that never was!

From the letter I reconstructed the message. Njooki, born again as Wamũingĩ, belonged to the people. By extension, this was true of the other children. I should not worry about them in isolation from all the other children and families in Kenya. By alluding to the local and international press, she confirmed what I had learnt from hints and oblique comments by the warders: my detention had raised some national and international concern. By expressing the hope that I was being treated like a political detainee, she was saying that I should insist on my rights as a political prisoner.

The letter considerably buoyed up my spirits. I showed it to other detainees. Thairũ wa Mũthĩga commented: 'It is good to have a politically conscious wife!' I could not help saying 'Amen'. She may not have been politically conscious, but she had started asking questions. Those outside the barbed wire and the stone walls must ask questions and demand answers. It's the only way to defeat the culture of fear and silence. And if a community of millions were to ask questions and demand answers, who would deny them?

Nyambura's letter had freed me from a certain fear. I was now psychologically and emotionally ready for the never-ending struggle with the stony dragon. I went back to cell 16, went back to Warĩĩnga and continued writing my novel with renewed vigour. On toilet paper.

Perhaps Njooki would one day read it and say: at least my father was ready to join all the Wamũingĩs of modern Kenya to say 'No' to the culture of fear and silence, and 'No' to exploitation, oppression and imperialist foreign control of a Kenya for which many from Koitalel to Kĩmaathi, had died.

CHAPTER SEVEN

Life in prison is not all endless confrontations and 'profound' meditations on history. It is basically a cliché: dull, mundane, monotonous, repetitive, torturous in its intended animal rhythm of eating, defecating, sleeping, eating, defecating, sleeping. But it is the rhythm of animals waiting for slaughter or escape from slaughter at a date not of their own fixing.

*

It has, though, its surface joys on deep sorrows: its surface laughter —sometimes very genuine and spontaneous — on hidden tears; its petty quarrels and friendships in a community of lonely strangers; its distinctions of nationality and class in a community facing a single enemy; its petty debating points; its gibes and innuendos that remain burning the brain like salt on an incurable wound, among people who know that their survival depends on not tearing one another apart as intended and encouraged by their captors; its moments of genuinely revealing dialogues against the knowledge that this is leading nowhere; its dreams against a background of a long continous nightmare that is prison itself.

I seek comfort in José Marti: good is the earth, existence is holy and in suffering itself new reasons are found for living.

*

On arrival at Kamĩtĩ, I am received by a prison superintendent in a greenish long-sleeved shirt and khaki trousers who ushers me into the chief warder's office. Beside him is a fat warder in khaki shorts and a green shirt. (Later I will learn that the green shirts come from South Africa via Botswana which makes me muse: does the South African police and prison service wear the same uniform as their Kenyan counterparts?) The superintendent takes down all the details — name, profession, social habits (Do you smoke or drink?), religion (None? Really?), location, district. He then assigns me a number, K677, in exchange for my name. The number means the sixth to be detained in Kamĩtĩ in the year 1977. The superintendent is young with a businesslike efficiency, but he is very polite. I have never in my mind associated prison service with youth, and it now looks to me as if the young superintendent has strayed into the place, a stranger. Business over, he raises his head — he has been sitting and I have been standing — and says: 'I have read all your books. I was planning to come to see *Ngaahika Ndeenda.* Then I read in the papers about the ban. Tell me, why really did they bring you to this place?' I say to myself: here now begins the long-awaited interrogation. But his voice sounds sincere.

'I don't know,' I tell him, adding, 'But it could be because of *Ngaahika Ndeenda.*'

'What's wrong with the play? What was it about?'

'Our history. The lives of peasants and workers.'

'What's wrong with that?'

'I don't know!'

'No, there must have been something else,' he says, as if he is talking to himself. The he suddenly shoots a question which is also a statement of his lingering doubts: 'Tell me the truth, was the play really being acted by workers and peasants?'

'Yes. They all came from Kamīrīīthū village!'

＊

As I am led into cell 16, literally opposite the chief warder's office, I keep on wondering if I will be the sole occupant of this doleful place, presided over by a youthful-looking superintendent and a jelly-fleshed warder. No other human sight, no sound. Amidst a sepulchral silence, the warder ushers me into my new residence and he locks the door from the outside. He then stuffs a piece of blanket into the slit on my door so that I cannot see anybody and nobody can see me. Then suddenly the sepulchral silence is broken with wild shouts, 'It's Ngũgĩ, it's wa Thiong'o', in Gĩkũyũ and Kiswahili. 'Wĩyũūmĩrĩrie! Jikaze! Gūtirĩ wa Iregi ūtūire!' continue the shouts. It's the other detainees. They had been locked in their cells to free the warders to impose a state-of-emergency type curfew in and around the prison. But the detainees had been peering through the iron-barred openings on the doors of their cells and some had witnessed my coming. It was Koigi wa Wamwere who, on recognizing me, started the shouts of regretful welcome. But this I don't now know and the voices, suddenly coming from the erstwhile silent walls, sound eerie. Later, the detainees are let out in groups. They remove

the piece of blanket, they crowd around the door, and they ask me
many questions all at once. But one question stands out above the
others: 'Tell us about *Ngaahika Ndeenda*. Is it true that it was acted
by peasants and workers?'

I am secretly thrilled by the knowledge that the Kamīrĩĩthũ
Community effort had broken through the walls of Kamĩtĩ prison to
give hope to political detainees, who before had never heard of
Kamīrĩĩthũ.

*

Yes, *Ngaahika Ndeenda* has preceded me in prison. Throughout
my stay, I'll get more inquiries about it. One comes from a warder of
Kalenjin nationality who tells me the play was read and translated to
him by his Mũũgĩkũyũ friend who worked at a coffee plantation
around Kĩambu. He tells me about the play and recounts the plot and
mentions the names of several characters. 'I hope that I will one day
be able to see a performance of the play,' he says wistfully.

I feel he is voicing the hope of many Kenyans and it feels good.
Truth, a peasant once told me, is like a mole. Try to cover it, and it
will still reappear in another place!

*

The welcome I received from the other detainees is touching.
Wasonga Sijeyo gives me a comb and a pair of tyre sandals. Martin
Shikuku gives me a hand-made cell calendar. Gĩkonyo wa Rũkũũngũ
the same. Adam Matheege, a *kũũngũrũ* uniform. Koigi wa Wamwere
a biro pen. Gĩcerũ wa Njaũ, a pencil. Thairũ wa Mũthĩga, a biro pen
Mũhoro wa Mũthoga, some writing paper with prison letter heads
Ali Dubat Fidhow, Hadji Dagane Galal, Hadji Mahat Kuno Roble.
Ibrahim Ali Omer, Mzee Duale Roble Hussein, they all try to find
something to give as a gesture of goodwill and solidarity. There's a
fellowship which develops among people in adversity that's very
human and gives glimpses of what human beings could become, if
they could unite against the enemy of humanity: social cannibalism
on earth.

*

I once, in 1963, opened a short story, *The Mubenzi Tribesman,* with
the sentence: 'The thing that one remembers most about prison is the

smell: the smell of shit and urine; the smell of human sweat and breath.' This was fairly accurate for a young imagination. Prison has its own peculiar smell: a permanent heavy pall of perpetually polluted air. On arrival at Kamītī, the smell hits me in the face, it descends on me, it presses me down, it courses down my nostrils and throat, I am gasping for breath, and I am really scared of an attack of asthma.

The smell of unsugared, unsalted, uncooked porridge is another. It is nauseating. I feel like vomiting. Was I a Mubenzi tribesman after all? Matheenge gives me a share of his own prescription of sugar (yes, it's true, sugar, soup of boiled beans without fat or onions — *Makerūro ma Mbooco* — milk, tea, rice are medicines given only on the orders of the prison doctor!) to ease me into the habit of eating *unga* for all seasons. Luckily I have never been choosey about what I eat.

There is also the smell of the warders and even that of the other political prisoners, and inwardly I am recoiling from the contact. Do they also feel the smell of the outsider? Is this how animals detect strangers in their midst? Later I stop smelling all the smells. No matter how I sniff now, I don't sense the smell. Did I earlier imagine it? And suddenly I realize that I am part of prison life. I am part of the life of the caged.

Perhaps one does not remember the smell after all. To adjust is human. But not to accept evil.

*

Or perhaps it is the civilian clothes (on top of my forced segregation) which separates us. I look hard at the other prisoners in their tyre sandals and their ugly white *kūūngūrūs* of collarless shirts and tight pants which match one's buttocks and narrowing thighs to the kneee. I watch how they circle one another aimlessly, how they walk to and fro within the same walls, and the image of madmen in a lunatic asylum, with their erratic aimless wanderings and gestures, steals into my mind.

Later, when I get into my own *kūūngūrū* white uniform and discard the civilian outfit, I feel one of them. The clothes, as Kamaarū would say, have made us all equal. After a time, I begin to feel 'natural' in them. I even begin to see huge differences between the immaculately clean *kūūngūrūs* and the dirty ones (before they all appeared of the same hue) and even to distinguish between the different cuts, really very minute, but there all the same.

When my period of internal segregation is over, I join in the same erratic, aimless circles and wanderings, going everywhere and nowhere. The compound is too tiny to give anybody the feel of a purposeful walk or even the illusion of one. I am now one of the inmates of this once famed lunatic asylum.

It is not a joke, really. The compound used to be for the mentally deranged convicts before it was put to better use as a cage for 'the politically deranged'. In a sense, we are truly mad. Imagine anyone questioning the morality of man-eat-man in a state of man-eaters? Imagine anyone questioning the ethic of eating human flesh when the western bourgeois civilization — God-given, universal and final in its American form — has taught its worshippers that social cannibalism is the highest good? Madness after all is relative. It depends on who is calling the other mad. In a state of madmen, anybody who is not mad is mad. This is the truth in Chekhov's literary masterpiece, *Ward 7*.

But human sanity will never be drowned in a pool of inhuman madness. For if a country has a class of man-eaters, then it has to have men to be eaten, and will these victims of others' greed always let themselves and their kind be eaten forever? The fact is that the objects of social cannibalism will never accept the morality of man-eaters as the all-time universal morality, not even if it comes disguised in draperies marked Free World, Christian Democracy, Christian Civilization, Social Democracy and other mind-dazzling labels and platitudes.

*

I arrive in Kamĩtĩ on Saturday, 31 December 1977. On 13 January 1978, four new detainees are brought in — Ahmed Shurie, Mohamed Nurie Hanshi, Mohamed Abdilie Hanshi, Mohamed Dahe Digale — all Kenyans of Somali nationality. Three days later on 16 January, the ex-senior chief of Garrissa, Sugow Ahmed Aden, also of Somali nationality, is brought in. I now feel an old boy in relation to the newcomers. But a paralysing thought keeps on nagging at me. Could there have been more arrests and detentions at Limuru? I ask some of the newcomers and they cannot recollect any such news. There is nobody else to ask. Not now anyway.

*

My first contact with — or shall I say the first communication from — the outside world is a formal note from our family and childhood friend, Ndeere wa Njūgi. It is a simple, to-the-point kind of letter sent through the office of the president and brought by hand by a police officer.

> Greetings from Nyambura Ngūgī and the family. The purpose of writing this letter is to request you to sign a few blank cheques which Nyambura could use to draw money when need arises. You took your cheque book with you.
>
> Everything is okay.

It is signed by Nyambura and by Njūgi. I know their signatures and they look authentic. The chief warder gives me back my cheque book — everything, including my driving licence and a few shillings, had been signed in and kept under lock and key — and I sit down and I sign all the leaves.

But I remain with the letter. I study it. Every word. Every line. The letter is typed on plain paper — without a letterhead. It is dated 10 January. The signatures are in ink. And they still look real. So Nyambura has already been in touch with the lawyer? A writer's imagination is always intensely fascinated by relationships — patterns of relationships — between objects and events in time and space. Certain symbolic, or seemingly symbolic, parallels, convergences, divergences, circles are irresistible to the imagination.

Njūgi, as he is commonly known, was the last person I drank a beer with, first at Ngara Road and then at Impala Hotel in Parklands on the night of my arrest. We had been together since five o'clock talking throughout about *Ngaahika Ndeenda* and speculating about the future of Kamīrīīthū. And now he is the first person I am hearing from!

His home — his parents' home, that is — is next to mine at Gītogoothi. So his letter takes me home to Nyambura, to the children, to Gītogoothi, to Bibirioni, to Kamīrīīthū, to Limuru, to the landscape of my childhood. Njūgi and I grew up together; I was a little older, and we went to virtually the same schools, ending up in Alliance High School, taught by virtually the same teachers and excelling in virtually the same subjects, English language and literature mostly. I had finally opted for literature and he for law.

There was a village teacher who once read to my Standard Four class at Maanguuŭ a composition I had written in the Gĩkũyũ language — this is how to write, he told them — but who became almost mad with anger when years later he heard that I had opted for English — mere words — instead of the more substantial professional courses like engineering, medicine or law. Really why don't you take law? Now I recall all this as I keep on fingering the letter. If I had taken law, or medicine, or engineering, or architecture, instead of mere words, would I today be in Kamĩtĩ?

Why not? Today more and more professionals are realizing that their sciences which should serve people — for really medicine, science and technology were developed by working people to free themselves from the capricious tyranny of nature — are benefiting only a moneyocratic idle class instead of the masses. Discoveries and inventions which are collective and social in origin end up as private appropriations of a few.

A fat-bellied, pipe-smoking fellow sits on another's back. Medicine, science, technology, instead of going to the aid of he whose back is sat upon, rush to the aid of the pipe-smoking fat-bellied fellow wearing a three-piece suit to ensure his continued health and strength and ability to sit on the back of the other. Armaments go to protect the fat-bellied moneyocrat against any challenges to the status quo. The law rushes to protect the property stolen by the pipe-smoking fellow from the hands of the other.

Some Kenyan professionals are beginning to realize and to see the utter immorality of that structure and of their own rôles in servicing the structure. And most of these are beginning, at the very least, to question and reject the comprador bourgeois ethic which declares on roofs and mountain-tops: that which is foreign is excellent; that which is national is backward.

Maybe even if I had taken law or medicine or engineering, I would have ended in Kamĩtĩ, for probably I would at one time have been tempted to shout: Professor Barnard, go home! Imperialist foreign experts, go home!

Well, I chose words. And now I am studying a few lawyer's words asking me to sign a few cheques to enable Nyambura to withdraw money for my children's school fees. When I am released I will learn that the cheque book sent for by Njũgi at the request of Nyambura was their first assurance that I had not been sent to Ngong Hills.

Then I did not know. But at the very time I was studying Njũgi's and Nyambura's signatures to convince myself of their authenticity, they were studying my signature at home to convince themselves of its authenticity.

Words? It depends on the reality they reflect.

*

In the period of my internal segregation, I keep on studying the detainees and I am amazed to find that the various detainees at Kamītī fall into groups that span the whole history of post-independence upheavals in Kenya. I am not here talking about whether the detainees were or were not involved in the upheavals which the KANU comprador regime saw as a challenge. I am not even concerned whether that challenge was real or imagined, but the excuses for detaining them can definitely be associated with the several major crises in Kenya's post-independence history.

There is the KPU (Kenya People's Union) crisis of 1969: this is represented by victim Wasonga Sijeyo. There was the crisis of the alleged military coup of 1971: Simba Ongongi Were is the representative victim. Then there was the J.M. Kariūki crisis of 1975: this had claimed the largest group of victims — Adamu Matheenge, Koigi wa Wamwere, Gīcerū wa Njaū, Mūhoro wa Mūthoga, Gīkonyo wa Rūkūūngū and Thairū wa Mūthīga. There was the post-J.M. crisis of parliamentary challenge in 1975: Martin Shikuku is the victim.

Then there has always been the question of national minorities, especially among the Kenya Somali nationality, leading into the crisis of territorial claims: the victims are Ali Dubat Fidhow, a KANU chairman; Hadji Dagane Galal Mohamed, ex-chairman of Garrissa County Council; Hadji Mahat Kuno Roble, a rich businessman; Ibrahim Ali Omer, a herdsman; Duale Roble Hussein, a herdsman/farmer; Ahmed Shurie Abdi, a chief; Mohamed Nurie Hanshi, a chief; Mohamed Abdilie Hadow, a Diwani; Mohamed Dawie Digale, a KANU chairman; Sugow Ahmed Aden, a senior chief.

And lastly, there was the peasant/worker consciousness, struggle and anti-imperialist challenge underlying all the above upheavals, and the Kamīrīīthū of 1977 was the highest representative of that anti-imperialist peasant/worker consciousness: I was its victim. There was another side to my detention: the growing anti-imperialist consciousness among university lecturers and students, and I was the sacrificial lamb!

Thought for despair? No! I am part of a living history of struggle. And without struggle, there is no life, there is no movement.

*

The thought is not original — I once read it in William Blake: without contraries there is no progression; attraction and repulsion, reason and energy, love and hate, are necessary to human existence. And later in Hegel: contradiction is the root of all movement and all life, and only in so far as a thing incorporates a contradiction is it mobile, does it possess impulse and activity. But it is true!

*

The warders talk of him with awe. The detainees talk of him with a mixture of bitterness, contempt and hatred. He is Edward P. Lokopoyet, the senior superintendent of prisons in charge of Kamītī Prison, and hence the detention block. Gradually I begin to comprehend the magnitude of this man's relentless tyranny over the political detainees.

For over two years, this officer has waged a war to break the detainees en masse physically and mentally. He has had them locked up in the cells for twenty-three hours a day for two consecutive years, a complete negation of every single prison rule and regulation. He might order uncooked food to be brought to them; food with bits of grass and sand thrown in; *ugali* cooked in warm water; beans and yellow vegetables enriched with worms and other insects; and whenever he comes into the compound (rare!) it is to reprimand detainees for not showing proper respect to oppressive authority. Tall, strong, dark and smooth faced, he struts about the compound, the very embodiment of all the written and unwritten oppressive laws of Kenya. He is himself the law. He is the mini-god and he is genuinely puzzled why these political pariahs do not see this and act accordingly. So he daily redoubles and trebles and quadruples the previous efforts to make them see the light and understand who he is and which forces in society he represents. It was during his reign that the chaining of detainees was started. It was during his sovereignty over Kamītī that the radio and newspapers had been withdrawn.

But these actions have only generated a huge antagonism from the detainees, who do not mince words in his presence. They keep on reminding him about the inevitability of change. He once lectured a detainee for taking the initiative of extending a hand to him in greeting. He, the detainee, should have waited to be greeted. The humiliating reprimand backfires. Now, whenever he himself takes out his hand to greet the detainees, they turn their heads the other way so that his hand is left hanging in the air.

The detainees decide to write a collective memorandum of protest against the intolerable conditions. Their letter, dated January 1977, is addressed to Mr Mūhīndī Mūnene, the security officer in charge of the detainees, through Justice Hancox, the chairman of the Detainees Review Tribunal:

> The inhuman and difficult conditions to which we are subjected now are an extreme hazard to the maintenance of our minimum physical and mental health, health that is already strained by its efforts to survive under the basic detention conditions, conditions that are abnormal to human living. Certain that the weight and roughness of these conditions are severely and cruelly bruising our physical and mental health, we are appealing to you to uplift these conditions now before they exact from our health the high toll of a conspicuous and irreparable damage. In appealing to you to free us from these conditions, we also appeal to you against the wisdom of thinking that damage upon physical and mental health must stick out a mile to count. Sir, by the time it sticks out a mile, it will no longer be damage but destruction and we hope and pray that this is not what the future holds in store for us.

But only a few eventually sign it: Major L.B. Mwanzia, Adamu Matheenge Wangombe, Ongongi Were, Gīcerū wa Njaū, Koigi wa Wamwere, Thairū wa Mūthīga. And one of those signing it, Major Mwanzia, is immediately transferred to Shimo-la-Tewa prison in Mombasa.

But the mutual hatred, contempt and antagonism continue. The letter is not answered. And nothing is done about their grievances about confinement, food, medication, mail, visits, handcuffs, radio and newspapers.

Gradually the antagonism begins to tell on him. His rare visits become even more rare. Now he sneaks in then quickly runs out as if safari ants were crawling all over the tiny compound. This however makes him even more repressive. He is incapable of seeing that there could be greatness in recognition of one's mistakes and failures. Now he uses his juniors to execute what he has mapped out in the office.

Because he himself is hardly there in the compound, the antagonism between him and the detainees works out, in practice, as an antagonism between the warders and the detainees. Abusive language, innuendos, gibes, outright denunciation: the tension building up could literally be cut with an electric saw and everybody is sure that sooner or later violence will erupt. At one time, so I am told, a more sensitive warder breaks down and weeps: 'Some of us are really sorry about all this. Please understand that we are only carrying out orders. If I should be sacked from my job, what will my children eat, where will they get their clothes and school fees? Where will they sleep?'

The other detainees tell me that the slight relaxation I see in the compound is because the ordinary warders have become bored and tired of carrying out the tyrannical commands of the prison sovereign. Of course, I do not see any relaxation, big or small. But if the harsh conditions of my three-week stay are any kind of relaxation, then their last two years were actual hell.

Wasonga Sijeyo, the longest resident at the compound, confirms this: 'I have been in colonial detention for five years. I have also been in this compound for nine years. But these last two years have beaten all the previous twelve years!'

*

This Lokopoyet steals into my cell one morning. He times the visit when all the other detainees are in their cells. He lectures me for an hour on the virtues of total submission. 'Don't copy some of these other detainees. Did you know any before you came here? Never mind. I will tell you the truth. They don't really want to go home. Let me tell you, if you behave yourself, who knows, you might go home any day. Some detainees have gone home after only two or three weeks. Others, as you can see, have been here for nine years. It is all up to you.' He tries out the divisive politics of flattery and threats. 'You see, you are the most highly educated person — well, I should say the only educated person, for what education have these others?

Some are not even politicians — and so if anything that requires brains happens here, it will be blamed on you.' As he is about to leave, he says: 'And remember, don't attempt to write any poems here. Not unless I have given you permission. And even then I must see the poems and approve!'

He walks out. The arrogance of power. The sheer confidence of ignorance. And suddenly I know that I *have to* write, I *must* write. My main problem will be finding ways and means of hiding the written notes. And if caught, well, I get caught!

Wrote William Blake: The prophets Isaiah and Ezekiel dined with me, and I asked them how they dared so roundly to assert that God spoke to them: and whether they did not think at the time that they would be misunderstood, and so be the cause of impositions.

Isaiah answered: 'I saw no God, nor heard any in a finite organical perception; but my senses discovered the infinite of everything, and as I was then persuaded, and remained confirm'd, that the voice of honest indignation is the voice of God, I cared not for consequences, but wrote.'

*

I will try a diary of life in prison. I'll record everything that happens: what I see, touch, smell, hear and think. But no matter how hard I try, no words will form on paper. I was never one for writing diaries and records and whenever I have in the past tried it — at Maanguuŭ and Kĩnyogoori Primary Schools, at Alliance High School, at Makerere and Leeds Universities — I have always had to give it up after one or two false starts. I am too close to the events for me to see them clearly, or for me to make out immediately what's happening to me.

Besides that, I find that here at Kamĩtĩ, in a certain sense, everything is so very ordinary — well, worse than ordinary, for time here is sluggish, space static and action a repetition of similar non-actions — that I have nothing outstanding to record. Yesterday as today: is that enough for a diary?

For similar reasons, I have never tried to write an autobiography — even when publishers have requested it — for my life has been ordinary, average really, and it would bore me to death. No, I'll let impressions form in my mind until they accumulate into a composite picture.

But I could write about premonitions, wish fulfilments, because these have always struck me as oddly inexplicable. My very first piece of writing to be published in *The Alliance High School Magazine* was based on a belief we used to have as children, that if you strongly wanted your aunt whom you had not seen in a long time to come, you could actually make her appear by dipping your head in a black pot and whispering to her. I think I did that once. And she came.

Many critics have pointed out the parallels between my own arrest and detention and similar but fictional events in the opening and closing chapters of my novel *Petals of Blood*. It opens with the arrest of a progressive worker — he is deceived into believing that he is wanted at the police station for a few questions — and it closes with his eventual detention on suspicion of being a communist at heart.

Or one Sunday a week before my arrest, and for the first time in my life, I drove past the outer gates of Kamītī prison, lingered there for a few seconds wondering what Kamītī really looked like, before continuing my slow drive to a friend's house at Kahawa. I was there for only a few seconds. Suddenly I felt sad and tired. 'You know,' I told him as we looked at books in his study, 'I feel as if I am living on borrowed time.'

But what I really want to write about is the day, in fact the Wednesday before my arrest, when the whole Limuru countryside seemed the most glorious landscape I had ever seen. I madly drove past Kikuyu, past Dagorretti Market, past Karen and on to Ngong Hills. The day was very clear, the sky a brilliant blue, and the landscape a luscious green. Down below was the whole expanse of Maasailand and the Rift Valley. To my left, facing Nairobi, I could see a very clear outline of Mount Kenya with its snow caps against the blue sky. The same for Kilimambogo . . . and the Akamba mountain ranges beyond Athi River . . . everything seemed to grow beautiful and clear under a skin-warming sunshine. I have never seen Kenya like this, I told my companion. Let's go back to Limuru via Gīthūūngūri . . .

I try to scribble something about this experience, and it sounds unreal, sentimental, and I am unable to write more than two lines. But throughout my forced stay at Kamītī, unable to see any green landscape, any contours of valleys and hills and mountains, I continue remembering the vision with a kind of gratitude.

*

Chief Mohamed Nurie tells me fantastic Somali folklore of heroic exploits by Kabaalaf and Egal Shidad. With little variations of word and place they are like those of Hare and Abunuwasi.

Hadji Dagan tells me about the real-life anti-imperialist military and literary exploits of Sayyid Abdullah Hassan, the great African patriot whose history Kenya shares with Somalia. Does he belong to Kenya or Somalia?

Kenya, Ethiopia and Somalia share common borders, some common nationalities and hence some common history. The united peoples' socialist states of Kenya, Ethiopia and Somalia, a union freely entered by the peoples of the three territories, holds a great future because of the past the three peoples share.

Idle thoughts: to whom would the imperialist powers sell the obsolete products of their war industries?

*

The trouble with you educated people is that you despise your languages. You don't like talking to ordinary people. But what use is your education if it cannot be shared with your own people? Let me tell you. You may possess all the book education in the world, but it's we, ordinary people in tattered clothes with bare feet and blistered hands, who have the real knowledge of things. If today I was to wear a suit, you would see me a different person, but it would not mean that I had suddenly acquired more knowledge and wisdom than I had when wearing tattered clothes. Have you seen any European calling himself Mutiso, Kamau, Onyango, Kiplagat or Simiyu? Have you seen Europeans bothering about our languages? Let me tell you something else. Yes, I may not have book knowledge, but even a child can give you a word which might benefit you. You people, even if you follow Europeans to the grave, they will never never let you really know their languages. They will never — and mark my words, don't look down upon a drop of rain — Europeans will never let you into the secrets held by their languages . . . What do you then become? Their slaves!

It is an ordinary Mũũgĩkũyũ warder talking to me, no, actually lecturing me, for I am speechless with disbelief. Is he trying to trap me into something indiscreet, anything? Does he know what he is talking about? Does he not know that I am here precisely because of trying to communicate with peasants and workers — ordinary people, as he calls them?

But there is a kind of frank bitterness in his voice that shows much genuine sincerity in his holding me and my 'class' responsible for the cultural plight of Kenya. I think he is utterly unconscious of the fact that what he is saying, were he to try and put it into practice, could land him in this very detention block.

I say he is genuine in his utter lack of consciousness of the heretical nature of his patriotic cultural position, because he is one of the few warders who seem to have been completely cowed by prison and authority. If you asked him about the weather outside, he would shrink back in fear, pleading: 'Please don't play with my job. It is where I get daily flour for my children.' So in saying this to me, it is probably because he thinks it a safe subject. Languages, culture, education? Who cares? I am content just to listen to his monologue.

What have Europeans done to you people that you follow them like dogs their master? What have they done to you that you despise your own tongues and your own country?

I cannot answer him. I am itching to tell him about the Kamīrīīthū experiment, but I know that if I so much as mention the name Kamīrīīthū, he will freeze in terror, change the subject, and move away from the door of cell 16. But his talk has stung me in ways that he will never know.

That night I sit at the desk and start the story of Warīīnga in the Gīkūyū language. It flows just like that, and for the first time since my incarceration, I feel transports of joy. That which I have always toyed with but feared — writing a novel in Gīkūyū — is happening before my own eyes, and I have government toilet-paper for writing material, and a government-paid warder as a consultant.

I am ever willing to learn. In prison, more so.

*

Throughout my stay in Kamītī, and looking at all the Kenyan nationalities represented in this compound, I note one dominant tendency. While in ordinary social talks, petty reminiscences and occasional jokes and family problems, people tend to retreat into their own nationalities, when it comes to serious issues — confrontation with authority, demands for our rights and justice — the walls of nationality break asunder and people group around given positions *vis-à-vis* the issues. Even when it comes to the interpretation of Kenyan history and Kenya's future, people tend to group around definite ideological positions.

I have seen a similar tendency among the warders of different nationalities. There are times when they express the bitterness of an oppressed, exploited class and they talk to us as if they see in us just members of an exploiting, oppressing propertied class who have only temporarily fallen from grace and out of favour with other brothers-in-the-eating of plunder.

*

Strange how a place acquires its own personality, history, even culture and special vocabulary. All those who have been in this compound became part of the spirit of our history as detainees. For those of us who are new, we can never hear enough about the personalities, characters, anecdotes, exploits, words, songs, sayings of those who were here before us and have now left. Jamaitta, Achieng Oneko, J. D. Kali, Ndhiwa, Mak'anyengo, Wawerũ Gĩthũũngũri, Kajiwe, etc., all these acquire legendary proportions in our imagination. Even some Senior Superintendents of Prison (S.S.P.s) and prison officers who have served in this block and have left, have become part of the block's history and legends. It is as if we are all part of an undeclared political fraternity.

*

If you were in prison for life or if you were shipwrecked on an island, what books would you like to have with you and why? That used to be a favourite question of literature teachers at Alliance High School, and later at Makerere College. The normal response was to mention, not really the books one would have liked to have — the situation envisaged by the question was anyway too remote even for imagination — but the novels or the volume of plays or poetry that one had studied in depth, on which one could do an adequate critical appreciation to earn one a good mark.

But here at Kamĩtĩ, the question is no longer academic and when I receive news that my books have arrived, I tremble both with excitement at the arrival of a package from home and with eagerness to know which books have been allowed through by the police and prison censors.

In Kamītī, there's no library of any sort. This is a great indictment of conditions in KANU government detention camps. The Bible and the Koran are the sole official library. A few detainees have had books sent them from home and they have lent me some. I have particularly enjoyed reading Shabaan Roberts' *Maisha Yangu, Masomo yenye Adili*; Dicken's *A Tale of Two Cities;* Miller's *Dreamers and Rebels*; Abbott's *Life of Napoleon*; Kwei Armah's *Fragments*; Aristotle's *Ethics*; and Brutus' *Letters to Martha*. Otherwise the titles and authors available are too few and too limited in emotional and intellectual range. So in asking for authors and titles from my home library I have taken into account both my needs and those of the other detainees. So the list includes several authors and titles I have read and taught at university.

I am happy, though, for a prison reunion with Voltaire; Balzac; Molière; Zola; Flaubert; Tolstoy; Chekhov; Gorky; Sembène Ousmane; Shakespeare; Bertrand Russell; Claude McKay; and to make new acquaintances like Amadi and Thomas Mann.

But suddenly, I stop, shocked by those titles and authors that are barred by the censors. Thus I learn: books about British colonialism in Kenya are not allowed; hence Macgregor Ross's *Kenya from Within*, a history book discussing British colonial fascism in Kenya in the 1920s, has not come through.

Books about economic exploitation, and the Boer fascist oppression of Africans in South Africa are not allowed through: hence Woods' *Biko* has been returned to sender. Books about slavery, racism and political oppression in the heartland of imperialism, the U.S.A., are not allowed: hence Haley's *Roots* has also been returned to sender. I now want to know more.

And from the other detainees I learn that any book discussing *socialism* (or simply with the title, *socialism*) is not allowed in; and of course any books bearing the names of Marx, Engels, Lenin, Stalin, not to mention Mao Tse-Tung, are banned from detention. I am also told that Abdlatif's poems, *Sauti ya dhiki*, based on his experiences as a political prisoner at Kamītī, and my novel, *Petals of Blood*, have been returned.

Now a few prison puzzles. Why has *Mwendwo nĩ Irĩ na Irĩĩri* been returned? The title? The language?

Why has William Ochieng's book, *The Second Word: More Essays on Kenya History*, been returned? Most of the books by William Ochieng which I had read before detention were based on a neocolonial interpretation of Kenyan history. Could this book be different? Or was there another reason for banning it? The fact that he now teaches at Kenyatta University College? The fact that he once taught at Nairobi University where I also used to teach?

But I am grateful for what has been allowed through, especially for Gorky's *Selected Short Stories* and *Selected Plays*. Truly beautiful is Gorky's story of Danko who, when his people are trapped in a big, dark and apparently impenetrable forest in their march toward liberation, courageously rips open his breast and tears out his heart and holds it high above his head to lift up their flagging faith.

'It shone like the sun, even brighter than the sun, and the raging forest was subdued and lighted up by this torch, the torch of the great love for the people, and the darkness retreated before it . . .'

The romantic story of Danko reminds me of one of Blake's proverbs: He whose face gives no light, shall never become a star.

Gorky has shown the way. Art should encourage people to bolder and higher resolves in all their struggles to free the human spirit from the twin manacles of oppressive nature and oppressive man.

*

J.M. Dent, publishers, have an interesting sentence in all the books that bear their imprint in what they call Everyman's Library. The book is supposed to be telling the reader: 'Everyman, I will go with thee, and be thy guide, In thy most need to go by thy side.' The line is taken from a medieval English morality play. But it is Wasonga Sijeyo who makes me remember the line.

Books, he tells me one day, books have kept me mentally alive. Without books, I don't know if I could have survived this long. If prison has taught me anything, it is a big respect for books. You know I never went to anybody's formal school. Not even once. All my education has been in the streets of struggle or else in detention camps.

He is very widely read with a keen informed interest in geography, astronomy, philosophy, biology (especially the character and behaviour of animals), world history, culture, literature, religion and of course politics. His knowledge of the material culture of the Luo nationality is truly phenomenal and I keep on urging him to write a book about it.

To me, as I see him devouring Russell's three-volume autobiography, Tolstoy's *War and Peace*, and Balzac's *Old Goriot* and *Eugénie Grandet*, he symbolizes the kind of brilliance and genius thrown to the fore in periods of genuine people's struggles. The 1952-62 Mau Mau armed struggle was such a period in Kenya's history and Wasonga Sijeyo was one of its direct products. I am sure, and I keep on telling him, that a story of his own life would be very instructive to Kenyan youth and he should write it down.

I wish, though, I had asked for Gorky's three-volume autobiography, *My Childhood*; *My Apprenticeships*; and *My Universities*. I am sure Wasonga Sijeyo would have readily recognized Gorky's universities.

*

But no book or volumes of books can be a substitute for the book of life. The fascination people find in newspapers is precisely the illusion of a daily participation in and a record of active life. Reading through a newspaper one gets glimpses of a tapestry of life as it is being daily woven by actions of numerous men and women.

In prison detention, where people are not allowed newspapers or the radio, the thirst and hunger for news are sometimes unbearable in their torturous insistence for satisfaction.

Thus gathering news at Kamĩtĩ is a psychological imperative, and the detainees have developed a fantastic instinct for nosing out and extracting news from reluctant warders. A detainee who goes out to hospital or to meet his family must be hawk-eyed. He must learn to tune and turn his ears with the deftness and alertness of a cat or a hare. Every word counts. Every building, vehicle, street, dress, colour of trees counts. When he returns to camp, each of these is discussed and analysed from every possible angle till they yield all their secrets. A similar process of course takes place outside the prison where radio and other media are so uninformative about the real events that people inevitably rely on inferences, deductions and the grapevine. This is what is erroneously termed as 'rumour-mongering' by the rulers. But in prison, as outside, these inferences are often true.

Sometimes a warder has gone out to buy, let's say, a toothbrush for a detainee. He might bring it wrapped in a piece of newspaper. Should he forget to remove it, then the piece of paper, however tiny, will be seized and once again, every word, every line, will be discussed and analysed until it too yields all the secrets, past and present.

One day, I get a dramatic illustration of news-gathering at Kamītī. I am in cell 16, my heart is down because after writing a whole chapter of my new novel without a problem, I have now come to a dead-end. Every writer of imaginative literature knows the frustration and desperation that seize a person during such moments. It is naturally worse in prison.

Suddenly Matheenge, who keeps teasing me that he is *the* original *Kamītī 6*, because his number is K6,75 and mine K6,77, bursts into my cell with a tiny piece of newspaper no larger than a few square inches. 'Look at this,' he shouts. 'I collected it from the rubbish-bin outside. I saw a warder throw in some rubbish, I went and saw this, quickly picked it up and hid it before he could see me. It says something about Gachago and Mūhūri and conviction and oh, yes, look there's a letter J. . . oh, wait, let the warders come on night duty.' At night two warders come. Then suddenly Matheenge calls out one by name:

'Hey! Have Gachago and Mūhūri started their years on the other side?'

'You mean the two M.P.s? They started some time ago.'

'How many years?'

'Five each. Plus a few strokes.'

'What for?'

'Coffee, of course. Magendo.'

Then suddenly the warder remembers that he is talking to a political detainee and he stops short.

'Who told you?'

'Never mind. Walls have voices.'

Tomorrow Matheenge will use this extra information to get more information and before a week the whole story will be out.

The news has an unsettling effect on me. Magendo in ivory, gem-stones, game-skins, coffee, maize, rice, sugar, *unga*, tea has been a way of life among the ruling circles in Kenya. Even the smallest child in a village could tell you the names of Big So-and-So, Tall So-and-So, Fat So-and-So, Moral So-and-So, Holy So-and-So, Upright So-and-So, who had camped at Chepkubwe waiting for his tons of coffee, later transported to Mombasa under police escort.

Why then pick on these two law-breakers? Or were they only two sacrificial lambs to propitiate an angry populace and buy time for a rotting, falling-apart system? Capitalism itself is a system of unabashed theft and robbery. Thus theft, robbery, corruption can never be wrong under capitalism because they are inherent in it.

Well, they are the structure. Without a systematic robbery of peasants and workers, a robbery protected and sanctified by laws, law courts, parliament, religion, armed forces, police, prisons, eduction, there is no capitalism. It is worse, the robbery, when a country is under the higher capitalism of foreigners which is imperialism. How else explain the fact that in a mainly agricultural country, peasants who farm often have to queue for yellow maize from America and Britain after what they have produced has been carted or sold or smuggled to those very countries? Lenin once defined imperialism as the highest stage of capitalism. Imperialism is the capitalistic robbery and theft of a country's wealth by foreigners aided, of course, by a few sell-out natives. Two M.P.s put in the cooler for small offences while the fat cats continue unabated.

And suddenly I discover the hitherto elusive theme of my prison novel. I grow literary wings. I am ready to fly. All because of a piece of newspaper little larger than a square inch retrieved from a rubbish-bin.

*

Detainees have also learnt to gather news from the warders by face-reading and their group behaviour. Certain kinds of groupings by certain warders have come to mean that some upheaval, good or bad for the detainees, has happened outside the block. A certain kind of laughter from the more cruel warders has come to mean that something not to the advantage of detainees has occurred, while a certain kind of sadness and fear on the same faces has invariably come to mean good news for the detainees. This intuitive news-gathering style is inherited by succeeding waves of inmates. An analysis of patterns of laughter and anger, of sadness and irritability, of gait and gestures, has become a daily ritual among detainees. I have been assured that this, augmented by judicious and well-timed questions, often yields very important news! And accurate! But I do not quite believe it at first and my scepticism registers on my face.

One day, Gĩcerũ wa Njaũ comes to my door and he tells me: 'I would like you to watch the faces of warders A, B and C. Observe the fear in their eyes. See how they walk? Some major event to our advantage has occurred.'

Throughout the day I maintain a careful watch on the said faces. Alas, they yield nothing to me. But later in the week news leaks out. The commissioner of prisons, Saikwa, has been dismissed, and

Lokopoyet, the S.S.P. in charge of Kamītī, has been transferred to another prison.

I have never seen anything like it. When the old S.S.P. comes to introduce the new S.S.P. (a Mr Mareka), and he announces his own imminent departure from Kamītī, the detainees actually clap in a collective spontaneous delirium of joy even before they know how the new S.S.P. will turn out to be.

For me, relief too. The old S.S.P. will never now demand to read and approve 'my poems'. I have never anyway written poetry, in or outside prison.

*

For a period, the reliefless senseless cruelty ends and Kamītī, under the new S.S.P., becomes, relatively speaking, a paradise.

The new S.S.P. ends the practice of locking up detainees for twenty-three hours a day. Even defiance of prison regulations and rules he will deal with reasonably. There will be no more collective punishment unless there is a collective insurrection. Our cells will be opened at six in the morning and locked at five in the afternoon. We shall now be in our cells for thirteen instead of twenty-three hours.

The new S.S.P. allows us to form our own committee for settling any disputes between us detainees, and as a vehicle through which we can present complaints that affect us all. Gīcerū and I will be on this committee throughout the rest of our stay. The other members, at different times, are Wasonga Sijeyo, Hadji Dagan, Mohamed Abdilie Hadow, and Ali Dubat.

The new S.S.P. orders the reconnection of the radio and for the first time we can hear Voice of Kenya and foreign news such as it is, and listen to sounds of music such as it is. We dance to the sound of music. On the concrete corridor. The new S.S.P. promises us a guitar!

The new S.S.P. allows us to start classes. Most of the Somali join English classes conducted by Mūhoro wa Mūthoga, popularly known as Fujika. Now he acquires another name — Mwalimu. His cell, no. 9, becomes a school.

The new S.S.P. allows us to buy our own newspapers: the *Weekly Review; The Standard; The Daily Nation;* and *Taifaeleo.* They are ruthlessly censored wherever there's a reference to any one of us, but that's a small price to pay for the privilege of a little contact with the outside world.

'During your reign,' Wasonga Sijeyo tells the new S.S.P. in a vote of thanks on behalf of us all, 'we shall be free!', meaning that his humaneness is a good omen.

*

That's how we come to learn about the release of Mohamed Babu from political detention; about Major Kisila and Captain Angaine; we learn of the Ogaden war; the uprising in Shaba Province against the Zairean comprador bourgeois regime of Mobutu, and the subsequent invasion and occupation of the area by the French to protect Euro-American investments.

That's how we come to learn about Professor Barnard's visit to Kenya as a guest of the attorney-general, Charles Njonjo, and about his open defence of racism and apartheid, and his insulting advocacy of ties between Kenya and the dying regime of South Africa.

I incorporate his visit into my novel.

*

It is in the newspapers that I one day see Mĩcere Mũgo, pictured during the '78 Kenya Schools Drama Festival at the British-run Kenya National Theatre, castigating the continued dominance of foreign imperialist cultural interests in Kenya, and my heart leaps in joy.

Mĩcere, a colleague in the literature department at the University of Nairobi, and I had co-authored *The Trial of Dedan Kimaathi* to rescue him from political and literary burial. Kĩmaathi was still buried at Kamĩtĩ prison. But he will for ever live in the collective memory of the Kenyan people. Like Waiyaki before him. Like Koitalel before him. Like Me Kitilili, and Otenyo and Nyanjirũ and many other patriots before him.

*

It is in the newspapers that I one day read news of Charles Njonjo's launching of Dawood's novel *No Strings Attached* (Spear Books, Kenya) at the ceremony in the Serena Hotel. I read with interest his unstinted praise of the novel, its good, correct, grammatical English, and his attack on those who launched books without first reading them, books moreover that attacked the government. I note that while reaffirming the right to freedom of expression, he warns Kenyan authors 'not to write about things which might embarrass the government in the eyes of the public'.

The novel is published by Heinemann and the reported occasion takes me back to the launching of my novel, *Petals of Blood*, by Mwai Kĩbaki, then Minister for Finance, in July 1977 at the City Hall, Nairobi. *Petals of Blood* had also been published by Heinemann and they had hailed the book as a major publishing event! Kĩbaki had certainly read the novel. He made a speech in defence of literary and intellectual freedom that made him the talk of the university community for the next few months. His words now come back to me with the terrible force of historical irony:

> It is true that writers all over the world want to write and comment on what is going on in their own country of origin. But one of the most terrible things about the modern world is how many writers have had to emigrate to another nation in order to be able to comment on what's going on in their own country of origin. And it is a tragedy because it means that societies are themselves becoming intolerant, whereas the true freedom in any democratic system should be — as we are trying to do in this country; we have not succeeded yet, but we are trying — that those who differ and those who take a different view of the society we live in must be able to paint what picture they see, so that we can have many, many pictures of the kind of Kenya we are living in now, because the efforts by some of the people in the media who write short quick stories, who try to present one picture only, is of course misleading . . . at least let us give encouragement to those who spend their lifetime writing, commenting on the society that we live in. There is not very much else that we can do but at least we can give them that particular kind of recognition . . .

Exactly five months later I was in Kamĩtĩ Maximum Security Prison for helping to write a play in the Gĩkũyũ language, *Ngaahika Ndeenda*.

Strange ways of encouraging Kenyan literature!

*

Fear of death suddenly dampens our happiness. Shikuku has been on a hunger strike for some days because the authorities have refused to allow him crutches to enable him to walk without crawling against the walls. Shikuku has been on other hunger strikes in prison whenever his rights to medical care and medical prescriptions have not been met. He fights for his rights and is admired for this by fellow detainees.

I had heard about hunger strikes before, but only in books and newspapers, never in real life. Every time Shikuku has been on a hunger strike, I thought he would die. In January, when most of the others were in Mombasa, he had come to my cell and had allowed me to read all his previous letters to the authorities related to his hunger strikes, just in case. . .

The police and the prison authorities would wait until he was on the verge of total collapse, then they would come for him and rush him to hospital where he would be forcibly fed through the veins. Two or three days later they would bring him back to prison.

But this time, it seems to us all, he is in a critical condition. They have kept him for four days. No food. No water. Fifth day. The same. 'They want him to die,' we whisper among ourselves. On the sixth day he collapses. We are all locked in our cells. They come for him with a stretcher.

We don't talk about it. But we are all sure that he is dead. A sense of impending doom grips the whole compound.

On the fifth day he is brought back. Without the crutches. But with promises. A few days later when it is clear that the crutches will not be forthcoming, Shikuku goes on yet another hunger strike.

On the fourth day of the strike, they come for him. But this time they don't bring him back to cell 11. They take him to an isolation cell in G block to live alone, and we never see him again until the day of our release. But we know he is alive because he keeps on sending warders for books!

A hunger strike is premised on a readiness to die if one's demands are not met, and also on the assumption that the other party fears the moral or political consequences of one's death. But what a terrible thing to watch death knocking at the door of a Kenyan simply because he has made a principled stand on national issues.

*

In detention, when one is not reduced to the level of a beast, one is certainly treated like a child. You cannot be trusted with sharp

eapons because you might take your own life. If you want to shave,
ou beg for a razor-blade from the corporal in charge and then must
romptly return it.

In defiance, I start keeping a razor-blade, hidden in the cracks of
y desk. It's simply a way of affirming my freedom and respon-
ibility over my life!

*

n earth tremor. (I later learned that a minor earthquake shook the
astern Highlands and Nairobi, measuring over 5 on the Richter
cale!) Wish it were a social tremor to bring an end to the system and
o this prison!

*

 james. Tenniquoit. Ludo. Chess. Draughts. Walks on the side-
avements.

*

Ve organize story-telling sessions. Ali Dubat and Wasonga Sijeyo
re mines of folklore.

*

inging too, Religious hymns. Popular tunes. Political songs.

*

here is a warder who hardly ever talks. But when we start reading
ews of the exploits of the Red Brigades in Italy, his mouth suddenly
pens. He can talk endlessly about them. With only one constant
efrain. 'And they are not touching the poor,' he would say, laughing
ntil tears flow down his cheeks. Then he would describe graphic-
lly, in minute detail, how they shot this or that rich Italian person, as
he had been present when the deed was done. 'And to know that
ey are not touching the poor,' he would repeat. About Kenya or
frica, however, he is absolutely mum. No words. No opinions.

*

The new S.S.P. releases old issues of *Time* and *Newsweek*. They are
given to Kamītī Prison by the United States Information Service in
Nairobi. For a week or so we revel in world events as seen through
American eyes. But the pleasure of a newspaper or a news-magazine
is reading between the lines, if you know the publisher's or the
writer's general view. There can be no totally objective newspaper
— much less an American one.

I come across a *Newsweek* carrying an interview with Kofi
Awoonor, the Ghanaian novelist and poet who had been incarcer-
ated by Achiempong for a year without trial. I first met Kofi at
Makerere, Kampala, during the historic 1962 Conference of
African Writers attended by, among others, Wole Soyinka, Chris
Okigbo, Chinua Achebe, Langston Hughes, Saunders Redding,
Ezekiel Mphahlele, Lewis Nkosi, Arthur Mamaine, Bloke
Modisane, Grace Ogot, Rebecca Njaŭ and Jonathan Kariara. I was
then a student at Makerere just beginning to write: one or two
published stories, two unpublished manuscripts, but with hope, great
hope for an East African literary renaissance. What I remember
most about the conference was the energy and the hope and the
dreams and the confidence: after all, we were part of a continent
emerging from a colonial era into . . . what? We never answered the
question, but the hopes and dreams and the confidence remained.
Now we have no doubt, two decades later, about the answer.

Now as I look at Kofi's picture in *Newsweek* at Kamītī Prison, I
remember that Chris Okigbo who led the conference with the
paper, 'What is African Literature?', is dead, a victim of an intra-
bourgeois war which, in the words of Kole Omotoso, was merely for
'redefining the land boundaries rather than redefining the quality of
life for those who live within the existing boundaries', a war in which
only the Americans, the British and the French emerged as victors;
that Wole Soyinka and Kofi Awoonor have served prison terms for
saying that things which are not right ARE NOT RIGHT; and that
many African writers have witnessed and recorded the terrible
anguish of Africans killing innumerable Africans so that Euro-
American capital can thrive on grounds made more fertile by
African flesh and blood!

Bitter memories but it's good just to see Awoonor's picture and
know that he is free and is continuing denouncing Africa's tin gods
who jump at any little criticism of their corrupt regimes. This earth,
our earth, my brother!

*

In another *Newsweek*, I come across a story about my detention. The main story had been censored out but they had forgotten that the story ran on to a different column on a different page. *Newsweek* quotes 'usually reliable' Nairobi intellectual circles as describing me as 'a naive ideologue' for not knowing the limits of dissent and therefore not living within the restrictive walls of self-censorship.

I laugh at this! A naive ideologue? For writing in a Kenyan language? For joining hands with peasants to build a modern patriotic Kenyan theatre? For communicating with at least a few peasants? This is not dissent even.Not really yet. Ideologue? And them, counter-ideologues.That's fair.

If sophistication means writing in a foreign language and taking a pro-imperialist anti-Kenyan line in national and international affairs, then avaunt! Quit my sight! Sophistication, go to hell! If naiveté means writing about the heroism of Kenyan people in their centuries of struggle against any and every form of foreign economic, political and cultural domination, then come naiveté, let me embrace thee for ever.

The Kenyan peasants were described as 'naive' by their educated brethren when they challenged the might of the British empire on whose shores the sun never set. The naive peasants took up arms against British imperialism in Kenya when their sophisticated brethren, fresh from seats of learning in Makerere/Harvard/Cambridge/London/Oxford and elsewhere, were crying out (in sophisticated languages of course): hold it, we have been taught that imperialism is mighty and we should willingly become its slaves and get international prizes for being its faithful spokesmen.

Intellectual slavery masquerading as sophistication is the worst form of slavery.

Viva the 'naive' peasants and workers of Kenya. Viva the glorious history of Kenyan people, I shout loudly in my heart in my cell later.

*

I hear a siren from the other side. It's a mournful, terrible sound, like a mother bereaved of all her children. Only that in this case I am told it's the prison alert for escaped prisoners.

I used to teach Dennis Brutus' book of poems, *Sirens Knuckles Boots*, but I never really understood the title. Now I do. I read his

Letters to Martha more avidly. His opening letter captures very acurately the emotions of a new political prisoner:

> After the sentence
> mingled feelings:
> sick relief,
> the load of the approaching days
> apprehension —
> the hints of brutality
> have a depth of personal meaning;
>
> exultation —
> the sense of challenge,
> of confrontation,
> vague herosim
> mixed with self-pity
> and tempered by the knowledge of those
> who endure much more
> and endure . . .

*

Tuesday, 13 June 1978: Gĩcerũ corners me and tells me: 'I would now like you to watch the faces of the same warders, A, B, and C. See how they walk? See how they laugh? It is not good for us!'

Yes. It is early in the morning. They are laughing and being a bit too jovial with detainees and they walk jauntily.

At three o'clock, we learn that the police have intervened. The radio is disconnected. And we can no longer buy or read news papers.

When he is later confronted by detainees about this vindictiveness, the detainees' security officer, Mr Mũhĩndĩ Mũnene, replies: 'What would then be the meaning of detention?'

Ah, well: it is at least good to know that the ill-treatment and torture in prison are not the results of personal aberration on the part of a few warders and officers, but that it is calculated and directed from the top.

But we shall never forget the relative humaneness of the new S.S.P.

*

We go back to our games, to our books, to our pens, to our religions, to our story-telling, to our monotonous lives, to our dreams of freedom.

*

Then Kenyatta died. And suddenly our dreams of freedom grew wings.

CHAPTER EIGHT

1

For those who wait in prison, as for those who wait outside prison, dreams of freedom start at the very minute of arrest. Something might just happen; maybe somebody will intervene; and even when everything seems against any possibility of release, there's the retreat to the final bravado: the plight can only end in either death or freedom, which I suppose are two different forms of release. So release of one sort or other is eventually assured.

But when? One of the cruelties of detention — unlike ordinary imprisonment— is precisely this *not* knowing when one will get out. For the ordinary convicted prisoner — we are not talking of the fairness or unfairness of the trial, the so-called justice involved — he knows the duration of his sentence and no matter how long it is, his emotions and intellect can adjust to it. Not so the political detainee: he can be released after an hour, a day, a week, or after fifty years! So whether he likes it or not, every minute, every hour of the day, the question lurks somewhere in his consciousness: could it be now, today? Every warder's clinking of chains, every unexpected knock at the door, brings this question to the fore: is it now, today? When? Some people ask: were you tortured in detention? But detention is itself torture and the greatest part of it is this ignorance of *when*. Yes, torture not only for those inside, but even for those outside!

Nyambura wrote me a letter on 19 September 1978, in which she told me about the progress of the children — Thiong'o, Kīmunya, Ngīna, Ndūūcū, Mūkoma and Wanjikū — in their different schools. Then she added:

'In your letter you told me that the state authorities have never asked you about your writings: what do they ask you when you go for questioning? I hear that all detainees are questioned or that their cases are reviewed every three or six months. How has your case been?'

She was asking about the Detainees' Review Tribunal, so much trumpeted by the Kenya ruling authorities whenever questions of release of detained persons were raised in world councils.

The following were the members of the Detainees' Review Tribunal: Justice Hancox (an ex-British judge of the Kenyan High

Court); Justice Cockar (a judge of the High Court); Mr Ransley (an advocate with Archer and Wilcock); Mr Karūgū (deputy public prosecutor — now attorney-general); Mr Kĩbara Muttu (a senior state counsel); Mr Karanja (deputy permanent secretary, Ministry of Home Affairs); Mr Mũhĩndĩ Mũnene (assistant commissioner of police); Mr Tsuma (principal, Shanzu Teachers' Training College).

The Detainees' Review Tribunal, which met every six months, served three political purposes: as a public relations team to allay national and international fears regarding Kenyatta's detention camps; as a screening team, just like those of the emergency era in colonial Kenya; and finally, but basically, as an instrument of torture, part of the state's psychological terrorism against the individual detainee and the nation as a whole.

As a hoax to national and world opinion, the tribunal was excellent: its very existence and its six-monthly motions of pretence at review —expenses and the trip to Mombasa fully paid — gave the intended impression that those not released had somehow not satisfied this very impartial tribunal. And to many, the fact that the Detainees' Review Tribunal was chaired by a foreigner was the final evidence of its impartiality. Thus its carefully nursed impression of impartiality, its quasi-judicial character (in theory a detainee could have the services of a lawyer) — tended to establish a prima facie case against the poor detainee. Either the detainee had refused to co-operate, or the tribunal, after carefully weighing the evidence, had, in its judicial wisdom, found such detainees still unfit for 'human' company. The detainee was tried (on unknown crimes of course) and found wanting.

The fact was that in its entire membership, the eight-man Review Tribunal was a wholly civil service affair. And the fact that it was chaired by a foreigner, far from inclining it towards impartiality would the more likely have inclined it towards partiality towards the state of which it was itself a part. In my case, my unstated reasons for detention were my consistent opposition to the foreign control of our economy and culture, and to the mental colonialism in the ruling comprador bourgeoisie that makes them have a childlike faith in foreigners per se, especially if such foreigners happen to be British or American capitalists. The foreign chairmanship of the Tribunal was, to me, one more proof of my correct position. Could one then expect a colonial foreigner to make a judgement against himself?

A foreigner, by the very nature of his position, feels only accountable to those who have given him the job. He tends to feel that it is not for him, a foreigner, to make controversial pronounce-ments on the basic questions of democratic and human rights in the country of his temporary but well-paid adoption. 'We gave them independence, let them make a mess of it if that's what they want,' tends to be the general attitude of those from an imperialist country working as 'experts' in a former colony. Yet they are thoroughly enjoying the fruits of that mess. Why care? Who cares? Such a foreigner might even pretend not to feel or to see the mess. At any rate, there is no way such a foreigner can feel loyalty to, or feel the pressures for democracy in, the Kenyan history of struggle. There is a chance that a Kenyan, depending on his class sympathies, might feel these pressures and loyalty and perchance his sense of patriotic duty might compel him to arrive at a position similar to the one held by the Indian supreme court: 'Preventive detention is a serious invasion of personal liberty and such meagre safeguards as the constitution has provided against the improper exercise of the power must be jealously watched and enforced by the courts.'

In our case, there was no hope of such a pronouncement. For even assuming that the tribunal was impartial, it had only advisory powers; its advice to the government was never made public, and it was never communicated to detainees.

It was in its proceedings, however, that the tribunal's rôle as a screening team came through. As far as I know, no detainee was ever told of the government's charges against him. The tribunal sat there and simply asked the detainee to tell them whatever it was that he wanted communicated to the government. It was a most weird experience. Not only was the detainee pre-judged to be the guilty party, but the burden of self-prosecution fell on him. In other words, the detainee was to be his own accuser, prosecutor and counter-witness. But even after going through all that, he could never be sure of release. He had to prove himself guilty beyond any and every reasonable doubt and to crown this with abject pleas for presidential mercy and clemency. Even then, he was not sure of release and after six months the tribunal would come for more proofs of one's assumed guilt and for more pleas for mercy without deigning to say what had been the reception of the previous self-prosecution and abject pleas. The Detainees' Review Tribunal then clearly saw its rôle as one of receiving a detainee's list of confessions and pleas, and carrying them to the government for a thorough scrutiny by the Special Branch.

Its being an instrument of mental torture consisted in its raising of false hopes. Twice a year, the Detainees' Review Tribunal would meet, raise people's hopes, and then dash them to the ground. Even when a detainee intellectually convinced himself — after four or six or twenty appearances — that the tribunal was at best an ineffectual body for a government cover-up and at worst a screening team, he still retained a faint hope that maybe this time . . . After three or five years, a number of detainees had arrived at a position where they resolved not to see the tribunal again, and had written to say so.

I appeared before the tribunal twice. The first appearance was after fourteen days at Kamĩtĩ in the S.S.P.'s offices and, incredible as it might seem, and despite what the other detainees had told me about it, I still went there with some hope: since what I had done had been completely above board in a democratic society, maybe someone might have thought it over and decided on the futility of detaining truth. Once the tribunal told me about the charges against me, I would be able to convince them of my innocence.

The first tribunal was chaired by Justice Cockar in an acting capacity — in the absence of Justice Hancox who was then reportedly on leave in Britain. After polite introductions, they simply stared at me. I asked them: Why was I detained? They did not know. What were the accusations against me? They didn't know. And now the chairman talked: Had I anything I wanted to tell the government?

The second tribunal, also at Kamĩtĩ — I, with a few others, was not taken to Mombasa as was the usual practice — was held in July and this time was chaired by Justice Hancox. This time I had written a memorandum, putting in writing my verbal complaints to the first tribunal, and expanding on them. I wanted to state my position vis-à-vis issues of languages, literature, culture and foreign domination very clearly and *very* finally. In my memorandum, it was the KANU government which was on trial. My detention for advocating a national culture, free from foreign imperialist domination, was major evidence against the regime. Again the same silent stares. And the same question: What more, apart from what was in the memorandum, did I want to tell the government?

The only difference between the first session in January and the second in July was in the chairmanship. Justice Cockar had been a bit more patient; he was at least willing, or seemed willing, to listen. He noted down anything that you wanted to say. Then the whole interview lasted slightly more than five minutes. Justice Hancox was impatient, yawned several times and kept on looking at his watch.

This time the interview lasted less than three minutes.

I always looked at the faces of other detainees and I could see the anxieties occasioned by the nearness of the tribunal. Dreams of freedom were eating into their peace of mind. I myself found it difficult to sleep on the eve of the two sessions. But after the interview, an incredible hollowness would seize me. It took more than two weeks to compose myself into waiting for the next session. I was determined, though, that the second appearance would, for me, be the last. I would thereafter join those who had said that they would not be a party to the gigantic judicial hoax. It was far better to nurse one's dreams of freedom in privacy and know that they were only dreams and wishes, rather than have them used against you, like Tantalus of old: you were shown the way to quench your thirst for freedom but on arrival at the gate the way was but an iron barrier and the Detainees' Review Tribunal merely watchmen at the gate.

Wasonga Sijeyo once called me aside and told me never to build any certainty of release on false hopes: 'It is good to have faith, to keep on hoping. For what is life, but hope? Never prevent a man from hoping, for if you do, you are denying him reasons for living. To hope for a better tomorrow, to dream of a new world, that is what is human. But don't be so certain of the hour and the day as to let it break you if the hoped-for freedom does not come at the expected hour and day.'

We sat on the pavement facing the stone walls that divided our compound from that of the Kenyans condemned to die.

Then he told me about his past experiences with dreams of freedom. On at least three occasions, he had been very sure of release. The first dream had its origins in a strong rumour from the warders at Kamītī and was given substance by certain assurances from the tribunal at its sitting in Shimo-la-Tewa Prison, Mombasa. He waited, unable to sleep, hope climbing on hope. Nothing came of it. The second had even greater substance. It was after a Luo delegation had visited Kenyatta. The delegation was promised Wasonga's release. A prison officer even told him to be ready for he could be summoned to Kenyatta's presence any day, any hour. For a week or so he lay awake, riding on tenter-hooks of hope. Nothing came of this. The third dream, almost a reality, was the furthest from reality, a nightmare really, and it was clearly meant to destroy him forever; for this time, he was told to get ready. He packed his luggage, all the precious little things that one accumulates in prison, and got into his civilian clothes. But at the gate, the officers looked at the official documents, and announced in hurt surprise at the late discovery of an elementary error that even a child could have detected,'Very sorry, Mr Sijeyo, but it was not you.'

Because of these, Wasonga was the most reserved and cautious whenever there were any individual or collective jubilations at rumours of imminent release.

2

One such premature jubilation was based on revelations from the Koran; what later came to be known as the Koran theory of freedom. Islam was introduced into the compound by members of Kenya Somali nationality.

Ahmed Shurie and Mohamed Abdilie led the daily festival of five prayer sessions (facing Mecca) and a feast of songs in Arabic and Somali. Before the arrival of the Somalis, the only religion was Christianity in the form of its two major sects — Catholic and Protestant, led by Father Lawless and Reverend Ngarī. Now the two major world religions — Islam and Christianity — and their two rival books of God, the Koran and the Bible, contented for adherents at Kamītī Prison.

Ongong Were and I were the only detainees who belonged to neither camp. Instead we would play a game of chess or else we would stand by and watch the proceedings from afar. Islam was the first and only one to make a dramatic conquest. Matheenge, previously a Catholic, became a Muslim. The ceremony of conversion took place on Monday, 30 January at 1.30 p.m. watched by all the detainees. He became Adam Ahamed and he wore a Muslim cap. But I did not see any Muslim become a Christian.

I was fascinated by the two religions and especially the differences between them. The Muslims at Kamītī believed literally in the Koran. I came to learn that the Koran was not just a book. Like the Torah of Judaism, it contained a way of life, a culture that regulated a person's daily actions, from the proper ways of making love to the proper ways of shitting and urinating. Though I thought that it could be reduced to ritual, Islam seemed the more demanding of the two religions: five prayer sessions a day and, at least for those aspiring to religious leadership, recital of the whole Koran from the first to the last page, once a week. For its adherents Islam was a world. The Christian Bible, on the other hand, did not contain a rigid way of life, a totality of culture or rules governing daily behaviour, and for its adherents, especially at Kamĩtĩ, it was not a world. It was certainly much less demanding in observance of ritual: there were group meetings only when the Protestant chaplain came to visit.

The Christian chaplain had told me: the Bible is a whole library. Twenty-eight books. You don't need any more. The Muslim sheikh used to tell me: the Koran is the only book you need. It contains all the knowledge there has been, there is, and there will be. Both claimed that *their* book was the book of God. But it was the Muslims who seemed to believe more in *their* book as the infallible word of God, a word-for-word transcript of a tablet in heaven, as revealed to the Prophet Mohamed by Gabriel, the angel, for they turned to it, read it, to find out what would happen tomorrow; for instance, who among the Muslim detainees would get a family visit and when.

Now Sheikh Ahmed Shurie read the Koran and he saw the stars scattering away and oceans rolling and it was revealed to him that we would all be released on Madaraka Day by the grace of Jomo Kenyatta, though the order would come from God.

Thus 1 June 1978 saw a high temperature of expectation, especially among the Muslims. Most of the non-Muslims expressed doubts about the veracity of the revelations, but we all hoped that the prophecy would come true and whether through revelation or coincidence, it did not matter. The calm dignity with which the sheikh kept on asserting the inevitability of our release, and the way he would smile confidence at the doubters, made some of us suspect that maybe some friendly warder had whispered vital news to him. But a systematic, though not open, inquiry among the other Muslims revealed that the entire revelation came through the Koran, which was a more reliable source of truth and prophecy. One Muslim detainee had even packed his luggage, ready to bolt to freedom at any hour of the day or night.

Nothing of our freedom came on Madaraka Day. But so sure was he of the truth of the relevation that even on 2 June — the newspapers had not yet been stopped — the sheikh asked that all the papers should be read carefully for any clue or hint about our impending release.

It turned out that Kenyatta's speech at Madaraka was the shortest ever and it contained not a single word about the fate of political prisoners. But reading between the lines we were all sure that Kenyatta was seriously ill.

3

It was about the same time that two doves started flying low over the compound, sometimes even perching and cooing on the high walls. Now emerged the dove theory of freedom. In Biblical Jewish mythology, the dove was the bird that brought the good news to Noah's Ark that all was now well with the earth and he could return home to land from his exile in the sea.

In some African mythology, the dove also plays an important rôle as the messenger of peace and hope. There is a beautiful Gĩkũyũ story in which dove, after being fed with castor-oil seeds by a pregnant woman whose life and that of her baby are threatened by a man-eater, Irimũ, agrees to undertake a journey to call her husband, a blacksmith, Mũturi, in his smithy, far away. It sings to him:

> Smith smithing away
> Caangarara — ĩca!
> Smith smith quickly
> Caangarara — ĩca!
> Your wife has given birth
> Caangarara — ĩca!
> With a man-eater for a mid-wife
> Caangarara —ĩca!

The dove sings so persistently and movingly that the smith at once goes back home and releases his wife from misery by killing the man-eater.

There is another story in which dove puts together the bones of a dead girl and moulds back her flesh using mud, then breathes life into her, and she walks back to her joyous parents with her former beauty multiplied tenfold.

Now at Kamĩtĩ it turned out that all the previous three consecutive releases — Achieng Aneko's, J.D. Kali's and Nthiwa's — were preceded by the mysterious sudden appearance of two doves, with one of them actually landing in the yard. One detainee believed that if one of these doves landed in the yard it would be a sure sign of the imminent release if not of all of us, at least of one, most likely himself — but a release all the same.

No doves landed in the prison yard. (When I arrived home after my release, I found doves in the yard. They had nested on the roof of the house. I asked Nyambura: 'When did these birds come here?' She replied, 'In January 1978, soon after your detention.') But the doves went on increasing in numbers, so that by December about twenty doves were making regular flights over the compound, eliciting many jokes about the dove theory of freedom, but also exciting fantasies of their flight in freedom. The dove theory of freedom and the heated controversy, fantasy and speculation it aroused — much more than that aroused by the Koran theory — recalled poem seventeen in Dennis Brutus' book, *Letters to Martha:*

> In prison
> the clouds assume importance
> and the birds
>
> With a small space of sky
> cut off by walls
> of bleak hostility
> and pressed upon by hostile authority
> the mind turns upwards . . .
>
> the complex aeronautics
> of the birds
> and their exuberant acrobatics
> become matters for intrigued speculation
> and wonderment . . .

Dennis Brutus, writing about his experiences in a South African prison in 1965, could now speak with an uncanny insight to us at Kamītī, Kenya, in 1978, penned in a similar inglorious spot.

However, it is poem eleven in the same *Letters to Martha* that best sums up our experience with these consecutive dreams of freedom:

> Events have a fresh dimension
> for all things can affect the pace
> of political development —
>
> but our concern
> is how they hasten or delay
> a special freedom —
> that of those the prisons hold
> and who depend on change
> to give them liberty.

And so one comes to a callousness,
a savage ruthlessness —
voices shouting in the heart
'Destroy! Destroy!'
or
'Let them die in Thousands!' —

really it is impatience.

The last one-line stanza is false as an explanation, though true as a
description. The essence lies in the second stanza. For Robben
Island in South Africa, as for Kamītī in Kenya, the poem bespeaks a
situation in which the release of political prisoners depends on the
subjective whims of a fascist bourgeois dictatorship. For these
prisoners, their final dream of freedom comes to rest on objective
change to give them liberty.

4

When I first arrived in Kamītī, the one question that nearly all the
groups shot at me was about Kenyatta's health. Quite innocently, I
would tell them that Kenyatta was in excellent health. On hearing
this, the group would drift away in silence without asking another
question. It was Thairū wa Mūthīga who was to later tell me the
reason: 'Believe me but we have lost any hope of release through the
tribunal or through presidential mercy. Since J.M.'s murder, no
detainee has been released . . . sorry, there was Ochieng Aneko but
we believe he was released to mollify public opinion after the
detention of Shikuku and Seroney. So our hope rests on Kenyatta's
death. You don't believe me? No detainee is going to be released
until after Kenyatta's death. That's our opinion anyway. So when
you told us that Kenyatta's health was excellent, you were crushing
our hopes without your knowing it.'

This theory of freedom — Kenyatta's death as the liberator —
gained in momentum, especially after the collapse of the Koran
Madaraka theory and the failure of the tribunal of January and July
to release anybody, especially those like Mwanzia (in Shimo-la-
Tewa), Ongongi Were, and Wasonga Sijeyo, going into their
seventh, eighth, and tenth years respectively.

On Tuesday, 22 August, we were locked in our cells at the usual
time of 4.45 p.m. As was my daily habit, except when stuck, I now

sat at the desk exorcising out of me all the images reflected in my mind during the day as I walked for exercise, or played tenniquoit, or chess, or listened to arguments or narrations or reminiscences. The novel had become my most important weapon in the daily combat with the stony dragon. A warder brought me a note from Wasonga Sijeyo: 'The greatest has fallen or he is about to fall. Keep this to yourself. Will confirm tomorrow.' He had been reading Ali's autobiography, *The Greatest*, and I assumed that he was talking about the fall of Mohamed Ali from the boxing throne. But why the uncertainty? He had either fallen, in which case it was news; or he had not, in which case it was speculation, and speculation was no news. And why the caution: 'Keep this to yourself'? I wrote back another note, for my suspicions and curiosity were now aroused and I could not wait until morning. 'Do you mean THE greatest in boxing?' The reply came through the wall. Just one word, 'No', and I there and then knew what was already public knowledge in Kenya, in the whole world, but for us detainees forbidden knowledge: Kenyatta was dead.

In the morning I cornered Wasonga. He confirmed it: Kenyatta had died in his sleep while on a 'busy working holiday in Mombasa'. His last companions were a group of foreign emissaries. 'But let's keep this to ourselves, for the time being. I myself will tell Koigi.'

It was a rule amongst us detainees that the sources of one's information were always to be protected: we did not want to jeopardize the job of any of our informants or cut off such sources of information.

It was a most terrible burden trying to keep this vital information from our fellow detainees — for it meant so much for each one of them — but we could not turn off the tap of information by making any indiscretion. For a day, the three of us carrying the burden would speak a thousand silent questions with our eyes or faces, but none had the answer. But gradually the news was passed to each detainee individually under the strictest promise not to show any feelings on our faces and in our voices, or in our behaviour towards officers and warders.

And so for three days a game of hypocritical silence was played in Kamītī: the warders pretending that all was as usual and we pretending that we did not understand their sudden absent-mindedness, their quick little surreptitious groupings, or their forced laughter. Now simple questions like: 'How is the weather outside?' or 'How is life outside?', spoken innocently, would suddenly acquire a special symbolism and you would see a warder cast a quick suspicious glance, or else wince before recovering and trying to laugh off the inquiry.

It was a most unreal situation. There was an important drama in Kenya's history being played outside the walls and here at Kamĩtĩ we were all pretences, actors in a theatre of extreme absurdity.

It was, ironically, the Protestant chaplain who broke the walls of this dance of absurdity. For some reason, the chaplain had grown more likeable over the year, and even those detainees who had known him in previous years said that they had noticed a change of attitude towards detainees. He had grown less ready to preach at them, as if he naturally assumed their guilt vis-à-vis the government's benign benevolence. He had stopped talking as if all they needed was to accept Jesus Christ as their personal Saviour, confess all their past political sins, and go back to Kenyatta's paradise, the envy of the rest of Godless Africa. Some of the detainees even started missing him and they would say: When is Reverend Ngarĩ coming? Or, Reverend Ngarĩ has deserted our compound these last few weeks.

Between him and me there had grown up a mutual acceptance of each other's position: he never again — after our initial encounter — tried to force his religion on me, and I in turn never questioned his right to believe in it. He would come, greet me, ask after my health, or comment on the game of chess, and go to his religious sessions with the others. He had, though, some kind of victory over me. He came one day with tapes containing a sermon by Reverend Gatũ and challenged me, on the basis of my stated premises, to hear it: had I not in January asked him about sermons by Kenyan nationals? I attended the session, the only one I ever did, and heard Reverend Gatũ at his oratorical best: he was attacking the leprosy of private property and property accumulation, basing his sermon on the text of Amon who had stolen a poor man's vineyard; I could hardly believe my ears!

When on Friday, 25 August, Reverend Ngarĩ came into the yard, he seemed disturbed. He did not go the rounds greeting people, he certainly did not greet me, and twice he came in and out within a space of fifteen minutes before settling down to the usual religious session. But it turned out not to be the usual religious session; and it was as if he sensed that the detainees had silently laid a trap for him: they wanted to see if he too — a proclaimed man of God — would participate in the grand deception of detainees. It was probably difficult for him, walking on the tightrope between his vows to his Christian conscience and his vows to his prison conscience. He resolved the conflict in prayer. In the course of the prayer and without mentioning names, he prayed God to keep in peace the soul of the leader who had departed from amongst us, and to guide the hand and heart of the one who had taken over the reins of power. Then he walked out of the compound to avoid responding to any direct questions!

Now the Muslims (and we, the two non-believers) surrounded the 'Christians' to make them describe to us every word of the chaplain, every change of nuance and tone of his voice, every word of his sermon, his gestures and behaviour, everything. It was as if the Koranic revelation had been or was about to be fulfilled, through a sermon from the Christian Bible.

Even after this, the theatre of absurdity went on, but this time all the actors were police, prison officials and warders. We were still officially ignorant of Kenyatta's death, and Moi's take-over. At one time, the warders were summoned by prison officials and put under the strictest discipline and threats of dismissal not to reveal anything about Kenyatta's death to us, or to reveal by word or gesture what was going on outside the walls. So a game of deadly wit started: now that we knew about Kenyatta's death through a prayer, we could talk about it openly and we no longer hid our feelings. Detainees would make inquiries as to whom they would now send their letters of supplication, and they would be told to write to Kenyatta. What address? State House, Nairobi, of course. So the joke started: 'I am writing to Kenyatta, the ex-detainee, c/o State House, Nairobi.' But the officials were really to blame for these trite jokes, because they grimly held on to 'their fact' that Kenyatta was not yet dead. How completely did they want a man to die in order to say he was dead?

When Ali Dubat, who had gone for an operation, was finally discharged from the hospital, he was not returned to the compound but to an isolation cell in G block. His fault? The natural possession of two ears. While in hospital a hysterical nurse had rushed in shouting the news of Kenyatta's death. He remained in that punishment cell until the day of his release three months later.

5

It is difficult to describe the feelings occasioned in me by Kenyatta's death. I had met Kenyatta only once in 1964 at Gatūūndū. I was then working as a reporter with the *Daily Nation*. The occasion was May Day 1964, and a group of peasants from Mūrang'a had come to donate relief money for their class counterparts in Nyanza, victims of floods at Kano plains. Oginga Odinga was present, a witness of this act of class solidarity. For some reason, I and the *Nation* photographer were the only journalists present. I still retain a photograph of Kenyatta, Odinga, and myself taken at the time by the photographer. I am standing, with a notebook and pen in hand, probably putting a question to the big two, the peasants crowding around us. It was a brief, a very brief first and last encounter.

But in my novels — *Weep not, Child, A Grain of Wheat,* and *Petals of Blood* — Kenyatta has appeared either directly as a historical figure or has been hinted at in the portrayal of some of the characters. In 1964 a publisher asked me to write Kenyatta's biography and for a time I played with the idea before rejecting it. I was not sure if I could get official permission and the family co-operation necessary for such a task. I also felt — which was true — that I was then too young, too inexperienced and too confused in social outlook to cope with the literary and political demands of putting together a definitive biography. The idea resurfaced briefly in 1968 when Ali Mazrui and I were travelling in the same plane from an international conference of Africanists in Dakar, Senegal, and we decided to attempt a joint biography. Mazrui wrote to Kenyatta, c/o President's Offices, Nairobi, to seek permission for that undertaking. He did not get it.

In a way, it was good that we did not get permission. Our outlooks would have clashed in the interpretation. Mazrui's analysis of the African situation starts with tribe, mine with class. To Mazrui, in all his books, imperialist languages and cultures created modern nations: tribes and tribalism tear these nations apart. In my opinion Mazrui sees imperialism as the true friend of Africa: progressive nationalism, socialism, communism are the true enemies of Africa.

But even without a clash of outlook, I am not sure if we could have done a finer job than Murray-Brown's *Kenyatta.* It is a revealing biography, less for his shallow interpretation but more for the impressive material he has unearthed and brought together between hard covers. Murray-Brown could not get at the Kenyatta brought to dramatic life by the very material he himself had assembled. The material and the history that occasioned and shaped the material were bigger than the author. A biographer — since there is no neutral biography — must first recognize the class basis (and hence the class world outlook) of his account, interpretation and evaluation of a life, any life, but more so of that of a leader of a society divided into definite economic classes.

In a class-structured society, a leader is not simply a leader of the whole nation, he is a leader of a class. A leader in power is a leader of the class in power, that is the class in control of the state. A leader of a struggle is also not simply a leader, but a leader of a class struggling to seize political power, i.e. the state. But in a struggle a leader, though a member of a particular class, can also stand at the helm of an alliance of classes to present a united front, either conscious or unconscious, against a common enemy. He is then a leader of a class and a leader of an alliance of classes. In such a situation, he articulates the maximum that unites the classes while manoeuvring to place his class in an advantageous position at the moment of victory. We encounter difficulties when dealing with the petty-bourgeois class, especially in a colonial context. Its intermediate position between peasants and workers (the oppressed, the exploited classes) on the one hand, and the imperialist bourgeoisie (the direct ruling power, the oppressing exploiter class) on the other, makes it a vacillating class with a vacillating world outlook simply because its economic base keeps on changing, making it sometimes stare at ruin (the lot of the masses), and at other times stare at prosperity (the lot of the imperialist bourgeoisie and its white-settler representatives).

When the people's power seems in the ascendancy, that's in times of intense struggle, it will move closer to the people and even seem to articulate their position and aspirations. When the imperialist bourgeoisie seems in the ascendancy, it will move closer to it, try some sort of accommodation and even articulate anti-people sentiments with a vigour only less intense than the one with which it had embraced the people's cause because of the naked racism (colour bar) in the colonial system. When in power, this class will embrace imperialism if it sees the masses demanding real changes. A leader of a people's movement who is of petty-bourgeois origins, training, or position must, like Cabral, recognize this reality if he is going to transcend it, by consciously rejecting his class to find a true and permanent, regenerative link with the people.

Kenyatta, a petty bourgeois to the core, who never consciously rejected that class base, was both a leader of an anti-imperialist alliance of classes and a leader in power. As a leader of an anti-imperialist alliance of classes, he kept on shifting his position, depending on the strength and weaknesses of the two mortally contending classes: workers and peasants, and the imperialist bourgeoisie. As a leader in power, he now championed the cause of his class and enabled it to play its historical rôle: with the colour bar out, i.e. with racial barriers to property accumulation removed, the Kenya petty bourgeois could now fully play the rôle previously played by the European and Asian representatives of the imperialist bourgeoisie — a compradorial rôle!

There were then several Kenyattas, but they can be reduced to four. There was the Kenyatta of the KCA era who made anti-imperialist statements and declarations valid for that time. He was then truly a spokesman of the peasants and workers and he took up the cudgels against the British imperialist bourgeoisie for its brutal, oppressive exploitation of the peasants of the various nationalities in Kenya: Wakamba, Aba Luhya, Dho Luo, Gĩkũyũ, Giriama, Masai, the lot. He articulated the need and necessity for a revolutionary unity of peasants and workers of Kenya to overthrow British imperialism.

Then there was the Kenyatta of the KAU era: this Kenyatta was a graduate of Malinowski's school of anthropology at London University, a cultural nationalist (he had written *Facing Mount Kenya* in which politics was deliberately cut out), who for fifteen years had quite literally been out of physical touch with the living struggles of the Kenyan people. KAU was a nationalist organization grouping a variety of classes under its constitutional non-violence umbrella. It had no quarrel with capitalism, only with the exclusion of Africans, on the basis of race, from fully participating in it.

The colonial African petty bourgeoisie welcomed it as basically their organization and instrument for a seizure of power. But in Mau Mau the peasants were finding their organization.

Then there was the Kenyatta of the KANU era: he was a prison graduate, an ex-detainee, who had once again been out of physical touch with the living struggle for nine years. Mau Mau, though forcing the political pace of events, had been weakened and the anti-imperialist movement was led by the petty-bourgeoisie of varying degrees of patriotism. Workers and peasants had no organization of their own — like Mau Mau — to force adoption of certain programmes by KANU. Mboya and others had made sure that workers and their organizations were excluded from active politics.

Then there was the Kenyatta of KANU in power, who made sure that the petty-bourgeoisie in its new rôle of a comprador was fully entrenched in the party organization, in administration, everywhere, and who made sure that anybody associated with militant nationalism or with true worker/peasant organizations like Mau Mau were never anywhere near the seats of power.

Thus in looking at Kenyatta, all the classes could see a bit of themselves in him: to the imperialist bourgeoisie he was their Kenyatta, but they were thinking of the Kenyatta in power who had ensured stability for their continued exploitation of the Kenyan people. To the comprador bourgeoisie, he was their Kenyatta; but they were thinking of the Kenyatta in power, the one who had not interefered with their traitorous tradition. To the nascent national bourgeoisie, he was their Kenyatta, but they were thinking of the Kenyatta of KAU days who wanted Kenyanization of capitalism. To the peasants and workers, he was their Kenyatta, but they were thinking of the Kenyatta of the militant 1930s and 1950s. But at the same time, all the classes were suspicious of him, they were aware of the other historical shades to his political character. Thus looking at Kenyatta, people tended to see what they wanted to see rather than what there was: petty-bourgeois vacillations and opportunism. Thus Kenyatta never formed a single political organization. He was always invited to lead already formed organizations: KCA, KAU, Gĩthũũngũri Teachers' College and KANU.

My reception of his death was then one of sadness: here was a black Moses who had been called by history to lead his people to the promised land of no exploitation, no oppression, but who failed to rise to the occasion, who ended up surrounding himself with colonial chiefs, home guards and traitors; who ended up being described by the British bourgeoisie as their best friend in Africa, to the extent of his body being carried to the grave, not on the arms of the Kenyan people, but on a carriage provided by the Queen of England, the symbolic head of the British exploiting classes. Kenyatta was a twentieth-century tragic figure: he could have been a Lenin, a Mao Tse-Tung or a Ho Chi Minh; but he ended being a Chiang Kai-shek, a Park Chung Hee, or a Pinochet. He chose the Lilliputian approval of the Blundells and the Macdonalds of the colonial world, warming himself in the reactionary gratitude of Euro-American exploiters and oppressors rather than in the eternal titanic applause of the

Kenyan people, sunning himself in the revolutionary gratitude of all the oppressed and exploited. For me, his death, even though he had wrongly jailed me, was not an occasion for rejoicing but one that called for a serious re-evaluation of our history; to see the balance of losses and gains, and work out the options open to us for the future of our children and country.

6

With Kenyatta's death, another dream of freedom possessed us all, and this time even Wasonga seemed to believe in the possibility. 'We shall not be here for more than three years from now,' he would tell us. Three years: not a particularly cheerful thought, but it was shorter than the ten years he had spent in the compound. Then suddenly a rumour started: we would be freed on Friday, 22 September.

The whole compound was gripped with feverish excitement and expectations. A week to go, and we would all be free to talk with our families, to see green life again, to hear the sweet laughter of women and children! Food became completely tasteless, and on Tuesday evening very few touched their prison food. We exchanged addresses and confidences, and promises of future meetings. We started talking of detention and Kamĩtĩ as things of history. Some detainees had already arranged for new tyre sandals which they would carry home as a remembrance of things past.

The morning of Friday, 22 September found us still in the grips of hope. There had been no official word but the rumour had become a reality. Why not? Every reasonable argument pointed to our release on that day. Some detainees had sat down, made a list of all cabinet members and tried to determine their voting pattern in terms of *yes* or *no* to our release on that day, and naturally the ministers in favour of our release outnumbered those against us. A detainee who cautioned realism in our expectations was shouted down and denounced as an enemy of the people.

It was a kind of collective madness, I remember, and when at about ten o'clock there was a vigorous banging on the outer door and a prison officer dashed in waving his staff of office, I said to myself at long last: God, freedom.

Quickly Koigi pulled me aside and whispered: 'Go and clean your room at once! There is going to be a search!'

No sooner were the words out of his mouth than we were all hounded back to our cells: if this meant release, it was certainly a rough way of bidding us farewell.

I had never seen a prison search before and though the other detainees told me that under Lokopoyot it had been a weekly ritual, I never really knew what it meant. My cell was the first to be raided: it was difficult to know what they were looking for. Razor-blades, nails, weapons of violence? Letters, diaries, secret communications with the outside world? Suddenly the sergeant saw piles of toilet-paper and pounced on them. Then, as if delirious with joy and triumph, he turned to the presiding officer and announced: 'Here is the book, sir, on toilet-paper.' 'Seize it!' the officer told him, 'the whole lot! Who told you to write books in prison?' the officer said, turning to me.

My novel written with blood, sweat and toil on toilet-paper had been seized! Only two chapters hidden in between the empty back pages of a Bible Koigi had lent me remained. The Bible lay there on the desk as if mocking me: 'If you had trusted all the Wariinga novel to me, you would have saved it all.'

It is only a writer who can possibly understand the pain of losing a manuscript, any manuscript. With this novel I had struggled with language, with images, with prison, with bitter memories, with moments of despair, with all the mentally and emotionally adverse circumstances in which one is forced to operate while in custody — and now it had gone.

Gloom fell over Kamĩtĩ. Every detainee had lost something. We had been deliberately lulled into slumber by the carefully circulated rumour of release. But most detainees had developed a fantastic cunning which had made them act like lightning and many had saved a lot of their prison notes. I had suffered the major loss and the other detainees clearly felt with me. I was grateful for the group solidarity. But it did not lessen the hurt.

The next three weeks were the worst of my stay at Kamĩtĩ. It was as if I had been drained of all blood. Nevertheless I made a new resolution: no matter what happened I would start all over again. I would reconstruct the novel in between the printed lines of a Chekhov, or a Gorky, or a Mann, or of the Bible (I would even ask the chaplain for three or four bibles of different sizes as evidence of a new-found devotion!), or of any book in my possession. It would not be the same novel, but I would not accept defeat.

I never had the occasion to try out my resolution though I did scribble the plot and the few sequences of events I could recollect in Chekhov's volume of short stories — *The Lady with a Lap Dog* — for, after about three weeks, on 18 October, the new S.S.P. returned the Waríĩnga manuscript to me.

'I see nothing wrong with it,' he said. 'You write in very difficult Kikuyu!' he added.

'Thank you!' was all I said, but he will probably never know the depth of the emotion behind those two words. Nor perhaps what his action meant for the birth of a new literature in Kenya's languages.

'But you should never have written it on toilet-paper,' he went on. 'I'll ask the chief warder to supply you with scrap paper — there is plenty of it in my office — so you can transfer the whole thing from toilet-paper.'

Write on, brother.
Write on!
My star still reigns!

CHAPTER NINE

Warĩĩnga ngatha ya wĩra... Warĩĩnga heroine of toil... there she walks haughtily carrying her freedom in her hands...

No!

There she walks knowing that... There she walks carrying... knowing...

No!

She walked outside knowing that greater struggles...

I try different combinations. Now and then I look at the walls for a word, a name, a sentence. The walls of cell 16 have become my dictionary of words and music.

Since the big fiasco of 22 September, dreams of freedom have given way to nightmares of a longer stay in this dungeon. Other dates on which freedom was expected, like Kenyatta Day, though not with the same intensity of 22 September, have proved to be receding mirages. The Koran no longer yields its secrets. The man of the Bible has not been seen. The doves keep on flying in increasing numbers but none lands. People are silent about predictions. I no longer mention my invitation to a roast goat party at my home on 25 December. Life has come to an ominous standstill. No more games of chess, ludo, draughts, tenniquoit. Walks on the side-pavements have become more popular. But now the main talk is about the necessity to brace ourselves for the nightmare of a longer stay in prison.

Although I too have been affected by the new mood of pessimism, every night I have kept faith with the Warĩĩnga novel. And since it is no longer a secret, I also have spent parts of the day-time writing it. Scrap paper has proved to be not as plentiful as I had been led to believe. Or the warder in charge is proving to be mean. Other detainees have been generous. Matheenge has given me all his reserve of paper: others have chipped in with the little they have.

But tonight I am back on toilet-paper. Of course there have been a few signs: we have been allowed to buy books through the warder in charge of the store. As a test case, Gĩkonyo places an order for *Petals of Blood*, and I for copies of Wole Soyinka's *The Man Died* and Meja Mwangi's *Going Down River Road. Petals of Blood* has been bought, and has been read by all the detainees who can read English. Also *Going Down River Road.* But a paperback copy of *The Man Died* is not available. Within the same last two months, a new doctor has come and examined us all. The commissioner of prisons has also called once and acceded to our request for tooth brushes and toothpaste.

And today, this morning, 11 December 1978, the S.S.P. agreed to virtually all our requests for sheets and a special diet from tomorrow, 12 December. But nobody dares trust the signs of the times no matter how potent, and the prevailing mood is one of gloom.

Waria . . . Njooki . . . my symbols of hope and defiance.

I hear the clinking of a bunch of keys. My cell is next to the tiny exercise-yard, so I always hear the noise of the main door into the block whenever it is being opened. Prison officers on night duty or corporals on night duty often make unexpected visits to see if the night warders are doing their watching duty properly.

Whenever I hear the clinking of keys and the noise of doors opening and closing I normally wake up, tiptoe to the door and through the bar-opening in my door I look at their faces and try to catch one or two words, all in an attempt to see if I can get news related to the world outside. I have never succeeded in getting any, but I keep on going through the ritual.

Tonight I just sit at my desk. To hell with the ritual! I don't care if the prison officer or anybody catches me writing the novel on toilet-paper. It is not my fault. I could not get enough scrap paper. The novel is virtually complete and I am possessed . . . imagination, once let loose, keeps on racing ahead, and the hand cannot keep pace with it . . .

Somebody is watching me through the opening. I know it, even before raising my head to meet the eyes of the new S.S.P. He lingers there as if he wants to speak to me. I walk to the door.

'Ngũgĩ, you are now free . . .'

I am the first detainee to hear these words. I shout the news across the walls . . . 'Free . . . We are now free . . .'

I have regained my name. I am no longer K6,77.

And when the door to cell 16 is finally open, the first thing I do is to rush to the compound to hug darkness (which I have not seen for a year) and to look at the stars.

We are free . . . We are free . . . and I feel certain that at home my mother, Nyambura, the children and the good people of Limuru and Kenya are gazing at the same stars!

SECTION TWO

LETTERS FROM PRISON

Prisons are built with stones of Law, Brothels, with bricks of Religion.

William Blake: *The Marriage of Heaven and Hell,* 'Proverbs of Hell'

> Through tatter'd clothes small vices do appear;
> Robes and furr'd gowns hide all. Plate
> sin with gold,
> And the strong lance of justice hurtless breaks;
> Arm it in rags, a pigmy's straw does
> pierce it.

William Shakespeare: *King Lear*

When I talk about ex-detainees, I would like the House to know that I am talking about innocent people who had been put in detention not because they had committed any crime against anybody. As a matter of fact, most detainees were in detention only because they had fallen out of favour with some powerful people somewhere. Others were in detention only because they had expressed patriotic and nationalistic views about certain aspects of our national life.

Koigi wa Wamwere, in a speech in Parliament on Wednesday, 3 June 1980

Under a shining bulb in my tiny cell at Kamĩtĩ, suffering seemed to have taken on the nature of infinity.

Wasonga Sijeyo, in an interview with *Viva,* 3 October 1980

If there is any country which wants torturers from outside, Kenya can supply them.

Martin Shikuku, in a speech in Parliament on Wednesday 3 June 1980

c/o Commissioner of Prisons
P.O. Box 30175,
Nairobi
13 November 1978

Dear Nyambura,*

I was suddenly full of joy when I opened your letter of 19 September and found the picture of Wamũingĩ: she looks healthy and beautiful! I hope that she will grow to live up to her name; to love and devote herself to the Kenyan people. Give her and the others all my love and tell them to continue working hard for themselves and for our beautiful motherland.

In you last two letters you seemed anxious about the way I am being treated. In your letter of 31 July, for instance you said that since you had gathered from both the local and the international press that I was under political detention you hoped that I was being treated as a political detainee and not as a criminal. Please remember: many so-called criminals are political detainees. You asked me if I was happy with the medical facilities. You also asked me about the Tribunal. Well . . . I am not in a position to talk about the conditions under which we live. But I think it fair to say the following:

(1) Since January 1978, I have been suffering serious toothache. One of my teeth is now rotten and hollow and I often have had to eat with one side of my mouth. My gums also bleed. I reported this to the prison doctor and he recommended that I see a dentist. He filled in the necessary consultation forms. When months later, the police came to take me out for dental treatment, they insisted on my first being chained as the condition for taking me to see a dentist. As I am not a criminal, either in practice or through conviction in a court of law, I refused to freely let myself be chained. As I would not have my body in chains, they refused to take me for medical treatment. On 15 June 1978, I wrote to Mr Mũhĩndĩ Mũnene, in his capacity as the security officer in charge of detainees, protesting against this and also requesting dental treatment. If for whatever fears, real or imagined, the police could not take me to the hospital without chains, then they should bring a dentist to my place of detention. Up to now I have not heard from him. And of course I have not been treated.

*This letter was not allowed through by the prison censors.

(2) Another day, in July 1978, I was told to prepare myself to come and meet you and the family somewhere outside my place of detention. It was early in the morning I remember. I was very happy because my last memory of you is still of that midnight hour of 30 December 1977 when the police raided our house and took me away as you stood by pregnant and helpless. I was very shocked when I was told that the condition for seeing you was my being chained. Once again I would not have my body in chains as a condition for seeing my family. Once again the police, who are directly under Mr. Mūhīndī Mūnene, refused to let me see you.

(3) We never get any news of what is happening in Kenya and the world. We get no newspapers or the radio, and the warders are forbidden to say anything about places outside our place of detention. So we live in a tomb of endless silence, gloom and ignorance. It's like time stopped moving and events stopped happening, well, history stopped at midnight on 30 December 1977.

(4) As for the Detainees' Review Tribunal, the less I talk about or even think about its composition, its mandate, and the conduct of its interviews, the better for my peace of mind. It is perfectly true that the Tribunal meets detainees every six months. I have appeared before it twice, the first time within the first fourteen days after my arrest. Every time they have asked me the same question. They stare at me and then the chairman asks me: 'And now Mr Ngũgĩ, what can you tell us so that we can in turn go and tell the Kenya government?' The whole thing hardly lasts more than three-and-a-half minutes. I have written them a memorandum affirming my position vis-à-vis questions of national literatures, cultures and languages in their struggle against domination by foreign cultures, and also affirming the responsibility of a writer to his nation and to his creative impulse. As Martin Luther once said: 'On this I stand, I can do no other.' The same applies for us writers in the Third World. I have always remembered those words of Wole Soyinka, the Nigerian writer: 'The man dies in all who keep silent in the face of tyranny.'

I hope that these few incidents will allay your fears and anxiety. Like you, I share the hope that one day we shall meet again and laugh and talk. I take comfort in the Gĩkũyũ saying: *Gũtirĩ ũtukũ ũtakĩa,* that there is no night so long and dark that it will never give way to the light of day. Like you I long for that day. But more than this is my faith and hope that democracy will one day reign in Kenya, and that Kenyans will then no longer be afraid of their thoughts and feelings; and that when that day comes, patriotic Kenyan writers will be able

o proudly reflect on the heroic struggles of their peoples without fear
of being arrested, detained and tormented: that they will be able to
write freely in their national languages and talk directly to their
people without fear.

I was delighted to hear that many friends have been coming to see
he new baby. That for me is something to remember and it gives me
courage. I was particularly touched by the greetings from Mrs
Namukwaya Zirimu. I got your letter at a time when I was thinking
about the death of her husband, Pio Zirimu, during Festac 1977 in
Nigeria, and about all the work he did for African theatre, languages
and literature. Give her my greetings.

I hope that Thiong'o and Kĩmunya are continuing with their
music. Greetings to all and to the children. Wanjikũ and Mũkoma,
now are they doing in their new classes? All the best to Ndũũcũ and
Ngĩna.

Yours,

Ngũgĩ

Kamĩtĩ Prison,
P.O. Box 30175,
Nairobi
15 June 1978

Mr Mũhĩndĩ Mũnene,
Security Officer,
Detained and Restricted Persons,
Nairobi

Dear Mr Mũnene,

Today, 15 June 1978, Mr Kimeto, the police superintendent who
arranges for detainees to see doctors in places outside Kamĩtĩ
Maximum Security Prison, and who also normally escorts them to
he same places, refused to take me to Kenyatta National Hospital,
Kabete Clinic, to have my abscessed and very painful tooth treated
as recommended by the prison doctor.

I am very concerned about the police refusal and Mr Kimeto's
cruel use of my failing health as a tool with which to torture me.

I complained about my tooth to the prison doctor a long time ago.
told him that the tooth hurt me a lot and that I was finding it difficult
o eat. I use only one side of my mouth in vain attempts to avoid the
sensitive tooth. The doctor looked at it and he immediately

recommended that I should be taken to Kenyatta National Hospital, Kabete Clinic, to get the necessary dental help. He promptly wrote out the consultation forms. Yet it has taken the state over a month to arrange for a visit to a dentist.

When at long last Mr Kimeto showed up this morning he insisted on personal humiliation as the condition for taking me to the hospital. He insisted on chaining my hands on top of the already strong prison and armed police guard.

Mr Kimeto was particularly arrogant and overbearing about the whole matter. He told me, in the presence of a prison officer, Mr Matano, and that of several detainees, that as far as he Kimeto was concerned, I was not a detained person but a common prisoner. He also told me to remember that even the first president of this republic was once handcuffed.

Whether or not Mr Kimeto chooses to imply that colonial conditions, colonial laws and colonial justice under a State of Emergency imposed by imperialism on an unwilling people are favourably comparable to conditions now prevailing in an independent Kenya without an openly declared State of Emergency is, of course, his own democratic right as a Kenyan national. He is entitled to his critical appraisal and evaluation of contemporary Kenya. Certainly he is well placed to know. But I do object to his implying that I have already been taken to a court of law, that I have been duly charged, that I have been found guilty and thereafter convicted to a prison sentence.

To set the record right, I was arrested in my house at Gĩto-goothi, Limuru, at midnight on Friday, 30 December 1977. The following day, Saturday, 31 December 1977, I was brought to the isolation block of Kamĩtĩ Maximum Security Prison where I have been confined to this day. I was never taken to court; I have not been charged with any offence against the existing laws of Kenya be they similar or not to colonial ones, and to date I have not been furnished with any detailed, concrete and specific reasons for my arrest and subsequent detention, apart from a vague, one-line statement alleging that I had engaged in 'activities and utterances which are dangerous to the good government of Kenya and its institutions.'

I have therefore been left to guess that the real reason for my arrest and detention was the fact that I was involved in the writing of a play in the Gĩkũyũ language, *Ngaahika Ndeenda,* and in its performance by a group of workers and peasants from Limuru to a wide and very appreciative and most enthusiastic audience at

Kamĩrĩĩthũ Community Education and Cultural Centre. For reasons best known to themselves, some propertied individuals who were obviously well placed in business and government circles objected to the fact that the play faithfully reflected certain social conditions, particularly the conditions of workers and peasants in Kenya today. I can only guess that it was the same group of the propertied few which was behind the moves and the pressures that led to the withdrawal of the licence to perform. The same group must have instigated my arrest and detention in order to create an aura of something sinister about my person and my writing. I guess that it would have proved embarrassing for the KANU government to have taken me to court and to charge me with being involved in writing a play which correctly reflects social conditions in the country. It would have been even more embarrassing for a KANU government to have held an open public trial accusing me of helping in the promotion of a genuine national theatre, national language and national culture. The fact is that my arrest was a complete travesty of simple justice and democracy. Not a single true Kenyan would have been deceived about the forces motivating my arrest and such a trial. Hence the convenience of detention where the government need only allege and not prove anything — conviction by innuendo!

But the fact still remains that my arrest and detention is an obvious attempt to suppress the rights of a Kenyan national to freely reflect on the social reality around him and to invite debate and discussion about that reality. Some people, it seems would rather smash the mirror that may show them the warts on their faces and then sit back with a smile of relief, saying: 'Thank God I now have no warts.' But no matter how many mirrors one may smash, one cannot wish away Kenya's social reality. Arresting and detaining writers who hold up the mirrors will not succeed any more than the ruling classes in medieval Europe were able to wish away the reality about nature and the natural universe by imprisoning the Copernicuses and the Galileos of the then emerging scientific world. Equally, my arrest and detention is a futile blow – but a blow all the same – struck against those of us Kenyan writers who are committed to the development of a Kenyan national theatre and a Kenyan national literature through the Kenyan national languages as the only correct basis for the evolution of a Kenyan national democratic and modern culture in dynamic opposition to the domination of our lives by foreign, particularly neo-colonial theatre, literature, languages and cultures. Then and only then can we as Kenyans proudly say: And this is ours at last, created by us for us Kenyan people.

I therefore reject Mr Kimeto's insinuations and only add this: I did not resist when the police raided my house at midnight and under false pretences took me away. And since I was brought here, I have not resisted any police and prison regulations. Further, I have no history whatever of escape or attempted escape; and I have no history of physical fighting with the police. Why should Mr Kimeto insist on humiliation as the condition for taking me to the hospital?

It is cruel enough, undemocratic enough, and therefore unjust enough that my human freedom has been so usurped, and that I have now been placed in a situation where I am humanly unable to take any responsibility over my body and my health. It is surely adding gross insult to gross injury to ask me to freely lend myself to actions that are meant to imply that I am such a dangerous creature as can only be led to its own welfare manacled and fettered in chains.

I still need medical attention. My tooth still hurts me. I still find it difficult to eat. If in the eyes of Mr Kimeto I have suddenly ceased being a writer and a teacher, and I have become a dangerously violent monster that must needs be chained, why should he not arrange for a doctor to come to Kamĩtĩ Maximum Security Prison where I am already securely caged behind several stone walls and iron bars and under daily guard for twenty-four hours?

I fully realize that the police are only the coercive arm of those that brought me here. Therefore in all matters where the police have the absolute authority of might over me, Mr Kimeto can always have me shackled. That too is suppression and I denounce it. But I am under your armed power and there is nothing I can do about it. Submission under those circumstances would not therefore mean acquiescence to the basic injustice. But I will not willingly and deliberately put out my hands to be chained as a condition and in exchange for my health and visits by my family.

But as I see it the matter is very simple. Since the police seem unwilling to take me to see a dentist, I would ask that you send a dentist here to treat me.

Yours,

Ngũgĩ wa Thiong'o

Copies to:
(1) The Chairman, Detainees' Review Tribunal

2) Mr J.J. Karanja, Ministry of Home Affairs
3) Mr Mareka, S.S.P. in Charge, Kamītī Prison

c/o Commissioner of Prisons,
P.O. Box 30175,
Nairobi
23 July 1978

Justice Hancox,
The Chairman,
Detainees' Review Tribunal.

Mr Chairman,
When I first appeared before this tribunal on 13 January 1978, I made some verbal presentation to do with my arbitrary arrest and detention and with the atrocious conditions at Kamītī Maximum Security Prison.

In particular, I protested against my arrest and detention without trial, and against the lack of a detailed and specific statement as to why I was arrested and detained. I also expressed my deep concern over the prevailing official cynicism towards culture in this country as it has been clearly shown by my arrest and detention for being involved in a cultural project which had been approved at all the necessary administrative levels from that of the assistant chief of Kamīrīīthū village right up to the office of the district commissioner, Kīambu. It was, in any case, a cultural project duly registered under one of the ministries of the Kenya Government, namely, the Ministry of Housing and Social Services.

I also complained about being confined in a dungeon for twenty-three out of twenty-four hours of the day; being fed on revolting food; and being denied access to the radio or to the newspapers.

Now I am once again before the same tribunal, a whole six months later, and nothing has really changed. Of the major complaints listed above, only confinement has been modified: we are now confined for thirteen hours instead of twenty-three as before, a welcome reprieve of ten hours. Otherwise I am still detained without trial; and I am still feeding on the same nauseating

diet. We got newspapers and radio for a time but then they were
suddenly withdrawn. Naturally I would like to know what you have
done about the above complaints, at any rate I am curious about the
results of the presentation since a whole six months have gone by
without a word from anywhere.

I have also since 13 January 1978 written a testament about my
position with regard to questions of language, literature and culture
in order to put in writing what I had tried to tell you verbally and to fill
in any missing links. I have also sent you a copy of the letter I wrote
to Mr Mūhīndī Mūnene, the security officer, on 15 June 1978
protesting against the police refusal to take me to hospital for dental
treatment, and in particular protesting against the police for once
again insisting on my grovelling in the dust as the condition for a
thirty or so minutes interview with my family. That in refusing me to
see my family, the police are also tormenting Kenyan nationals who
are themselves not detained, is apparently of no consequence to the
Kenya police. Or is my family 'guilty' by biological association? I
would like to have it put on record that up to now I still have not been
allowed any dental treatment; that I have not yet had any reply to my
letter, or even a simple acknowledgement of its receipt; and that for
six months since I was cruelly torn from my home and forcibly
stripped of my democratic and human rights, I have not been
allowed to see my family.

Naturally I would like to know if you have received the two
documents: the copy of my letter addressed to Mr Mūnene and my
testament addressed to you.

I would now like to turn to that testament of 23 June 1978, and
introduce it with the following brief anecdotes. They are all taken
from memory and so I hope that you will excuse the manner of my
telling them, and doubly so if you already know them or if you have
read them in books where they are more elegantly told. The first two
relate to the issue of national languages in the struggle to free them
from the stranglehold of foreign languages and cultures. The two
come from India, a country which has had to face the same problems
of multi-languages, foreign and national.

Once when he was only beginning to write and even so writing his
poems in English, Balwani Gargi, the now noted Punjab writer,
visited the great Indian writer and Nobel prize winner, Rabindranath
Tagore, then in the sunset of his days. Tagore received the young
man warmly but he was very surprised to learn that Gargi wrote all
his poems in English.

'What language does your mother speak?' asked Tagore.

'Punjab,' replied the young writer, not knowing what would follow.

'Then,' replied Tagore, 'go back to your mother if you have not yet learnt the language. Learn it and write in it if you want to be a poet. Otherwise write in any language — Spanish, Chinese, German, anything, it does not matter, but you will not be writing for the Indian people.'

The second anecdote tells of an Indian Catholic priest who, while studying in Rome, was once introduced to the Pope as a gifted linguist. The priest knew many Indian languages and virtually all western European languages including one or two dead ones. But the Pope was only mildly impressed:

'Do you know your mother tongue?' asked the Pope.

'No', replied the priest a little embarrassed.

Quickly, the Pope made the apt comment: 'Then you don't know any language at all.'

The next and last two stories are to be found in many fables. But they relate well to the only two possible uses of language: for masking the truth or for unmasking the truth; for putting clouds over reality or for clearing away fogs and clouds so that reality can be seen in all its ugliness and beauty.

The first is the very well-known story* about the vain emperor who wanted a special suit made for him, a suit that would be the most unique in all the land, if possible in the whole world. So he ordered tailors from abroad. The foreign tailors immensely flattered the emperor's vanity by telling him that they would make him a suit that only the wise could see.

At long last the tailors reported the suit ready. On the day of the birthday celebrations, the emperor removed all his clothes and the tailors dressed him in the new suit that only the wise were allegedly able to see.

On horseback, the emperor rode through the cheering crowds who had gathered in the national arena to see the emperor in his unique birthday suit. The counsellors outdid one another in praising the suit to beyond the sky, each discovering unique features in the suit. They even congratulated themselves in having so cleverly anticipated the wishes of the emperor in recommending a foreign firm of tailors.

*The retelling, in a neo-colonial context, of the tale by the nineteenth-century Danish writer Hans Christian Andersen.

Court poets composed and sang songs of praise to the colours, harmony and rhythm of the suit. Court historians were busy writing up instant treatises and learned manuals on the historical peculiarity and significance of the suit. Court lawyers were busy drawing up documents of legal possession and also a bill of property rights as these related to the emperor's new clothes. Court economists wrote of the economic viability of these unique products of this unique alliance between foreign tailoring industries and their local middlemen and on the beneficial economic fall-out of foreign technical know-how on the up and coming local talents. Court newspapers wrote banner headlines such as: SUIT TAILORED TO SUIT US. SUIT TAILORED AT HOME — FROM ABROAD. A NATIONAL SUIT —A MEASURING SUIT FOR LOCAL INDUSTRY etc. They wrote stirring editorials that called upon the emperor's subjects to emulate the very high standards — international standards — set by the foreign tailoring interests. Court chaplains hailed the brotherhood of men as symbolized by the beneficial co-operation between foreigners and the emperor's subjects in the tailoring of the suit and called upon God to bless further efforts in that direction. And lastly, court politicians were equally busy arguing and quarrelling with one another about the political significance of an emperor wearing such a unique suit on his birthday, and they were even more sharply divided on the nature of the special political features unique to that country's system of government as revealed by the emperor's new suit. And of course the spectators grew hoarse as they shouted every imaginable quality into that suit.

But suddenly, above the hubbub of general acclamation rose a child's dissenting voice:

'Mummy, mummy, look, the emperor is naked, the emperor is naked.'

His mother tried to silence him. The child persisted in its cry: 'But the emperor is naked, he is indeed naked.'

As if scales had suddenly been removed from the eyes of the beholders, everybody started seeing and saying what all along had been obvious to the naked eye.

Whereupon the counsellors in consultation with the three wonderful tailors decided that every child and every person who could not see the suit had to have a surgical operation on their eyes — at each victim's expense.

The last story is very similar except for a little twist at the end. It

oncerns a certain stranger who went into a certain country and built
a house, but he soon claimed that an angel of the Lord had come to
visit him. The angel was in one of the rooms but he was only visible to
those without sins. And so everybody, including the king and his
counsellors, who went into the room later claimed that each had seen
and talked with the angel.

Later the stranger went to the king and he told him that he, the
stranger, had come to present him with a coat, a gift from the angel,
only that once again, the coat was only visible to those without any
sin. And once again everybody in the king's courtyard and royal
entourage outdid one another in praising the coat and the large
pockets, for no one wanted to be thought a sinner by telling the truth
of what he really saw.

Indeed they were caught in a trap. For having deceived
themselves into the first lie about seeing and conversing with an
otherwise invisible angel, they had now to continue adding to the lie
and living the lie by accepting the very logical possibility of an
invisible visible gift from the same invisible visible source.

Only one of the king's wives — the most despised — dared say the
truth: she could not see the coat and she doubted it was there at all.
Amid angry attempts to silence her, she still maintained that she
could not see any coat, that indeed there was no coat. She challenged
the counsellors into a simple test: since the coat was supposed to
have big pockets, let them put stones into them. If the stones fell
through or if the stones remained inside the coat, then the truth would
be known. But the counsellors would not hear of any tests.

Instead, the counsellors after consulting the stranger turned round
and accused her of being a sinner. The proof of her sins was the fact
that she was unable to see the coat. Some of them claimed that they
had known all along that she had always been disloyal to king and
country. 'Confess, or be doomed,' they told her. But she was
speechless with angry and fearful wonder. This was the second and
final proof of her guilt. Whereupon they tried her and after carefully
weighing all the evidence, they sentenced her to stoning and then into
exile from king and country. This was the start of one of the biggest
witch-hunts in that country for the sinful and disloyal subjects, and
the proof of a person's guilt was his stated inability to see the coat,
and even more conclusive his failure to make a truthful confession of
the original sin that made him unable to see the coat.

The woman's story and her eventual state reminds me of Brecht's
Galileo beseeching the official philosophers of his time to look

through the newly invented telescope and only believe the evidence of their eyes about the motion of the heavenly bodies. But they would not deign to look and they proceeded to urge for Galileo's exile, detention or death.

Any Kenyan writer worth that name can only hold to the position of Tagore vis-à-vis the centrality of our national languages in our literature. This may sound strange coming from the lips of one who has been writing novels, plays and stories in a foreign language for the last seventeen years. But then I am not saying all this, in fact I have never tried to make any criticism, from a holier-than-thou position. Believe me when I say that I often write from the depths of personal anguish and I don't stop to ask for whom the bell tolls for I know that it also tolls for me. I am therefore not sparing myself. My seventeen years of writing in a foreign language has not brought us anywhere near the foundations of a true Kenyan literature for Kenyan people. Nor is this a sudden obsession or whim. I do not wish to bore you with my personal literary history. But I can say that I have been sufficiently disturbed by the issue of languages for me to have stated in a lengthy newspaper interview at the University of Leeds, England, in 1966, that I had reached a point of crisis where I felt that I could not continue writing in English; that if writing in English and thus depriving a large section of the Kenyan masses of the results of my creative imagination was my only alternative, I would stop writing all together. But I had not properly argued out the case until early 1976 when I gave a public lecture at Kenyatta University College entitled 'Return to the Roots: The Language Basis for a Kenyan National Literature', in which I called on Kenyan writers to return to the sources of their beings in the languages of their peasant mothers and fathers, to thoroughly immerse themselves in the rural community life of our people, and to seek inspiration from the daily rhythms of life and problems of the peasants. The same issue of national languages as the basis for a national literature was going to be the main theme of the second Oluadah Equiano Memorial Lecture which I had been invited to give at the University of Ibadan, Nigeria, this very July. Instead I am arguing the same case at Kenya's Kamĩtĩ Maximum Security Prison! Ironically not for fellow Africans in Nigeria, but to you, chairman of this tribunal, of British ancestry.

Finally, any Kenyan writer worth that name can only hold to the position of the little child and the despised woman vis-à-vis the use of one's chosen language to faithfully recreate in imaginative literature the evidence of our eyes, noses, ears, heads and mouths on the reality of the world in which we live.

In other words for a Kenyan writer, for instance, to write about the fact that many Kenyan children are today going without food and clothes and shelter and other needful facilities, while a few others in alliance with foreigners have all these in abundance and more, is only calling our attention to what is obvious to the naked eyes of the day. But such a writer must go beyond this and seek the truth in the continuity of the Kenyan history of struggle.

But my main contention is that we cannot wish away man-made ugly facts of life, such as children eating from dustbins, by pretending that what *is not is,* and that what *is* is not; or by putting those calling us to believe only the evidence of our eyes into prisons and detention camps, torturing them with rotting food, denial of news and information about their country, diseases, and with forcibly breaking their families by keeping them apart and incommunicado.

Denying people their basic democratic and human rights is hardly the best way of serving Kenya, our beloved motherland!

Ngũgĩ wa Thiong'o

c/o Commissioner of Prisons,
P.O. Box 30175,
Nairobi
23 June 1978

The Chairman,
Detainees' Review Tribunal

Dear Sir,

MY TESTAMENT

On Friday, 31 December 1977, at about midnight, a force of the regular and the secret police, armed with guns and in several vehicles, raided my house at Gĩtogoothi, Bibirioni location, Limuru, and woke us up. They ordered me to show them the room where I kept my books. I took them to my library study where they rummaged through the shelves and collected many books into a heap. Although they could see that there were hundreds of titles by different authors from all over the world, they seemed particularly keen on any book that bore the names of Karl Marx, Friedrich Engels, and Vladimir Lenin. They also pounced on a few other titles by other authors, including twenty to thirty copies of bound cyclo-styled typescripts of the play in the Gĩkũyũ language, *Ngaahika Ndeenda*.

They then told me to accompany them to the police station so that I could be present as they counted and recorded the titles they had collected. I invited them to use my table to count the books and record the titles. They refused and now said that I had to accompany them to the police station. Was I then under arrest? I asked them. No, no, they protested. They were merely taking me for routine police questioning, they said, adding that they would bring me back to the house the same night. Someone laughed.

They stopped briefly at Tigoni Police Station. Then they took me to Kĩambu Police Station where a few minutes later, a man who identified himself as Police Superintendent Mbũrũ came and told me that I was under arrest and that it had been decided to send me to detention. The same man now took me in another car to Kilimani Police Station, Nairobi, where I was thrown into an empty cell.

I tried to sleep, but it was all in vain. I knew now that this was an abduction by the state and judging by recent events anything could be done to my person. I recalled the brazen lies of the government police only a few hours earlier and I felt bitter. I had been rudely and crudely wrenched from my home, family and work. Was I so dangerous a monster that I had to be lured from my family and Kenyan people by lies? What harm would it have done to the policemen's famed *utumishi kwa wote* by telling me the truth and allowing me a few seconds of grace to settle one or two things with my wife? For instance, she had no money. I carried the cheque book. She was pregnant and she had children in the house. Would the state, of which the police were the armed expression, have suddenly collapsed had they been just a little considerate about ordinary human feelings, like not wanting to unnecessarily hurt and oppress the immediate innocents who would be hit by the hurried, secretive, lying and abrupt manner of my arrest?

On the morning of 31 December 1977, at about 10 o'clock, a man who identified himself as Mr Mũhĩndĩ Mũnene, and who I much later came to learn was the senior assistant commissioner of police, Nairobi area, and also the detainees' security officer, served me with a detention order signed by Mr Daniel Arap Moi as the then Minister for Home Affairs. A few minutes later I was treated to a most incredible — if slightly ludicrous — show of psychological terror. I was truculently handcuffed by a gruff unsmiling policeman, shoved into a vehicle between two policemen armed with a rifle and a machine-gun and seemingly at the ready for combat, and was then whisked off across Nairobi to the gates of my present place of detention. The same gruff, murderous policeman grabbed me by the collar of my shirt and pulled me out of the car. I was handed over to the prison authorities. No words, no questions, no explanation, nothing. I was in cell 16 in the isolation block wedged, I now gather, between the block for madmen and the block for those already condemned to hang. It was almost a stolen act from the pages of a nightmare. Only that now, instead of fiction, it was me, Ngũgĩ wa Thiong'o, to whom the whole nightmare of arbitrary arrest, state terror and summary detention was happening, and the scene was not a territory of imagination, but Kenya twenty-five years after Operation Anvil, in the final quarter of the twentieth century.

Reading the detention orders was once again like reading a page out of a nightmare.

For instance, I at first avidly read that one of the provisions of the Kenya constitution was that a detained person shall, 'as soon as reasonably practical and in any case not more than five days after the commencement of his detention, be furnished with a statement in writing in a language that he understands specifying in detail the grounds upon which he is detained'. That sounded well and clear. I turned to the statement. It simply alleged that I had engaged myself: 'in activities and utterances which are dangerous to the good government of Kenya and its institutions. In order to thwart your intentions and in the interests of the preservation of public security, your detention has become necessary.' I read this over and over again, turning from the provisions of the constitution to the 'detailed' statement and back, trying to unravel the mystery:

. . . *in a language that he understands:* well, despite my ten years of teaching literature in English, I still found the language of the statement least understandable to me!

. . . *activities and utterances:* how for instance was I to interpret this? What activities? What utterances? For presumably not all my activities, in sleeping and waking, and not all my words, spoken and written, were allegedly dangerous to the good government of Kenya and its institutions. Or were they all? For all time?

... to thwart your intentions: what intentions? Who was this with a gift of second sight who claimed an ability to read my mind and know my intentions? One of the most contentious and hardest problems in literary criticism which I have taught for some years is precisely the determination of an author's intentions in a given piece of work. Hence the vast differences in the interpretation of even a single work by an author. It looked as if I was, in effect, being charged with just more than the crime of harbouring secret thoughts and wishes . . . I was being detained on somebody else's assumed knowledge of (my) innermost thoughts and desires.

Could anything be more incredible as reasons for taking away the human and democratic rights of a Kenyan national than those contained in that statement?

But on further reading the other sections of the detention order, I felt relieved. I read that 'no more than one month after the commencement of his detention and thereafter during his detention at intervals of not more than six months, his case would be reviewed by an independent and impartial Tribunal established by the Chief Justice from among persons qualified to be appointed as a judge of the supreme court!' I therefore looked forward to my first appearance before the Tribunal under your chairmanship with great interest. I was hopeful that you might enlighten me.

I was undaunted in my hopes even after reading further that the Tribunal's recommendations were not binding on the authority that ordered my detention, the KANU Government.

I was still undaunted even after meeting you and seeing that the Tribunal was heavily weighted in favour of the civil service — the administrative expression of the state — with you as a judge of the high court; a deputy Permanent Secretary in the Ministry of Home Affairs; a senior assistant commissioner of police (the same who served me with the detention orders); a state counsel; a school headmaster; and a practising lawyer. I thought that the closer to the authors' of my detention the Tribunal was, the clearer, fuller and better would be your knowledge of the reasons for my arrest and detention. I assumed that you would enlighten me so that I could get a chance to refute any false claims and allegations, clear any possible misunderstandings, add information or at least be in a position to frankly discuss and thrash out the whole issue. My spirits were high!

It was therefore with profound shock that I was hit by your very first question: What had I to tell the Tribunal? I had all along taken it for granted that you would do the telling. Now you were asking me to tell you. When I asked you to tell me why I was arrested and detained, you told me that it was all in the detention order, that you knew no more about it than what was contained in the statement. And yet the statement was precisely part of the problem.

It seemed to me then, and it seems to me now, that what was expected of me was a mournful, repentant confession before a screening team, or else an assumption of the position of the persona in the Babylonian psalm inspired by a terrifying consciousness of unknown sins against a terrible God:

> The sins I have sinned, I do not know;
> The offence I have committed, I do not know;
> The uncleanliness which I have trodden, I do not know;
> Wash me clean, God, from sins I do not know;
> Though my sins be seventy times seven.

I do not accept that position — confession or penitence — simply because there is nothing to confess and nothing to be penitent about.

I am not therefore pleading for mercy: it is I, as a Kenyan national, who has been wronged and who now cries aloud for democratic justice.

In freedom, I used to see as through a film darkly: in prison I see in the clearer light of the 100-watt bulb in my cell that never lets me sleep; I see in the clearer light of the eyes of the keys-jangling guards who have completely stripped me of any privacy in eating, washing and shitting; I see it in the clearer light of the sickening nauseating food that I daily have to force down my throat; I see it in the clearer light of this Bleak House, this human zoo, where every hour I only look at stone and dust and iron bars, and more stone, dust and iron bars; I see it in the clearer light of the callous police use of disease as a means of torture; I see it in the clearer lights of the endless acts of humiliation meant to strip me of the last vestiges of humanness — like being chained as a condition for being treated in a hospital or being chained as a condition for seeing one's family; above all, I see it in the bright light of my certain knowledge and total conviction that the forces that pressed for and obtained my arrest and detention are the ones killing democracy and human freedom in this country.

I am now without any illusions about the Kenyan situation.

Baudelaire once said of a character: 'He is very old, for he has lived three days in one.' I should say that I have 'aged' considerably for I have lived several years in six months.

I now know, or rather can see, that the police force both regular and secret, the law courts, the prisons, the administration, are all coercive arms of the state. The question is: What kind of state? Run by whom for whom? Is it a democratic state run by a KANU government on the side of democracy and democratic freedoms, or is it another kind of state — an autocratic state in the interests of the kind of forces and class that had me arrested and detained simply because I had written the truth about certain aspects of Kenyan life?

I have not been charged or told so, but I am convinced in other words that I am where I am because I have written about and believed in a Kenya for Kenyans, because I have attempted to hold up a mirror through which Kenyans can look at themselves in their past, their present and perhaps in their future. I am here because a tiny section of that society — but more influential because of the political and the ill-gotten economic power it wields over the labouring majority — has not particularly liked the image of its rôle in Kenya's history. They have therefore struck with vengeance at the hand that raised a mirror which showed them what they did not like to see, or what they did not like seen by the ordinary folk. To them, the hand which held the mirror and the mirror itself, were what created the reality therein reflected. There is a slightly humorous story which used to circulate in central Kenya about a senior colonial chief who, on hearing through the radio that Jomo Kenyatta was finally being released and returning to Gatūndū, smashed the radio to pieces, accusing it of creating tales. Then he said: 'I have stopped the silly radio from bringing him back!' Some people, it would seem, are more comfortable with the outlook of such a chief.

In particular, I believe that I am where I am because I was involved in the writing of a play in the Gĩkũyũ language, *Ngaahika Ndeenda,* a play that looks at the Kenyan history of struggle against imperialism with pride, delineating the traitorous rôle of those who sold out and the heroic rôle of those that held out; a play which correctly reflects the true social conditions in Kenya today, especially in its comparative depiction of the styles of life of the 'privileged' thieving minority and the labouring majority. In his press interview with the *Nairobi Times,* the D.C. Kĩambu, who stopped the public performance of the play, exemplified the mental outlook of the above chief when he said that the play was calling for a class struggle in Kenya. Can anything be more ridiculous? How could the play call for something which was already there? The play did not nvent classes in Kenya. Classes and class struggles have been the central facts of Kenyan history for the last eighty-seven years. (Even he KANU government acknowledges this by setting up three 'overnment organs: an employers' organization (FKE) and a workers' organization (COTU) and an industrial court to arbitrate between the first two.) What would an industrial court be doing if here was already harmony between the two sides? The fact is that with such an outlook we would have to ban nearly all the classics of European and American and African and Asian Literature —world iterature.

But my main sin, it would seem from the comments of the same D.C., lay in helping in the writing of a play for peasants and workers n a language spoken and understood by them, and in having the play performed by workers and peasants to applauding thousands.

Another sin it would seem, lay in the drama proving that given the chance, Kenyan workers and peasants can rise to heights hitherto unknown and undreamt of in the area of modern performing arts; and n it also proving that the lives of peasants and workers, the anguages they speak, the rhythms of their speech and gait and daily work and homely chores; the conflicts in their lives arising out of the tension between their expectations moulded by their experiences of he past, and their knowledge of the stark reality of the present — the ension, if you like, between their future and their present rooted in he past — that all these and more are the stuff out of which we must build a national theatre, a national literature, and a dynamic national culture. Need we ever again kneel before foreign gods and languages and other people's icons of culture?

Not so long ago, in the 1940s in fact, the celebrated Martiniquan poet and playwright, Aimé Césaire, found it necessary to refute the claims of the ruling classes of the leading imperialist nations of the world, that they had reached the acme of civilization and that all the nations and classes of the world had only to follow the paths already trodden by the masters, in the immortal words:

for it is not true that:
the work of man is finished
We have nothing to do in the world
We are parasites in the world
Our job is to keep in step with the world.
The work of man is only just beginning.

from *Return to my Native Land,* Penguin edition)

He went on to argue that, to paraphrase him, no race or nation possessed the monopoly of beauty, of intelligence, of force.

In Kenya, in our own country, isn't it strange that the call to ape foreigners and be satisfied with paths already trodden by our erstwhile British masters comes from some Kenyans? For I know that lies similar to the ones that Césaire felt called upon to refute have been bandied around in Nairobi and in the foreign-owned Kenya Press about the possibilities of Kenyan theatre; the classic statement about this came from no other than Dr Taaita Toweet, then minister for housing and social services, when in about 1975 he scoffed at what he thought was a ridiculous call for a true Kenyan theatre: Where is this Kenyan theatre? he asked contemptuously. I believe that in a small way the drama at Kamĩrĩĩthũ Community Education and Cultural Centre successfully proved that in the area of modern theatre we certainly need never be parasites in the world, only keeping in step with foreign theatres and cultures. Members of this Tribunal should have been there to see at least one or two sections of the play as performed by the group of Limuru workers and peasants; the *Gĩtiiro* opera sequence, written word for word at the dictation of an illiterate peasant woman from Kamĩrĩĩthũ village and performed step by step according to her choreography, was one of the finest aesthetic experiences on the Kenyan stage and one of the brightest moments in the show. The D.C. Kĩambu never saw a single performance, and still he banned the play. Maybe those who took the final decision to have me interned never saw the show. They must therefore have acted on the pressures exerted by some powerful propertied elements in this society who feel uncomfortable, or who get scared, when peasants and workers whom they have come to regard as only fit for picking tea leaves and coffee beans, prove that out of their own internal resources and the passions born of their unique experience of history, they can outshine the best that can be produced by parroting foreigners, and by following submissively the trodden paths of foreign education, foreign theatres, foreign cultures, foreign initiatives, foreign languages.

At any rate, it was because of my involvement in that collective enterprise for a national theatre in a national language for a national audience, that I am now languishing in a detention prison. I am unrepentant. I do not regret even a single minute of my many Saturdays and Sundays and evenings that I worked with the peasants and workers at Kamĩrĩĩthũ, and learnt far more than I ever gave to them in the whole area of our music and dance and drama and language. I also learnt from them the meaning of sheer selfless dedication to a communal effort. The KANU Government can detain me for life, if they so wish. But I know they cannot destroy the Kamĩrĩĩthũ idea.

For I have accepted the lot of all writers who try to hold a clear mirror unto the motions of human thought, human society and history in general. This is not the first time that writers have been held for saying, like the child in the story, that the emperor is naked. Indeed South African writers have been jailed and killed and exiled for this. But I never thought that a Kenyan government would ever link Kenya, our dearly fought for motherland, to that unholy camp of tramplers on human lives. But it has happened. We who write in Kenya, in Africa, in the Third World, are the modern Cassandras of the developing world, condemned to cry the truth against neo-colonialist and imperialist cultures and then be ready to pay for it with incarceration, exile and even death.

What really galls me is the hypocrisy in the whole process of gagging me as shown in the said 'detailed' statement, and I accuse the KANU Government of lying to the Kenyan people:

This KANU Government says it loud and clear on all world councils and platforms that it believes in democracy. It inveighs against those regimes that suppress human rights. Indeed Kenya is a member of UNO, UNESCO and other kindred bodies. Article 19 of the universal declaration of human rights states very clearly that 'everyone has the right to freedom of opinion and expression'. Yet today I and others are behind iron bars for exercising that right. Kenya is currently holding the presidency of UNESCO. UNESCO is very emphatic about cultural freedom and in particular the right of writers to free creative expression without state harassment. More than this, the same government that has interned me had itself licensed the play *Ngaahika Ndeenda!* Can anything be more incredible than the situation in which I now find myself?

The KANU Government says it believes in integrated rural development. Indeed one of the government's rallying calls at public rallies is for people to return to the land. Yet when one writer takes the government at its word and returns home to work with peasants and workers over a community project that is trying to put into practice that noble ideal of integrated rural cultural development, he is immediately apprehended and detained. Just for the record, Kamīrīīthū Community Education and Cultural Centre was legally registered as a self-help project under the department of community development in the ministry of housing and social services.

I was particularly drawn to the project because of its attempt to build a community centre on the basis of a Harambee of sweat and talents as opposed, if you like, to the usual Harambee of money donations from 'me and my friends' in the glaring presence of TV cameras and hand-clapping in apparent gratitude for this charity from a few and their undisclosed friends. At Kamīrīīthū, it was going to be mainly a contribution of sweat and talents: everyone, at any rate, had to work, to give physically and mentally to the common pool of ideas and labour. Again members of this Tribunal, were it not for their understandably heavy commitments 'tribunalling' over so many detainees, should have been there to see the open-air stage with a seating capacity of more than a thousand, one of the biggest in the country and certainly the only one of its kind in the republic. It was all designed and entirely built by the village peasants and workers. This is cultural 'upliftment'!

I was also drawn to the centre because of its belief in community education which, incidentally, I assumed was in line with declared KANU Government policy. It seems as if one should not assume anything in present-day Kenya. The action of the government in taking such a drastic step to suppress, or at least in practice discourage, the spread of community education reminds me of the words of the emperor of Austria when during the Congress of Laibach in 1821, he took time off to talk to professors at the University of Laibach and voice the mortal fear monarchs then held: 'Be careful, and do not teach your pupils too much. I do not want learned or scientific men. I want obedient subjects!'

The KANU Government says it believes in the social welfare of the people. Yet when a play is viewed by thousands who have no other sources of entertainment apart from churches and bars, that play is immediately banned at the instigation of a depraved group that has golf, the cinema, tennis, squash, swimming pools, as well as cathedrals and night-clubs, etc., at its disposal. And as if to add insult to injury, the performance of the play is stopped under the euphemism of public security. Yet during the rehearsals of the play — which were open to the public — and throughout the actual performances in October/November 1977 — a period of five months in all — not a single brawl ever took place, not even a single case of drunken interference, despite the fact that there was never a single police guard.

Finally, the KANU Government says it believes in national cultures and at least in one national language. Yet look at our newspapers: they are foreign owned and run. Look at our publishing houses: they are foreign owned. Look at our cinema industry: it is virtually all foreign controlled. Look at our so called Kenya Cultural Centre and the Kenya National Theatre: who occupies the major space there? A foreign cultural mission, i.e., the British Council. What plays are normally staged there? Such unpalatable junk as *Carmen; The King and I; Jesus Christ Superstar; The Desperate Hours; Boeing, Boeing; Godspell* and the like, often with imported directors and orchestral pieces. All are cheap theatre and all are foreign, and all are done by foreign-based groups. Yet not a single play of theirs has ever been stopped or banned, not even such racist offerings as *The King and I*. But when patriotic Kenyan-based drama like *The Trial of Dedan Kimathi* is written, and although in English, it becomes a struggle to get even a one night's footing in that 'national' building. Yet the Kenya Cultural Centre and the Kenya National Theatre are all under the ministry of housing and social services. Now theatre in Kenya, Nairobi in particular, is virtually all in a language foreign to peasants and workers in Kenya. Yet when the very first modern and major play in a (Kenyan) language — other than Swahili — is written and performed, the licence to perform is withdrawn.

Pride alone, pride in what is Kenyan surely demanded not that the effort be suppressed, but that it be given all the help, all the necessary encouragement. There is surely no pride whatsoever in suppressing the development of our languages and then claiming the foreign as ours. In this respect Shabaan Roberts has written apt words:

> Na juu ya lugha, kitabu hiki (changu) husema katika shairi jingine kuwa titi la mama litamu (lingawa la mbwa), lingine halishi tamu. Hii ni kweli tupu. Watu wasio na lugha ya asili, kadiri walivyo wastaarabu, cheo chao ni cha pili dunia — dunia ya cheo.

One sure way of developing languages is to actively encourage popular drama and literature in those languages. Indeed the major languages in world history have not been so solely on account of the number of people speaking them but because of the literature they have carried. But foreign languages, no matter how highly developed, will never be Kenyan languages. Foreign theatre and foreign literature, no matter the weight of philosophy they may carry, will never be Kenyan theatre and literature. Foreign cultures, no matter how rich they are, will never be the national cultures of Kenya. And foreigners, no matter how brilliant and gifted and dedicated and selfless, can never, never develop our national languages, our national theatre and literature, and our national cultures for us.

When I first appeared before you in January this year, I stated that my arrest was a sad but eloquent commentary on the whole official attitude to culture in this country. I can now go a little further and say that my arrest and detention in the circumstances described above inevitably raises the more basic questions: on whose side, in whose interests is this KANU Government running the state as far as culture and languages are concerned? Is it on the side of foreign languages and culture, or is it on the side of Kenyan national culture and languages? If KANU and the government are on the side of foreign culture and languages, they should once again remember the three basic prides of a nation as described by Shabaan Roberts in his poem; 'Fahari ya Taifa':

fahari ya kila mtu, kwanza ni taifa lake,
Ataingia misitu, na bahari azivuke,
Kutimiza wake utu, afe ama aokoe;
Pasipo hofu ya kitu halipendi liondoke

Fahari ya kila mtu, ya pili ni nchi yake,
Mtu hakubali katu, kutawaliwa na pake,
Hilo haliwi kuntu, halina heshima kwake;
Pasipo hofu ya kitu halipendi litendeke.

Fahari ya kila mtu, ya tatu ni nchi yake
Kuwaye chini ya watu wageni wa nchi yake,
Ni jambo gumu kwa mtu, japo vipi aridhike;
Pasipo hofu ya kitu hulipenda liondoke.

In other words the first and second and third prides of a people are country and nation, country and nation and yet again country and nation. Language and culture are two of the basic components of a nation.

If on the other hand, KANU and the government are on the side of a national patriotic literature that instils great pride in the country and the nation as described by Shabaan Roberts, then *must* they face up to the practice and implications of that choice.

A national culture (and literature, theatre and languages are integral components of culture) must reflect the entire national situation, rooted as it is in the concrete experiences of the various nationalities that make up the Kenyan nation. Modern Kenyan national culture will then be a symphony played by a huge orchestra of all Kenyan communities in harmony. The symphony will be conducted in the all-Kenya national language — Swahili — while the regional parts of the orchestra will be conducted in the languages of the various peasant communities.

But whatever the choice of an all Kenyan national language, and whatever place we give to the other national tongues relative to the one for all Kenya, *their* theatre, *their* literature must inevitably reflect people's fundamental aspirations for a national economy that provides each Kenyan with adequate food, decent shelter, decent clothes, and ensures purposeful economic, political and creative participation in the national life. In such a situation, or in pursuit of such goals, Kenyan national literature would inevitably be patriotic and profoundly opposed to any foreign domination in any sphere of our lives and thoughts.

The flowering of such literature in Swahili and in all our other languages, thus making Kenya a many-coloured cultural garden, requires an open-minded outlook on the part of Kenyans.

Those in power now should perhaps heed the following words of Aristotle on truth:

> The investigation of the truth is in one way hard, in another easy. An indication of this is found in the fact that no one is able to attain the truth adequately, while on the other hand we do not collectively fail, but everyone says something true about the nature of things, and while individually we contribute little or nothing to the truth, *by the union of all a considerable amount is amassed* . . . It is just that we should be grateful, not only to those with

whose views we may agree, but also to those who have expressed superficial views; for these also contributed something by developing before us the powers of thought.

Finally I would like to state that my detention avails nothing, if it is meant, as I am convinced it is, to consciously and deliberately suppress the genuine voices of Kenyan national literature, national theatre, and national culture. It avails nothing because I have seen with my own eyes that there are many more writers where this one came from: in the bosom of every Kenyan peasant woman, in every corner of Kenya, in every nationality. This generation of Kenyan writers must do for our languages, our literature, our culture what OTHERS HAVE DONE FOR THEIRS!

Not to do so would be to betray the fundamental thrust and flow of the Kenyan history of struggle: from the time of Arab and Portuguese invaders through the reign of British imperialism, to the present era of mounting struggle against neo-colonialism.

It has been more than seven centuries of a long and glorious history of heroic struggle against foreign invaders and their local allies, a struggle waged in sweat and blood for the economic and political control of the labour of millions, the sole creator of cultures.

Kenyan writers have no alternative but to return to the roots, return to the sources of their being in the rhythms of life and speech and languages of the Kenyan masses if they are to rise to the great challenge of recreating, in their poems, plays and novels, the epic grandeur of that history.

Instead of being suppressed and being sent to maximum security prisons and detention camps, they should be accorded all the encouragement to write a literature that will be the pride of Kenya and the envy of the world. But perhaps I err; for to be so detained tempers them; to be detained means we have made a start.

That is my Testament. On it I stand.

Yours,

Ngũgĩ wa Thiong'o,
23 June, 1978

Adam Mathenge wa Wang'ombe,
c/o The Commissioner of Prisons,
P.O. Box 30175,
Nairobi
21 August, 1977

The Security Officer,
Detained and Restricted Persons,
P.O. Box 30051,
Nairobi

Dear Sir,

Re: Appeal for Proper Medical Treatment

Since I was detained in June 1975, I have consistently been
pleading that I be taken to Kabete Orthopaedic and Dental
Clinic so that my severely aching back can be X-rayed and given
electro-therapy treatment.

Prior to my arrest and detention, I suffered from this
backache, but unlike now, I used to get regular treatment from
the Nakuru Provincial Medical Hospital where I was undergoing
electro-therapy every three or four months. This treatment was in
the process of curing my backache but since it was deliberately
withdrawn from me two years and two months back upon my
detention, the backache has most likely deteriorated to, I am
afraid to say, a near irreparable extent.

Why I have been denied proper treatment, I can only guess,
for guess I surely will.

Instead of being taken to Kabete Clinic for orthopaedic
treatment, I am being subjected to treatment for mental
instability, from Kenyatta National Hospital.

How do I know this?

First: I have noted correctly and without a doubt, that from
the attitude of the doctors towards me, these doctors are under
the impression that I am mentally disturbed. On entering the
presence of one doctor on 12 July 1977, I was greeted with:
'Relax, relax Mr Mathenge, we have the case history of your
disease. So when you talk to me, please feel at home!'

It is clear from the words of this doctor that some government
authority had misinformed him as to my mental state. Against

this, I could not help but remonstrate on the spot: 'Doctor, I am not crazy as you have been led to believe.'

Second: earlier on, on 11 August 1976, I was taken to a gynaecologist to be treated for my backache! All the medicine that the specialist for women's diseases could offer for my ailing back was a couple of brain-tranquillizing Ativan tablets.

Third: both on the 11 August 1976, and the 12 July 1977, I was given at Kenyatta National Hospital, Ativan and Valium brain-tranquillizing tablets and Beufen pain-killing tablets. I cannot be given brain-tranquillizing tablets unless I am assumed mentally disturbed. And if Beufen tablets were given for backache treatment, they were given more to deaden the ache than to eradicate its organic cause.

Four: when in hospital, the escorting police officer acts the patient to the doctor on my behalf. He explains my disease to him and he is told whatever information the doctor should give me as the patient; information which is never passed on to me by the said escorting police officer.

Five: handcuffing me in hospital is but an effort to portray in practice to the doctors that I am a violent lunatic. Otherwise why should I be handcuffed while in hospital in the first place, I am not detained because I was a violent criminal or a criminal at all.

And as if treating me like an insane person and denying me proper medicine for my ailing back is not enough, it takes me more or less a year between the time I request to be taken to hospital and the time I am taken to hospital, to be given the false impression of being under proper treatment when in fact I am not. Additionally when the said brain-tranquillizers and pain-killers are prescribed for me, their supply is so much delayed that once I was compelled to get them from home, in itself an intolerable form of oppression for one in detention.

As a victim of all this administrative and medical hanky-panky and deprivation, I have been driven willy-nilly into drawing the painful conclusion that:

One: somebody somewhere is refusing to treat my disease so that it can be rendered chronic and incurable by the lack of treatment and myself crippled by the disease for all my life after detention, and;

Two: the proper treatment for my disease is being unjustly withheld from me so that the disease may continue to be used as a come-handy, God-given instrument of political torture.

However, the main purpose of writing this letter is to plead with you that:

First: I be immediately taken to Kabete Orthopaedic and Dental Clinic for X-ray and electro-therapy for my ailing and crippling backache.

Second: I be granted the right to explain my disease to the doctor and receive directly from the doctor information relating to the nature and treatment of my disease.

Third: I be supplied by the government and without any delay, whatever medicines have been prescribed for me by the doctors.

Fourth: that the nonsense of treating me for mental instability as a smoke-screen for denying me proper treatment for my ailing back, may be withdrawn.

Fifth: that giving the doctor the impression that I am crazy and violent, by handcuffing me be withdrawn as well.

In the hope that you will be kind enough to relieve me of this most oppressive burden;

I remain, Sir:

Yours faithfully,

(Signed) Adam Mathenge
21 August 1977

c.c. The Chairman
  Detainees' Review Tribunal
  Nairobi

SECTION THREE

PRISON AFTERMATHS

Our release from detention was unconditional. When being released, nobody told us we were being released on any condition. We were not told that we will not get jobs on release and we were not told that there were certain things we were supposed to do before we could get jobs. This is why it is very surprising to see that, although some of us have been able to get back our liberties, freedoms and rights, some of us are still suffering from the denial of these rights. A job should be considered a right and never a privilege in a democratic country.

However, today there are still people in this country who believe that jobs are privileges to be given to friends and those people who agree with them politically.

Koigi wa Wamwere, in a speech in Parliament on Wednesday, 3 June 1980

We need complete freedom, not half freedom, not three-quarters freedom, not even five-eighths freedom, but complete freedom. Complete freedom is what we are struggling for.

Kīmani Nyoike, in a speech in Parliament on Wednesday, 3 June 1980

The test of the well-being of our society therefore shall be that the rule of law shall prevail, that we be guided by principles and principles alone and preservation of our public institutions as they are, so that personal vengeance has no place in our society, that the humblest man has his right to be protected by the state so that no one shall be persecuted or have his liberty taken away or be embarrassed for his thoughts or opinion, or because someone dislikes him, unless he is subversive or he has committed a specific crime known to the laws of our country.

A speech in Parliament by James Karūgū on succeeding Charles M. Njonjo as the new attorney general, as reported in the *Weekly Review* of 30 May 1980

The regulations that appear on the next pages, plus the detention order shown in the frontispiece, were issued to me by Mr Mūhīndī Mūnene at Kilimani Police Station on Saturday, 31 December 1977, just before I was taken to Kamītī. I was required to sign them.

THE   PUBLIC   SECURITY   (DETAINED AND

RESTRICTED PERSONS) REGULATION 1966

STATEMENT TO BE DELIVERED TO DETAINED PERSON WITH A

COPY OF THE DETENTION ORDER (reg. 10(1)   )

(to be delivered as soon as reasonably practicable and

in any case not more than five days after commencement

of detention.

TO .....NGUGI WA THIONGO......................................

        a detained person by virtue of a

        Detention Order dated the 29TH DECEMBER, 1977

This statement is written in the ENGLISH

language, which you have stated you understand.

The detailed grounds on which you are detained are:-

                        P.T.O.

You are detained on the followin g grounds:-

1) You have engaged yourself in activities and utterances which are dangerous to the good Government of Kenya and its   institutions.

In order to thwart your intentions and in the interest of the preservation of public security your detention has become necessary.

Signed ....

Date ....12./.7.).........

Serving Officer ....

Date ....

Time ....

Place ....POLICE STN.

The Provisions of section 27(2) and (3) of the Constitution of
Kenya concerning review of your case are as follows:-

   27. (2) Where a person is detained by virtue of such a
law as is referred to in subsection (1) of this section the
following provisions shall apply, that is to say:-

     (a)   he shall, as soon as reasonably practicable
         and in any case not more that five days after
         the commencement of his detention, be furnished
         with a statement in writing in a language that
         he understands specifying in detail the grounds
         upon which he is detained;

     (b)   not more than fourteen days after the commencement
         of his detention, a notification shall be published
         in the Kenya Gazette stating that he has been
         detained and giving particulars of the provision
         of law under which his detention is authorised;

     (c)   not more than one month after the commencement
         of his detention and thereafter during his detention
         at intervals of not more than six months, his case
         shall be reviewed by an independent and impartial
         tribunal established by the Chief Justice from among
         persons qualified to be appointed as a judge of the
         Supreme Court;

     (d)   he shall be afforded reasonable facilities to
         consult a legal representative of his own choice
         who shall be permitted to make representations to
         the tribunal appointed for the review of the case
         of the detained person; and

     (e)   at the hearing of his case by the tribunal appointed
         for the review of his case he shall be permitted to
         appear in person or by a legal representative of his
         own choice.

        (3) On any review by a tribunal in persuance of
this section of the case of a detained person, the tribunal
may make recommendations concerning the necessity or expediency
of continuing his detention to the authority by which it was
ordered, unless it is otherwise provided by law, that authority
shall not be obliged to act in accordance with any such
recommendations.

MINISTER FOR HOME AFFAIRS

The
University Administration:
An Instrument of Suppression?

Just before my detention I was employed at the University of Nairobi. I was an Associate Professor in Literature, employed on permanent terms because I was a Kenyan national. Nowhere in my terms of service was it ever mentioned that political detention would be a factor in terminating the services of an employee. But as the correspondence on the following pages indicates, the University of Nairobi, after an extraordinary silence of eight months after my release, wrote to tell me I had been dismissed through an Act of State on the day I was detained. But the Kenya government had denied, through a statement to parliament, that it had anything to do with the matter. This is a very bitter consequence of detention, and it affects every detainee. Thus in Kenya the torture of a detainee continues even after his release . . .

The correspondence also shows the other side of the picture: the tremendous support for detainees from the overwhelming majority of Kenyans and, in my case, the relentless struggle waged by students and staff of the university to let me resume my duties.

30 January 1979

Vice-Chancellor
University of Nairobi

Dear Mr Karanja

      Re: Resumption of my Duties as Associate Professor in the
      Department of Literature, University of Nairobi

I was released from detention on December 1978. For the last one month and a half, I have been resting at home, in Limuru.

I would like to know the university's position and attitude toward my resuming my teaching duties at the university.

Yours faithfully,

Ngũgĩ wa Thiong'o

c.c. (i) Dean, Faculty of Arts
(ii) Chairman, Dept. of Literature

P.O. Box 384
Limuru

9 July 1979

The Chairman
University Academic Staff Union
Nairobi

Re: Resumption of my Duties as Associate Professor,
Department of Literature, University of Nairobi.

In view of the fact that you, as a Union, have taken up the case of my resumption of my duties with the University of Nairobi as Associate Professor in the Department of Literature, duties which were interrupted by my arbitrary arrest and detention between 30 December 1977 to 12 December 1978, I thought that I should acquaint you, for the record, with the efforts that I have so far made to contact the university over the matter and the university's responses.

I may point out that I did not resign from the university and that up to now I have not been formally dismissed from the university. During my six years or so of continous service with the university I did all I could to contribute my best to the Department of Literature and to the university as a whole.

(1) After my release from detention on 12 December 1978, I waited to hear a word from my employer, i.e., the University of Nairobi about when or under what circumstances I should resume my duties in the department. I never received a word, any word, from the university.

(2) On 30 January 1979, I wrote to the then Vice-Chancellor, Dr J Karanja, stating my interest in resuming my duties and asking for a clarification of the university's position about it. I copied the letter to the Dean, Faculty of Arts, and the Chairman, Department of Literature.

I never got a reply. Not even an acknowledgement.

(3) On 31 May 1979, I wrote to the Chairman of the University Council, drawing his attention to my unacknowledged letter of 30 January 1979, and asking him to tell me the university's position and attitude toward my resuming my duties in the university. I copied the letter to the following: the Vice-Chancellor, University of Nairobi; the Registrar, University of Nairobi; the Chairman, University Academic Staff Union; Dean of the Faculty of Arts, University of Nairobi; and the Chairman, Department of Literature, University of Nairobi.

Up to now I have not had a reply from Mr B.M. Gecaga. Not even an acknowledgement.

(4) On 13 June 1979, following a telephone call from the Registrar, I went to see the Vice-Chancellor, Professor J. Mŭngai.

The meeting took place in his office about 2.30 p.m. in the presence of the Registrar, Mr Gĩcũhĩ.

It was a cordial, relaxed and friendly meeting. I did not get any impression of a personal or an academic hostility towards me. On the contrary, the Vice-Chancellor assured me of his and the university's readiness to take me back. But the matter was beyond the university.

The following is the gist of our conversation. I hope it is a fair summary and I am sending a copy of it to the Vice-Chancellor and the Registrar:

(A) The Vice-Chancellor told me that what he was about to tell me was virtually what he had already told a delegation of the University Academic Staff Union which had been to see him about my case.

(B) He said that he had taken the initiative to call me to his office and he was taking on the responsibility for doing so.

(C) He wanted to give me a brief outline of what the university had done since my arrest and subsequent detention:

(i)   The university had tried to find out why I had been detained, and they were told that that was a matter of public security.

(ii)   The university then did its due. The university paid my wife my six months' salary. The Registrar said that the six months' salary included terminal dues.

(iii) Just before my release from detention, the university had written to the government seeking their guidance over my affair in the event of my release. The university was told that my detention was an 'Act of State' which automatically dissolved all previous contractual relationship between me and the university.

(iv) Strictly speaking therefore, the University had no legal or any contractual basis for dealing with me.

(v)   My case was therefore beyond the university, it was a matter of public security, and I should get a clearance from somewhere. An act of state was above everything else.

(vi) The University could re-advertise the post and I could re-apply; the University could even invite me back directly: that was simple and mechanical. But in the absence of a clearance, nobody was even sure whether I could or could not take the job once offered.

(D) My own responses were as follows:

(i)   I had not resigned from the university. I had not been dismissed. I still regarded myself as being employed by the University of Nairobi. Since my detention and subsequent release I have never seen anything in writing from the university about any aspect of this matter. For instance, although I was aware of the six months' salary from January to June 1978, because my wife told me about it, the Registrar's mention of terminal dues was the *very* first I was hearing about it. I said that I was disturbed by the whole game of silence regarding my case as evidenced by the non-reply to my letters.

(ii) As far as I knew, my release from detention had been without ANY conditions either written down or verbal, direct or indirect. I could not therefore see what my contractual relationship with the university, my employer, had to do with public security.

(iii) On what basis could I go about seeking clearance? From whom? For what? Somebody might think I was crazy if I went to him and said 'Please give me a clearance!'

(iv) Over my detention I still regarded myself as the wronged party. I still held my position regarding the necessity of a truly patriotic Kenyan national theatre firmly rooted in the peasant cultures and languages of the various nationalities that make up Kenya. I was still opposed to the domination of our cultural life by foreign theatres and languages, and hold that Kenyan national languages and Kenyan national theatre centres should be allowed to flourish freely and to stage plays which truthfully reflect Kenyan social realities and patriotic Kenyan history.

(E) The Registrar left. The Vice-Chancellor and I continued discussing more general topics of languages, theatre, science, the university, and community involvement, etc.

(F) I thanked the Vice-Chancellor and left.

(5) Sir, what I would really like to get from the university in writing is a statement telling me if I have been dismissed or not. If I have been dismissed I should be told why. If I have not been dismissed, then I should be told when I should resume my teaching duties. If on the other hand there are other reasons why I am not allowed to resume my rightful position at the university, then I should also be told so in writing so as to end the game of speculation and uncertainty.

(6) The present game of literary silence is unfair to me, to my family, and to the Kenyan public who keep on asking me: Why have you not gone back to the university?

I would like to thank, through you, all the staff who have expressed their concern over the plight and rights of their academic colleague.

Yours faithfully,

Ngũgĩ wa Thiong'o

c.c. (i) The Vice-Chancellor,
          University of Nairobi
     (ii) The Registrar,
          University of Nairobi

THE KENYA GOVERNMENT
MINISTERIAL STATEMENT TO PARLIAMENT
ON 31 JULY 1979

MR OLOO-ARINGO: Mr Speaker, I beg to ask the Minister for Education the following question by private notice:

Why has Professor Ngũgĩ wa Thiong'o not been reinstated to his former position at the University of Nairobi, despite requests from students and staff of the university and the people of Kenya who know his contribution to the resurrection of the African cultural heritage?

THE ASSISTANT MINISTER FOR EDUCATION: (Mr Wanjigi): Mr Speaker, sir, I beg to reply.

I think there is some misunderstanding between Mr Ngũgĩ wa Thiong'o and the university authorities regarding the terms under which Mr Thiong'o will be re-employed in the university.

Mr Thiong'o feels that he should be reinstated under the old terms and conditions of service whereas the university authorities, quite rightly, say that his contract expired: he was paid his full terminal benefits and should reapply as a new person.

MR OLOO-ARINGO: Mr Speaker, is the Assistant Minister aware that

Professor Ngũgĩ wa Thiong'o was detained and as a prisoner of conscience, has not been convicted in any court of law and therefore he cannot be treated as a criminal to be denied the opportunity to serve his country at the university? Does he agree with me that he has not himself violated the terms and conditions of service under which he was employed and that he was forced to do so because of detention, which was beyond his control?

MR WANJIGI: He has not violated his contract terms, and that is why he was paid the full amount of the contract even six months after he had left the university. So, as far as the employer is concerned, there is nothing wrong. Even these civil servants who have resigned to contest parliamentary seats, if they do not make it, they will have to reapply to be accepted into the civil service as completely new people. The same thing applies to my good friend. He is a good friend of mine as he is a friend of anybody else.

MR IVUTI: Mr Speaker, when the Assistant Minister says that there is a disagreement between the Professor and the university administration, and the university administration itself says that they would like to reinstate but they are not allowed to do so, where is the truth; is it that there is some disagreement or is there some fault away from the university?

MR WANJIGI: Mr Speaker, I must not be misquoted. I said that there is some misunderstanding, not that there is any disagreement.

MR MIDIKA: Mr Speaker, the Assistant Minister says rightly that there is some misunderstanding, but the Hon. Member said that as representatives of the people we have heard that the university authority says that they would wish to take the Professor back but they are not allowed to do so by somebody else. Who is that somebody else? If the contract expired but the Professor can be taken back, as the Assistant Minister is saying, why has he not been taken?

MR WANJIGI: Mr Speaker, I am going to be held responsible only to what I have said. What Mr Midika and anybody else has heard is none of my business. I said that there is a misunderstanding as regards the terms of employment, and if you have heard anything else which the university is saying it is none of my business.

MR OLE KONCHELLAH: Mr. Speaker, sir, can the Assistant Minister tell the House when Professor Ngũgĩ's contract expired and when he was paid?

MR WANJIGI: Mr Speaker, I am sorry I need time to answer that question. However, I know that he has been paid the full contractual obligations but as to what date that was done I need time to check on it.

MR OLOO-ARINGO: Mr Speaker, this university comes directly under the Ministry of Education, and it is the Ministry of Education that answers for the university in this House. Can the Assistant Minister take steps to ensure that people, such as Professor Ngũgĩ, who are of world eminence, with training that can help our country, are not allowed to go and spend their lives in exile and contribute to the development elsewhere instead of contributing to the development of our own people?

MR WANJIGI: Mr Speaker, we would be as keen to have Professor Ngũgĩ teach in our university as anybody else, but as I have said, there are two sides of the coin which must be reconciled.

MR SPEAKER: Let us go on now.

UNIVERSITY OF NAIROBI

Registrar's Department

Professor Ngũgĩ wa Thiong'o,   P.O. Box 30197
P.O.Box 384,   Nairobi
Limuru   3 August 1979

Dear Professor Ngũgĩ wa Thiong'o,

Please refer to your letter dated 30 January 1979 addressed to Dr J.N. Karanja the former Vice-Chancellor, and to another one dated

30 May 1979 addressed to the Chairman of the University Council. I am now writing to reiterate what the Vice-Chancellor Professor Mungai informed you on 31 May 1979 in his office and in my presence regarding your former contract.

Following your detention, the university sought legal advice which indicated that in the circumstances the contract between yourself and the University of Nairobi was dissolved by an Act of State the day you were taken away and detained, namely with effect from 1 January 1978. Strictly speaking, therefore, the university should have paid all your benefits accrued up to the day you were detained. However, at a meeting of Council held on 2 February 1978, the Council decided to pay you terminal benefits up to 30 June 1978, a period equal to the period either party would have been required to give notice of termination of contract under normal circumstances. On enquiring from the government authorities as to how this information could be transmitted to you, the university was informed that as a detainee, no communication would be allowed between you and the university. Consequently, your wife was given this information verbally by the Registrar and the Finance Officer in the Registrar's Office. As you already know, the six-month salary and terminal benefits were effectively paid as directed by Council.

In effect, therefore, your contractual relations with the university were ended by the Act of State. However, the university is planning to advertise vacant posts in various faculties, including the Faculty of Arts, and you may be interested to apply for a suitable post.

Yours sincerely,

E.N. Gicuhi
Registrar

c.c.   Chairman of Council
       Vice-Chancellor

P.O. Box 384
Limuru
18 August 1979

The Registrar,
University of Nairobi,
P.O. Box 30197,
Nairobi

Dear Mr Gĩcũhĩ,

I am in receipt of your letter of 3 August 1979, which presumably is the university's offical reply to my letters of 30 January 1979 addressed to Dr J.N. Karanja, the former Vice-Chancellor, and of 31 May 1979 addressed to the Chairman of the University Council, in both of which I had sought to know the university's position regarding the resumption of my duties as Associate Professor in the Department of Literature.

I would like to thank you for at long last letting me know that acting on some legal advice from unspecified quarters, the University of Nairobi had, as early as January 1978, decided to dismiss me from my job through the invocation of an Act of State.

I note with regret that it has taken the university about eight months to let me know in writing information you must have known for the last one and a half years. Why, if I might ask, was this information deliberately withheld from me? You say in your letter that while I was in detention you could not transmit this information to me because the Kenya Government did not then allow any communication between me and the university. Very well. I came out from detention, freed without any conditions, on 12 December 1978. Yet it is only now, August 1979, a whole eight months or so after I have been set free, that you are passing this very important information on to me.

In your letter you say that you are only reiterating what the Vice-Chancellor, Professor Mungai, informed me in his office and in your presence on 31 May 1979. In case it may have escaped your memory, let me remind you that I never met the Vice-Chancellor and yourself on 31 May 1979. But I presume that you are referring to a similar meeting held in the Vice-Chancellor's office on 13 June

1979 following a telephone call to my house from you, as the Registrar. You will remember that after the Vice-Chancellor had told me that my case was beyond the university and that it was a matter of public security and that I needed clearance from somewhere, I asked him whether that could be put down in writing so that I would be able to act on a written document. What did he tell me? That nothing between me and the university could be put down in writing. You, I remember, supported that view. You also remember that when you, in particular, vaguely made reference to some terminal benefits, I told you that that was the very first time I was hearing about these so-called terminal benefits.

In your letter you say that I was dismissed from my job through 'an Act of State'. What is this 'Act of State' which dissolves all legal obligations between two parties when one of them is detained? In case it may have escaped your notice, I may draw your attention to the fact that I was on permanent and pensionable terms of service and nowhere in those terms of service is there a single reference to an Act of State that would automatically dissolve mutual legal obligations between the university and myself. While in your letter you say that my contractual relations with the university were ended by 'the Act of State', an Assistant Minister of Education, Mr Maina Wanjigi, in a Ministerial statement to parliament on 31 July 1979, made no mention of this mysterious Act of State. On the contrary, he made it clear that the whole matter lay with the university authorities as my employer.

In your letter you refer to terminal benefits paid to me. By this I presume you are including the six months' salary (January – June 1978 inclusive) that you paid into my bank.

I would like to state that my wife has told me quite categorically that when she came to your office some time in February or March 1978, you only told her about this six months' salary. She has told me that no conditions were put to the payment of the six months' salary. Once again, you deliberately avoided putting anything in writing. Yet now in your letter you claim that you told my wife that all those were charitable dues following my unilateral, arbitrary and illegal dismissal by the university through a mysterious Act of State. Let me assure you that my wife would never have accepted any acts of charity from the university and she would never have been a party to any transactions which could have implied in any way that my services were being terminated.

I note bitterly in fact that not a single payment was ever

accompanied with a cover note if only to have things on record, that every single payment into my bank from the university was always under a cloak of literary silence and secrecy.

I will give you an example: following the ministerial statement in parliament on 31 July 1979 about terminal benefits, I went to my bank and I asked them to give me photostat copies of every and any payment advice notes and vouchers of any money entered into my account for year 1978. It was only then that I noted that my accound had been credited with a sum of K.Shs. 30048/80 (K.Shs. Thirty-thousand and forty-eight shillings and eighty cents) from the Universty of Nairobi on 18 December 1978, exactly six days after I had been freed from detention. Could this be what you mean in your letter when you talk of *terminal benefits* besides the six months' salary? Again this money was paid under a strict cloak of silence and secrecy. Why? On 18 December 1978 I was already at home and free, and you knew it. Why did you not let me know in writing? And now you have the bravery to claim that you informed my wife verbally about this payment! I ask you: who was it easier to tell this to, my wife who was not an employee of the university, or myself who was the party involved?

Even up to now I have not yet got any official communication from you as to what this payment of 18 December 1978 constitutes. Does it, for instance, constitute the next few monthly payments after June 1978? Or does it constitute the terminal benefits referred to in your letter? How was it possible for a whole national institution to pay any sum of money without advising the person to whom the sum was paid? What could be the motive? For lack of any official and written communication from the university I had always taken that sum to be payment of book royalties from my publishers. The university's secrecy and silence can only lead me to conclude that your actions were a calculated deliberate move by university authorities to trick me (or my wife) into participating in, and therefore seeming to be party to, unilateral and arbitrary and illegal acts on the parts of the university, especially my summary dismissal.

What is not in doubt however, is that your reference to terminal benefits is evidence of the fact that the university has terminated my services.

I would like to protest in the strongest possible terms against this unilateral, arbitrary and illegal act of the universty against one of its employees. Your action is not only a gross breach of contract, but it is also oppressive.

By taking the kind of action that you have taken, the university has joined hands with those forces in the country which are against the position I have consistently held about the necessity of a patriotic Kenyan theatre, literature, and a culture free from any and every form of foreign domination and control, a culture that reflects and draws its strength and inspiration from the heroic struggles of Kenyan peasants and workers against all forms of internal and external exploitation and oppression.

Yours,

Ngũgĩ wa Thiong'o

c.c. (1) Chairman of Council
      (2) Vice-Chancellor
      (3) Chairman,
           University Academic Staff Union,
           P.O. Box 31873,
           Nairobi

PRESS RELEASE – 20/8/1979

UNIVERSITY ACKNOWLEDGES SECRET, ARBITRARY DISMISSAL

The Assistant Minister of Education, Mr Maina Wanjigi, gave a ministerial response to parliament on 30 July 1979, regarding my employment status with the University of Nairobi. That statement, whether by accident or intention, grossly misrepresented, and in important details, falsified the case. I wish to state and document the case so that the Kenyan public is not misled in this matter.

(1) In his statement, the Assistant Minister, for reasons best known to himself and to the university authorities, told parliament that my contract with the university had expired. The fact is that being a citizen, *I was on permanent and pensionable terms of service and*

ot on contract. The question of the expiry of 'the contract' does not therefore arise.

2) In the statement, Mr Wanjigi told parliament that I had been paid full terminal benefits. But what Mr Wanjigi failed to tell parliament was that any payment of any terminal benefits by the university to a person on permanent and pensionable terms of service could only mean, in this case, that the University of Nairobi had unilaterally and arbitrarily terminated my employment. Yet as the Assistant Minister himself admitted, I had not broken any of the terms of service.

3) The Assistant Minister also gave the false impression that the university had issued me with new conditions under which I could resume my duties at the university and which I had refused to meet or fulfill. The fact of the matter is that up to the time of the ministerial statement to parliament on 31 July 1979, I had not received *any* written conditions, old or new or modified, which I was supposed to meet in order to resume my duties at the university.

4) The university's adamant refusal to communicate with me in writing is borne out by the following facts:

(a) On 30 January I wrote to the then Vice-Chancellor, Dr J.N.Karanja, seeking a clarification of the university's position and attitude toward the resumption of my duties. I never got a reply. Not even an acknowledgement.

(b) On 31 May I wrote to the Chairman of Council, Mr B.M. Gecaga, about the same issue. He never replied to the letter. He did not even acknowledge its receipt.

The question of 'some misunderstanding' between me and the university does not arise. Or could it be that the then Vice-Chancellor and the Chairman of Council misunderstood my letters and sought refuge in literary silence?

5) It is true that on 13 June 1979, following a telephone call at my house from the Registrar, Mr Gĩcũhĩ, I went to see the new Vice-Chancellor, Professor J.M. Mũngai. But he had only invited me to his office to tell me that my case was beyond the university, that it was a matter of public security, and I needed a clearance from somewhere. He told me in the presence of the Registrar that I had

been detained by an 'Act of State', that this dissolved all previous contractual relationship with the university. I asked him to put that in writing. He said that nothing involving me and the university could be put in writing.

In view of the above, I can only conclude that there was a collusion between the university and the minister to give false impressions to the Kenyan people about my position in this matter.

(6) However, the ministerial statement did at long last force the university to come out of their self-imposed literary silence and to respond in writing to my letters of 30 January and 31 May 1979, and for the first time, to concede openly their unilateral, arbitrary and unjust position regarding my status with the university. To wit:

In a letter to me dated 3 August 1979, signed by the Registrar, Mr E.N. Gĩcũhĩ, and which finally reached me on 13 August 1979, the Registrar has informed me that the University of Nairobi with no recourse to higher authority dismissed me on 2 January 1978, the day that I was arrested and subsequently detained. Let me quote from the letter:

> Following your detention, the University of Nairobi sought legal advice which indicated that in the circumstances the contract between yourself and the University of Nairobi was dissolved by an Act of State the day you were taken away and detained.

After a slightly lengthy section telling me how the university went about silently, gracefully and charitably terminating my service including the paying of terminal benefits — that is without their even informing anybody about it in writing — the letter ends by reiterating the fact of my arbitrary and unilateral dismissal. I quote:

> In effect, therefore, your contractual relations with the University were ended by the Act of State.

(7) THE UNIVERSITY THEN SECRETLY, UNILATERALLY AND UN-JUSTLY HAD DISMISSED ME NEARLY TWENTY MONTHS. It has taken them eight months to state what presumably they must have known since January 1978, and in so doing they have invoked a new extra constitutional legal status created by an 'Act of State'.

8) The letter from the Registrar says clearly that I was dismissed from my job through an 'Act of State'. What is this 'Act of State' that dissolves all legal obligations between two parties when one of the parties is detained? In my terms of service, there is not a single mention of any 'act of state' that would automatically dissolve mutual legal obligations between the university and myself. I also know of no constitutional clause that stipulates loss of my rights of contract employment or otherwise once detained. My terms of service only refer to dismissal on criminal conviction. Yet in my case I was never formally charged in a court of law with any offence, I was never convicted of any criminal offence under the existing laws of Kenya, indeed up to now I have never been given any reason for my arbitrary arrest and subsequent detention. My release was without any verbal or written conditions.

9) By invoking a mysterious 'Act of State' (presumably only known to the university and to their legal advisers) and by claiming that I needed clearance from unstated quarters, the university authorities apparently are trying to imply that my case was beyond solution by any authority in Kenya. The university, to defend its arbitrary actions, is in fact implying that I am a *stateless person.* Presumably the university authorities realize the full implications of their statement.

10) The ministerial statement obviously contradicts the letter from the university Registrar, Mr Gĩcũhĩ. Mr Wanjigi says that the whole matter is between me and my *employer*, and by implication, any termination of my duties is the *entire responsibility of the university.* But Mr Gĩcũhĩ's letter says that the whole matter is an 'Act of State', and the responsibility for my dismissal must be borne by this 'Act of State'. Where is the truth?

11) The university and the ministry should tell the Kenyan people the real truth regarding my position, so that the present air of falsehoods and uncertainty is cleared once and for all.

12) Let me finally say that over my detention, I still regard myself as the wronged party. I still hold my position regarding the necessity of a truly patriotic Kenyan national theatre firmly rooted in the peasant cultures and languages of the various nationalities that make up Kenya. I am still opposed to the domination of our cultural, economic and political life by foreign interests. I still hold the position that Kenyan national theatre centres should be allowed to

flourish freely and to stage activities which truthfully reflect Kenyan social and political realities and history.

I look forward to a time when no Kenyan shall lose his job for saying that Kenyan cultures must be free from foreign domination; a time when no Kenyan shall lose his job for demonstrating that Kenyan cultures that glorify the grandeur of our past struggles and achievements and that show the great possibilities open before us all, Kenyan people, can bloom in great dignity and beauty if given the chance!

Ngũgĩ wa Thiong'o

20 August 1979

UNIVERSITY OF NAIROBI

P.O. Box 30197
Nairobi
20 September 1979

Professor Ngũgĩ wa Thiong'o
P.O. Box 384, Limuru

Dear Professor Ngũgĩ wa Thiong'o,

Thank you for your letter dates 18 August 1979.

I would like to take this opportunity to apologise for the typographical error regarding the date of our meeting in the Vice-Chancellor's office, which you correctly state took place on 13 June and not 31 May 1979.

Yours sincerely

E.N. Gĩcũhĩ
Registrar

BRIEF REPORT ON USU'S STRUGGLE TO HAVE PROFESSOR NGŨGĨ RESUME HIS DUTIES AT THE UNIVERSITY

) 19/4/72 The Union was registered as a *Union* but prior to this, it had been registered as an Association. The Union worked up to 1975 without the University Council's recognition.

) 1976 Officials resigned unconstitutionally through pressure from University authorities.

) 1976 – February 1979
The Union was dormant.

) 10/1/78 Professor Ngũgĩ wa Thiong'o, Chairman of the Department of Literature and a member of USU (University Staff Union), is arrested.

) 15/1/78 The press announces detention of Professor Ngũgĩ. No reasons for detention are given.

The following weeks, intermittent student demonstrations expressing resentment at Professor Ngũgĩ's detention and demanding his release.

Members of the Department of Literature send a delegation to the Vice-Chancellor and demand Professor Ngũgĩ's release.

Student agitation continues while academic staff members keep silent. The University of Nairobi makes no official comment on the fate of its member.

) 12/12/78 Professor Ngũgĩ released from detention. University students make a jubilant procession through the city. They are joined by members of the public.

) 13/12/78 Professor Ngũgĩ addresses the university staff and students and receives a tremendous reception from the community. Students make a procession through the city. They are joined by members of the public.

) January – February 1979
Mass student meetings continue to call for Professor

Ngũgĩ's resumption of duty to office. University authorities keep silent on the issue. Students send a petition to the Chancellor. Student leaders make several requests to the university authorities for Professor Ngũgĩ's resumption of duties. University academic staff members make no official comment. The university remains silent.

(9) 28/2/79 Finally the academic members of staff take a step towards the fate of their colleague. A special conference of the then UASU took place. Former official resignations were constitutionally accepted. A new Executive was elected by this special conference and a resolution was unanimously passed as follows:

> 'That this Special Conference meeting of 28/2/79, having duly elected an Executive Committee and being gravely concerned about the non-resumption by Ngũgĩ wa Thiong'o of his duties, hereby mandates the said committee to take up with the relevant authorities the question of the re-engagement of Professor Ngũgĩ wa Thiong'o as a matter of singular and utmost urgency. This special conference further directs the said Executive Committee to report back as soon as possible and in any event in not later than two weeks' time.'

(10) 5/3/79 To act on this resolution the Executive Committee met and discussed the resolution.

(11) 8/3/79 The Executive Committee met the then Vice Chancellor, Dr J.N. Karanja, and after the introductory formalities, the Committee raised and discussed the Ngũgĩ issue.

(12) 14/3/79 There was a special conference of the then UASU which endorsed the petition reproduced here below and mandated the Executive Committee to procure signatures from the members of academic staff. The conference also accepted the content of memorandum of councils (Nairobi and Kenyatta University

sity College) asking them to stand up and defend
Ngũgĩ's contract and rights.

**PETITION TO H. E. THE PRESIDENT, THE CHANCEL-
LOR OF THE UNIVERSITY OF NAIROBI IN REGARD OF
PROFESSOR NGŨGĨ WA THIONG'O SUBMITTED BY
ACADEMIC MEMBERS OF STAFF OF THE UNIVERSITY**

'We the undersigned, being members of the academic staff in the University of Nairobi and
Kenyatta University College and all being colleagues of Professor Ngũgĩ wa Thiong'o *do petition*
your excellency in your capacity as Chancellor of
the University to allow Professor Ngũgĩ wa
Thiong'o to resume his teaching duties at the Department of Literature in the University of Nairobi. We
do so on the grounds that he is a patriot and a scholar
who greatly loves his country; he is an outstanding
teacher with proven capability to contribute to the
development of our society — he is the only Kenyan
creative writer of international repute . . . he can only
participate fully in nation-building by taking his
place in the university. We have sent a memorandum expressing similar sentiments to the Council,
Nairobi University and the Council, Kenyatta
University College. We are sure, your excellency,
that in the interests of this nation in general and those
of the university in particular, you will favourably
consider this petition.'

(13) 4/4/79   The first memorandum to the Council sent to the
Vice-Chancellor.

(14) 5/5/79   The amended copy of the memorandum sent to the
Council.

(15) 16/5/79   The Executive Committee resolved to postpone an
appointment with the Chancellor and brief the new
Vice-Chancellor, Professor J.M. Mungai, on all the
developments and congratulate him on his new
appointment.

(16) 28/5/79   The Chairman and Secretary-General met the new
Vice-Chancellor and stressed the urgency of Pro-

fessor Ngũgĩ's case. They got a date for the entire
committee to discuss the issue with the Vice-
Chancellor.

(17) 31/5/79 Professor Ngũgĩ writes to Council expressing readiness to resume duties.

(18) 6/6/79 The Executive Committee meets the Vice-
Chancellor and is told that the issue of Professor
Ngũgĩ resuming his duties in the university rested
with people other than the university authorities. His
situation, the Committee was told, was an Act of
State.

(19) 7/6/79 – 16/7/79
Executive Committee seeks appointment and audience with the Chancellor without success.

(20) 13/6/79 The Vice-Chancellor in the presence of the Registrar
told Professor Ngũgĩ that his case was beyond the
university and that it was a matter of Public Security
and that he (Professor Ngũgĩ) needed clearance
from somewhere.

(21) 16/6/79 Special Conference of the Union rules that the
petition be sent to State House by hand in the event
an appointment and audience with the Chancellor
was not seen forthcoming. The conference further
ruled that a press conference be called to inform the
Kenyan public that members of staff have petitioned
the Chancellor.

(22) 16/7/79 The petition to Chancellor. Sent to the office of the
Comptroller of State House. The press conference
took place an hour later in the Junior Common
Room. The press statement noted, above all:

'Professor Ngũgĩ has devotedly served Kenya as an
outstanding national scholar: he has continuously
struggled for the true development of national cultures of Kenya against domination by foreign
cultures. In this struggle, from pre-independent
Kenya up till now, he has stood as a firm patriot in
the eyes of the broad national population of our

country. We hope that the Chancellor will use his
good offices to facilitate Professor Ngũgĩ's redemp-
tion of duty in the University.'

(23) 17/7/79 Up to date, Kenyan general public begin to openly
show support for the petition in view of the fact that
Professor Ngũgĩ has been expressing national sentiments in his stand on national cultures and languages against foreign domination.

Letters to the editor in the press reflect the national
feelings on the case of the writer.

(24) 30/7/79 Members of Parliament ask the Assistant Minister
of Education why Professor Ngũgĩ is denied the
opportunity to resume his duties in the University
despite requests from students and lecturers at the
University *and the people of Kenya*.

The Minister's response grossly mispresented, and
in important details, falsified the case. He was acting
on information given by the university.

(25) 31/7/79 Professor Ngũgĩ discovers, after the ministerial
statement in Parliament that he had been paid
terminal benefits, that the University had paid the
benefits, on 18/12/78 by a voucher presented to the
Bank on 14/12/78.

Professor Ngũgĩ was released from detention on
12/12/78.

(26) 3/8/79 The Registrar, University of Nairobi, writes to
Professor Ngũgĩ and informs him that the University, acting on some legal advice from unspecified
quarters, had, as early as January 1978, dismissed
Professor Ngũgĩ from his job through the invocation
of an Act of State.

(27) 18/8/79 Professor Ngũgĩ replies to the letter from the Registrar. He abhorred the secrecy and silence in the
matter and ended his letter by stating:

'By taking the kind of action that you have taken, the

university has joined hands with those forces in the country which are against the position I have consistently held about the necessity of a patriotic Kenyan theatre, a literature and culture free from any and every form of foreign domination and control, a culture that reflects and draws its strength and inspiration from the heroic struggle of Kenyan peasants and workers against all forms of internal and external exploitation and oppression.'

(28) 20/8/79   Professor Ngũgĩ gives a press statement and tells the Kenya public the truth: that the university has acknowledged his secret, unilateral, unjust, arbitrary and illegal dismissal. Professor Ngũgĩ concluded his press statement patriotically: 'Let me finally say that over my detention, I still regard myself as the wronged party. I still hold my position regarding the necessity of a truly patriotic Kenyan national theatre, firmly rooted in the peasant cultures and languages of the various nationalities that make up Kenya. I still hold the position that Kenyan national theatre centres should be allowed to flourish freely and to stage activities which truthfully reflect Kenyan social and political realities and history.

I look forward to a time when no Kenyan shall lose his job for saying that Kenyan cultures must be free from foreign domination, a time when no Kenyan shall lose his job for demonstrating that Kenyan cultures that glorify the grandeur of our past struggles and achievements and that show the great possibilities open before us all, Kenyan people, can blossom in great dignity and beauty if given the chance!'

(29) 22/8/79   The report that far appeared in the then UASU's newsletter no. 1 of 1979.

(30) 22/8/79   The university's legal position in dismissing Pro-
– up to date   fessor Ngũgĩ has been investigated, researched into and legal opinions sought. The verdict is this: the university's legal position is *plainly erroneous in law* because of the following legal reasons:

(a) The defence of 'act of state' is used by governments or agents of government. Nowhere has it been shown that in dismissing Professor Ngũgĩ the university was acting as an agent of the Kenya Government.

(b) It is settled law in this country (as it is in Britain) that if a wrongful act has been committed against a person, the wrongdoer cannot set up as a defence the Act of State.

(c) The University of Nairobi under s. 3(2) is liable in its corporate capacity and the University of Nairobi Act, 1970, does not state otherwise.

(d) The Preservation of Public Security Act under which Professor Ngũgĩ was detained nowhere provides for the university's legal position.

(e) The issue of whether or not the university wrongfully dismissed Professor Ngũgĩ can be raised, heard and disposed of in a court of law on the basis of the contract between Professor Ngũgĩ and the university. That is not possible in issues involving Acts of State.

(f) Professor Ngũgĩ had no contractual relations with the Kenya Government regarding his job.

(g) There is in law no Act of State between the government and its citizens.

(h) The Act of State is not the university's act and so it cannot claim such a defence, this being only open to the goverment or its officers.

(31) November 1979

The university advertises for a post of Professor, Department of Literature, Faculty of Arts. Professor Ngũgĩ subsequently applies and his application is acknowledged. The matter awaits the usual procedures of short-listing, interviews. Everyone is hopeful because Professor Ngũgĩ stands out as the right applicant at whatever level, national and international. And the Union reiterates its position as concisely expressed in the position above.

(32) April 1980

Professor Ngũgĩ's novels (*sic*), *Ngaahika Ndeenda* and *Caitaani Mũtharaba-inĩ* appear in the shops. According to press reports, the books have been very well received by the people of Kenya. They are a great contribution to the anti-foreign languages struggle by Kenyans who rightly advocate the development of Kenya's national languages free of foreign domination.

The books also emphasize one other important thing. Professor Ngũgĩ is being denied his means of livelihood. This is what the Union has been struggling against. And Professor Ngũgĩ, the great patriot that he is, refuses to leave Kenya to earn a living but instead writes for all patriotic Kenyan people. This is a great inspiration to us all.

(33) 1/5/80   This report is prepared.

Willy Mutunga,
Secretary-General, USU

The Last Word?

Resolved accordingly [i.e. by Parliament]:

THAT, while thanking His Excellency the President for releasing all detainees, and given that some of the detainees who were released in December 1978 and their families have suffered economic hardships within the duration of their detention and are still unemployed and looking for jobs, this House urges the Government and the private sector to assist the ex-detainees to obtain the jobs they qualify for to enable them to earn a living.

From *Hansard*, Wednesday, 11 June 1980

The University Staff Union has given the University Council a deadline by which to decide some pressing questions.

The Union wants a decision by August 1 on salaries, Professor Ngũgĩ wa Thiong'o, the medical scheme, discrimination against middle grades, and academic freedom.

From the *Daily Nation*, 17 July 1980

President Moi yesterday said that the Union of Kenya Civil Servants and the University Staff Union will be banned.

The President said the government was taking care of the civil servants by improving their wages and their welfare and did not understand why they should continue politicking.

He said the two unions represent workers who are employees of the government and should stop politicking.

He said the government was looking after its employees properly.

From the *Sunday Nation*, 21 July 1980

President Daniel Arap Moi is having his say about ex-detainees long after Parliament passed a private members motion by Koigi wa Wamwere (Nakuru North) calling upon the government to make it easy for ex-detainees to find employment. Last week when speaking to a church group in his home town in Kabarnet, the President startled many Kenyans when he said ex-detainees who were detained after Kenya received her political independence, would be the last to be considered for available jobs. Moi said he could not be expected to give such people priority in jobs since they had been 'undermining' the government of the late President Jomo Kenyatta. 'Was President Kenyatta's government a colonial one to deserve such agitators?' he asked. 'Is my government a colonial one?'

From the *Weekly Review*, 11 July 1980

A Worker's Voice

While you're alive, don't say never!
Security isn't certain
And things won't stay as they are.
When the ruling class has finished speaking
Those they ruled will have their answer.
Who dares to answer never?
On whom is the blame if their oppression stays? On us!
On whom does it fall to destroy it? On us!
So if you are beaten down, you just rise again!
If you think you've lost, fight on!
Once you have seen where you stand, there is nothing can
    hold you back again.
For those defeated today will be the victors tomorrow . . .

Bertold Brecht: *The Mother*